Unification of Tort Law: Causation

EUROPEAN CENTRE OF TORT AND INSURANCE LAW

Principles of European Tort Law **Volume 4**

Other titles in this series:

The Limits of Liability: Keeping the Floodgates Shut – Edited by J. Spier – 1996 – ISBN 90-411-0169-1

The Limits of Expanding Liability: Eight Fundamental Cases in a Comparative Perspective – Edited by J. Spier – 1998 – ISBN 90-411-0581-6

Unification of Tort Law: Wrongfulness – Edited by H. Koziol – 1998 – ISBN 90-411-1019-4

Unification of Tort Law: Causation

J. Spier (Editor)

F. D. Busnelli/G. Comandé
H. Cousy/A. Vanderspikken
S. Galand-Carval
K. D. Kerameus
H. Koziol
U. Magnus
J. Neethling
W. V. H. Rogers
G. T. Schwartz
J. Spier/O. A. Haazen
P. Widmer

KLUWER LAW
INTERNATIONAL
THE HAGUE – LONDON – BOSTON

Published by Kluwer Law International
P.O. Box 85889
2508 CN The Hague, The Netherlands

Sold and distributed in North, Central and South America by
Kluwer Law International
675 Massachusetts Avenue
Cambridge, MA 02139, USA

Sold and distributed in all other countries by
Kluwer Law International
Distribution Centre
P.O. Box 322
3300 AH Dordrecht, The Netherlands

Library of Congress Cataloging–in–Publication Data is available

This book is published with the financial support of the European Commission within the network 'Common Principles of European Private Law' (= part of the program "Training and Mobility of Researchers"), the Austrian Ministry of Science, the Austrian Ministry of Justice and the Swiss Ministry of Justice.

ISBN: 90-411-1325-8

Kluwer Law International incorporates the publishing programmes of Graham & Trotman Ltd., Kluwer Law and Taxation Publishers and Martinus Nijhoff Publishers

Preface

This book is the fourth volume of the European Group on Tort Law (the Tilburg Group). After a series of meetings, which resulted in 'The Limits of Liability, Keeping the Floodgates Shut' and 'The Limits of Expanding Liability, Eight Fundamental Cases in a Comparative Perspective', it was decided to embark on drafting European Principles of Tort Law. The first book in this 'new series' was 'Unification of Tort Law: Wrongfulness', edited by Helmut Koziol.

We realise that the drafting of a body of European principles of tort law is quite an exercise. It takes some time to achieve that goal. Consequently, we had to face the question whether we should publish the final principles together with a comment thereto at a much later stage or rather keep those interested informed on a regular basis, as the work progresses. The latter approach has been chosen.

Publishing the various topics after their respective completion undoubtedly has advantages. First, we think that the national reports, based on a mix of theoretical topics and often leading cases, are already in themselves sufficiently important for the outside world and may serve as an up-to-date overview of the law of torts in a large number of countries.

Secondly, by publishing the national report prior to the principles we hope to stimulate a discussion on the conclusions that we have reached mid-way, and so to improve the quality of the final principles. For that purpose, we do not merely publish the reports, but we add a comparative analysis which sheds light on the solutions we think best at the present stage. On the basis of suggestions by others and after reconsideration by the time the entire field has been covered, the final principles will be drafted and published.

Our group aims at drafting European principles. Yet, we are most grateful that eminent tort law experts from the USA and South Africa are members of our group, notably Gary Schwartz (UCLA), Dan Dobbs (Tucson) and Johann Neethling (Pretoria).

The other members of the group are Francesco Busnelli and Giovanni Comandé (Pisa), Herman Cousy (Leuven), Bill Dufwa (Stockholm), Michael Faure (Maastricht), Olav Haazen (Tilburg), Viggo Hagstrøm (Oslo), Helmut Koziol (Vienna), Konstantinos Kerameus (Athens), Ulrich Magnus (Hamburg), Miquel Martin Casals (Girona), Horton Rogers (Nottingham), Jorge Sinde Monteiro (Coimbra), Jaap Spier (The Hague), Geneviève Viney and Suzanne Carval (Paris I), Pierre Widmer (Lausanne) and Michael Will (Geneva).

The next volume in this series will be about damages, and will be edited by Ulrich Magnus.

In our 'Preliminary Observations' of 'The Limits of Expanding Liability', we wrote that our group aimed at establishing an international research centre in the area of Tort and Insurance Law. We are proud to say that at the beginning of this year, the European Centre of Tort and Insurance Law was founded in Vienna; Helmut Koziol – who greatly contributed to its realisation – leads the Centre as its Director.

We are very grateful for the financial support received from the network 'Common Principles of European Private Law', which is sponsored by the European Comission. The network in which participate as partners Barcelona, Berlin, Oxford, Lyon, Münster, Nijmegen and Turin is part of the program 'Training and Mobility of Researchers' (TMR). We are also most grateful both to the Austrian Ministry of Science and to the Austrian Ministry of Justice as well as to the Swiss Ministry of Justice for the generous financial and moral support of this project.

Finally, we express our gratitude for the most valuable help of Dr Klaus Vogel and Mag. Martin Kauz to make the manuscript ready for the publisher and to Mag. Barbara Steininger for her help to correct the proofs.

Jaap Spier, Olav Haazen

The Hague, April 1999

Contents

Causation: Questionnaire and Cases

Causation: Questionnaire and Cases

Part I

1. Causation as a requirement

(a) Is there a requirement of 'causation' in your law?
(b) If so, is it a one or a two step approach?

E.g. 'a cause in fact', a 'preliminary filter', a difference between causation as a requirement for establishing liability and determining the amount to be paid or between factual and legal causation?

2. Relevant factors/reasons/criteria

Assuming that the first step (if any) has been taken, what reasons/factors are to be taken into account in establishing the scope of causation?

- conditio/causa sine qua non;
- (reasonable) foreseeability;
- remoteness;
- probability;
- adequacy;
- common sense and/or policy arguments;
- reasonableness;
- proximity;
- proximité temporelle;
- causa proxima;
- disproportion de gravité entre deux fautes concurrentes;
- protective purpose of the violated rule.

Are you of the opinion that the relevant factors in your legal system are sufficiently clear/well-defined to solve individual cases? If not, do you consider this a disadvantage? If so, could you please provide additional criteria/factors which would increase predictability?

3. Specific legislation

Please mention legislation establishing specific rules concerning causation, e.g. about joint and several liability of joint tortfeasors. Please stick to your national legislation and disregard treaties and conventions.

4. The borderline between causation and causation or other factors

It will not always be easy to argue whether, let alone why, specific cases are to be addressed from the angle of causation or from the related perspective of damage.

Would you approach the following cases as a matter of causation and/or damage and/or the scope of the protective rule:

(a) x poisons a horse in a stable with a slowly working poison. Before the poor animal dies,

J. Spier (ed.), Unification of Tort Law: Causation, 3–7.

Y sets the stable afire. The horse perishes in the flames.[1] Who could be sued: X and/or Y and why?

(b) X has been exposed to asbestos dust during his work for three subsequent employers (A, B and C). Ten years after retirement he falls seriously ill. Inhaling asbestos dust does not affect a person's health unless the total amount of dust exceeds a certain level. It has to be assumed that the fatal threshold was crossed when X was employed by C. X sues A, as B and C went bankrupt. A argues that he is not liable because the damage was caused by crossing the threshold (in other words: when X was employed by C). Please disregard prescription and assume that A's liability as such is not disputed.

(c) an attorney (A) makes a mistake by not lodging an appeal in time. His client (C) sues him for damages. A argues that the appeal would have been rejected.

(d) A statute requires a carrier by sea to keep animals in pens. The purpose of this requirement is to prevent the spread of a disease. While P's animals are being carried on deck without pens they are swept overboard in a storm. If they had been penned they would not have been lost. Alternatively, the unpenned animals are lost because the ships sinks in the storm.

Part II Cases

Single event occurrences

1. D collides with a coach with US attorneys (P 1/10) who earn quite a lot of money, as we know. They are all seriously injured. The loss of income of all the attorneys amounts to at least $ 250.000.000. P 1/10 sue D.

2. P is struck in an accident for which D is liable. P has a predisposition. As a consequence of this predisposition P remains unable to work, while he otherwise would have recovered in several weeks. P sues D for the loss of income.

3. T has stolen a car and causes an accident to P. O, the owner of the car, negligently did not remove the key from the lock, despite the fact that many cars are stolen in the area. P sues O, because T is not worth suing.

4. The power supply of an entire neighbourhood has been cut off by the negligent act of D, a building company. The cables belong to the supplier of energy. A factory plant (P1), its customers (P2) and their customers (P3) suffer damage – P1, P2 and P3 sue D. It has to be assumed that P1's engines were damaged.

5. The defendant negligently places unlabelled rat poison on a shelf full of food. The shelf happens to be near a stove that gives off heat, and the heat quickly causes the poison to explode, injuring the plaintiff.

6. A bus is damaged in a car accident caused by D. While the bus is under repair, P, the owner of the bus, uses a reserve bus and sues D for part of the costs of buying and maintaining the reserve bus.

---

1 The example is borrowed from Iulianus, D. 9.2.51.2.

7. In a railroad accident caused by the negligence of A, B is injured and, moreover, is left in a position of peril. C, coming onto the scene, attempts to rescue A. In the course of this rescue effort, C is himself injured. C brings suit against A.

8. Because of the negligence of D, A's only kidney is badly damaged. A will not survive without a kidney transplant. P is an appropriate match. P permits the surgical removal of his own kidney, so that it can be transplanted into A. P sues D for all the pain and discomfort associated with the surgery.

Intervening events

(a) Natural event occurs independently of the act of any human being

9. D, a plumber, negligently causes fire in P's house. Before repair, the house is completely destroyed by an earthquake. P sues D, who argues that P did not suffer damage, as his house would have been destroyed anyway.

10. A ship was damaged in a collision for which the defendant's ship was wholly responsible. After temporary repairs which restored the ship to a seaworthy condition, she set out on a voyage to the USA, a voyage which she would not have made had the collision not occurred. During the crossing of the Atlantic she suffered extensive damage due to heavy weather, and on her arrival in the USA the collision damage was permanently repaired at the same time as the heavy weather damage was dealt with. The owner sues D for the entire damage.

(b) The event consists of the act or omission of a third party

11. P is seriously injured by a car accident caused by D. It would take him about a year to recover. An ambulance brings P to the hospital. On the way to the hospital, the ambulance is hit by:
(a) a car, driven by a drunk driver X;
(b) an avalanche.
P's injury further increases; he will now need three years to recover. Is D also liable for the loss of income over the last two years?

12. Dl's vehicle broke down and he negligently failed to take steps to remove it from the highway. His car was struck by D2's truck. The latter came to rest at the opposite carriageway, where it was struck by P2 and P3. D2 had been driving recklessly. P2 and P3 sue Dl.

13. D, a driver, knocks down P, a pedestrian, whose wallet is stolen while he is lying injured. P sues D.

(c) The event consists of the act or omission of the plaintiff himself or is attributable to a cause which can be imputed to him

14. P is seriously injured by a car accident, caused by D. He would never sufficiently recover to take up his work again. In the hospital he has a heart attack. Had it not been for the accident, he would have become unable to work for the rest of his life. P sues D for the loss of income.

15. P loses one leg as a consequence of a traffic accident. D is liable for this accident. He dies eleven years later in a fire in his house, because he was not able to leave the house fast enough. P's widow sues D.

Loss of a chance

16. Doctor A negligently fails to diagnose the cancer in his patient B. At the time of the negligent failure, B's chances of survival (had proper treatment been given) were 40 percent. By the time the proper diagnosis is provided, B has no chance of surviving. After B's death, B's heirs sue Doctor A.

17a. 1 per cent of the residents of a small town with 10.000 inhabitants (notably: 100 persons, Pl/100) fall ill due to a very dangerous illness. The percentage is extremely high, as 0.05 per cent would be 'normal' (i.e. 5 persons). This may be caused by negligent emissions from D, a neighbouring factory, it may also be mere coincidence. Pl/100 sue D for the entire amount of their alleged damage.

17b. The normal rate for a particular form of cancer is one person per one thousand residents. Because of D's negligent emissions, the cancer rate goes up to three persons per thousand. All three victims sue D. (This hypothetical raises the issue of proving causation by statistics. It also raises the question whether all three plaintiffs can sue, even though only two are apparent victims of the defendant's negligence.)

17c. The normal cancer rate is two persons per one thousand. Because of D's negligent emissions, the rate goes up to three. All three sue D. This raises the issue whether the defendant escapes liability despite the evident causation of harm – because no one victim can make a 'more-likely-than-not' causal showing.

Concurring causes

18. Dl and D2 each pile a ton of rubbish against P's wall which, in consequence of the total pressure, collapses. P sues Dl for the entire damage, D2 not being worth suing.

19. Dl, D2 and D3 are hunters. In a wood, frequently visited by walkers, they negligently try to bring down a bird. Instead, one shot hurts P. It is unknown whether the fatal shot was fired by Dl, D2 or D3. P sues Dl, D2 and D3 not being worth suing. Does it make any difference whether or not they act in concert?

Please assume that the case is about tort law and (consequently) disregard funds dealing with hunting accidents.

20. At the same time A and B discharge poisonous waste into a river. All of the fish die. The waste water of A as well as that of B was sufficient to kill the fish. P, the owner of the fishing rights, sues A.

21. Several manufacturers (D1/D20) negligently[2] manufacture a drug. Dl has a marketshare of 50.01 per cent; D2 a marketshare of 15 per cent; the remaining companies have

2 Negligence possibly is not a requirement for liability (yet in view of prescription, it may be). To avoid discussion about liability, it has been added.

marketshares ranging between 0.5 and 3 per cent. D20 probably has a marketshare of approximately 0.5 per cent. The drug causes serious injury, which has a long incubation period. It occurs after 10 years. Pl/25000 are seriously affected by the drug. However, after such a long period, they are no longer able to identify the manufacturer of the drugs bought by them. It has to be assumed that the total harm can be attributed to Dl/D20, while each of them cannot have caused the same.

(a) Pl/25000 sue D20, the other manufacturers not being worth suing;[3]
(b) Pl/25000 sue D2, the other manufacturers not being worth suing;
(c) Pl/25000 sue Dl, assuming that their chances are most favourable in doing so.

Please disregard prescription.

22. Mountain climber P is hurt by a falling rock. At the same time a second rock nearly hits him. The falling of the rocks is caused, on one hand, by negligence of D, and on the other hand, by a chamois. It is unknown which rock hit P. P sues D.

23. Ship A (SA) crashes into ship B (SB). It is demonstrated that the accident causing extensive damages to both vessels can be attributed to the captain of SA only for 20 per cent, the remaining 80 per cent must be attributed to exceptional unpredictable weather conditions, fog, heavy sea.

Can SB sue the captain and/or the owner of SA for damages? In case of an affirmative answer, does SA have to pay the entire damage?

Miscellaneum

24. D1, driving too fast in the fog on the motorway runs into the back of the vehicle in front, bringing both vehicles to a halt. In the ensuing seconds another ten vehicles, driven by D2–D11 are involved in further collisions attributable to the initial obstruction, causing death, injury and property damage to the participants. Some of these vehicles are being driven at a proper speed but are nevertheless hit by vehicles coming from behind. After the first collision, it is not possible to allocate blame to individual drivers.

3 This is not likely, of course. Yet, the example aims to show the most farreaching consequences.

Country Reports

Austria

Causation under Austrian Law

Helmut Koziol

Part I: General Questions

1. Causation as a requirement

Liability of a person for a certain damage can only be established if there is a connection between this person and the damage. According to §§ 1294, 1295 General Civil Code (ABGB), the 'Beschädiger' (damaging party) has to compensate the damage which he has 'zugefügt' (inflicted) on the claimant. Therefore, only that person can be liable who has caused the damage.[1] But it is not a requirement that he actually caused the damage himself; very often it is sufficient that his sphere was the cause.[2] This is the case, for example, in the area of vicarious liability (§§ 1313a, 1315 ABGB) or of strict liability for dangerous objects such as railways and motor vehicles (see Eisenbahn- und Kraftfahrzeughaftpflichtgesetz).

It is common opinion that in the field of tort law the theory of causation is a theory of liability which has to solve the problem of attributing damage; therefore, a natural concept of causation can not be decisive.[3]

In Austria the 'Äquivalenztheorie' (theory of equivalence) prevails: Every fact is causal which was a sine qua non condition for the damage.[4] But it has to be stressed that, on the one hand, there are important exceptions to the tenet of causation and, on the other hand, causation is only a preliminary filter. The former applies in cases in which several actors are involved or 'potential' causes are given (see sec. 3); the latter applies insofar as liability normally can not be established without causation, but not every damage caused by the tortfeasor has to be compensated, even if he acted negligently or wilfully and knowingly (see sec. 2).

2. Relevant factors in restricting liability for caused damage

Liability for all damage caused by the tortfeasor is considered unreasonable. Under Austrian

1 *Cf.* F. Bydlinski, *System und Prinzipien des Privatrechts* (1996) pp. 186–187.
2 *Cf.* R. Bienenfeld, *Die Haftung ohne Verschulden* (1933) pp. 119 et seq.
3 F. Bydlinski, *Probleme der Schadensverursachung* (1964) p. 4; Th. Mayer-Maly, Zivilistische Kausalitätstheorie in Bewegung, [1965] *Juristische Blätter* (JBl), 441.
4 *Cf.* H. Koziol, *Österreichisches Haftpflichtrecht* I (3rd edn. 1997) nos. 3/5 and 8 et seq.

J. Spier (ed.), Unification of Tort Law: Causation, 11–21.

law two theories are accepted in eliminating those categories of damage not subject to compensation: The theory of adequate causation and that of protective purpose of the violated rule.[5] The Austrian Supreme Court (Oberster Gerichtshof, OGH) applies both of them.[6]

(a) Adequacy

The tortfeasor only has to compensate adequate damage, i.e. damage that is not too remote. An exception has to be made if a protective statute forbids a certain behaviour in order to protect certain assets: The wrongdoer who violates such a law must indemnify even remote damage of a protected asset. Some hold that the restriction of compensation is also not applicable if the tortfeasor acts with intent. On the other hand, it should be pointed out that the prevailing opinion upholds the theory of adequacy applicable not only in the area of liability based on fault, but also in the area of strict liability.[7]

Adequacy is established if the damaging event was generally suitable for increasing to a considerable extent the possibility of such a damage as occurred. Whether this was the case has to be judged by an objective ex ante examination. As the defenition is very broad, courts seldom negate adequacy; therefore, in its present form the theory is of hardly any use in restricting liability.

Austrian lawyers do not see the idea of adequacy as being part of the theory of causation, but rather as an independent theory that tries to limit liability on the basis of weighing the interests.[8]

(b) Protective Purpose

The doctrine of 'Rechtswidrigkeitszusammenhang', or the more general 'Schutzzweck der Norm' (protective purpose of the violated rule), is accepted by the prevailing opinion in Austria.[9] This theory is a result of the generally accepted method of interpreting the law according to its purpose ('teleologische Interpretation').[10] The protective purpose is relevant in two or even three respects:[11] Firstly, the wrongdoer has to compensate only the losses of those persons which the law is intended to protect; secondly, he has to indemnify only that damage which the violated rule is intended to avoid. One can add that, thirdly, the damaging party is only liable if he caused the damage in a way that is forbidden by law.

The doctrine of the protective purpose of the violated rule is applied especially in cases of infringement of statutes with protective purpose (§ 1311 ABGB), but also in any case of

5 For more details, *see* H. Koziol (supra note 4) nos. 8/2 et seq.

6 Adequacy: Oberster Gerichtshof (Austrian Supreme Court, OGH) in [1992] JBl, 255; [1995] *Zeitschrift für Verkehrsrecht* (ZVR), no. 73; protective purpose: *Entscheidungen des Österreichischen Obersten Gerichtshofes in Zivil- und Justizverwaltungssachen* (SZ), 62/73 and 63/166.

7 P. Apathy, *Kommentar zum Eisenbahn- und Kraftfahrzeughaftpflichtgesetz* (6th ed. 1998) § 1 no. 10.

8 *Cf.* F. Bydlinski (supra note 3) pp. 59–60.

9 *Cf.* E. Rabel, *Das Recht des Warenkaufs* I (1936) pp. 495 et seq.; W. Wilburg, *Die Elemente des Schadensrechts* (1941) pp. 244 et seq.; H. Koziol (supra note 4) nos. 8/17 et seq.

10 *See* F. Bydlinski, *Juristische Methodenlehre und Rechtsbegriff* (2nd edn. 1991) pp. 453 et seq.

11 *Cf.* M. Karollus, *Funktion und Dogmatik der Haftung aus Schutzgesetzverletzung* (1992) pp. 339-340; OGH in SZ 55/190; SZ 56/80; SZ 66/77; SZ 67/39.

breach of a duty of care. Furthermore, the purpose of the law has to be taken into consideration if the law provides strict liability; one has to determine whether there is a connection between the particular danger justifying strict liability and the damage caused.

(c) The flexibility of the criteria

The predominant opinion holds that adequacy and purpose of the violated rule are strict and inflexible criteria. But Wilburg[12] argues convincingly that they are flexible: He stresses that adequacy is a relative concept which allows for gradations. He believes that the tortfeasor has to compensate more or less adequate damage according to the weight of the particular factors establishing liability. Therefore, the borderline of adequacy has to be extended further if the tortfeasor acted with intent than if he behaved slightly negligently. The radius of adequacy depends, furthermore, on the weight of wrongfulness and on the protective purpose of the violated rule.

In the same sense the scope of the protective purpose of a statute is flexible: Frequently, one can detect a hard core of damage which must be compensated in any case and this is surrounded by a broader peripheral area that is not as obviously included by the protective purpose. Depending on the weight of the factors establishing liability, more or less broad limits have to be set on the protective purpose.[13]

If one accepts the flexibility of adequacy and protective purpose of the violated rule, I feel that these factors are sufficient and suitable for reasonable restriction of liability for the damage caused.

3. Specific legislation

(a) §§ 1301, 1302 ABGB

According to §§ 1301, 1302 ABGB, joint and several liability is imposed on joint offenders regardless of whether the damage caused by each and every tortfeasor is determinable. Bydlinski[14] points out that, as a rule, it is impossible to prove whether the joint decision really was a conditio sine qua non for the damage that occurred or whether one or more of the group would also have caused the damage on their own. Therefore, Bydlinski stresses that only 'potentielle Kausalität' (potential causality) can be determined and the joint offenders are liable merely on account of presumed causation.

Furthermore, § 1302 ABGB holds that even independent offenders are jointly and severally liable if the damage caused by each one is not determinable.[15] Therefore, here again, every tortfeasor is liable on account of a mere presumption.

---

12 W. Wilburg (supra note 9) pp. 242 et seq.; *also* espoused by F. Bydlinski (supra note 3) p. 62; M. Karollus (supra note 11) pp. 380 et seq.; H. Koziol (supra note 4) nos. 8/15–16 and 8/21; OGH in [1998] JBl, 113 and 114.

13 *Cf.* OGH in SZ 65/8.

14 F. Bydlinski, Haftung bei alternativer Kausalität, [1959] JBl, 10–11; F. Bydlinski, Mittäterschaft im Schadensrecht, [1959/60] *Archiv für civilistische Praxis* (AcP) 158 at 411–412.

15 *Cf.* Bydlinski [1959] JBl, 11–12; OGH in [1982] JBl, 266; SZ 59/7.

(b) Analogy to §§ 1301, 1302 ABGB

By analogy with §§ 1301 and 1302 ABGB, common opinion[16] in Austria holds that joint and several liability[17] also has to be established if several tortfeasors who have acted in fault have possibly caused the damage, but there is no way of determining which of them actually caused it (see case 19). In such cases of 'alternativer Kausalität' (alternative causality), causation can not be proven, but in the concrete situation each of the tortfeasors acted dangerously in the highest degree and may potentially have caused the loss. As the causal connection can not be proven, liability is based merely on potential causation. In establishing liability the weakness of this factor has to be compensated by a higher weight of other factors. Therefore, Bydlinski[18] stresses that the damage only then is attributable to the tortfeasors if in the concrete situation each of them acted dangerously in the highest degree; in other words, adaequacy in the highest degree is a requirement.

One of the arguments used in favour of joint and several liability of the alternative causal tortfeasors is that it is more reasonable to burden the tortfeasors, who acted wrongfully and with fault, than the claimant, who was undoubtedly injured by a liable tortfeasor.

In case one of the alternative causal wrongdoers indemnifies the claimant, he has recourse to the others,[19] so that in the end each of them has to compensate the same amount. There is a discussion in progress on liability in such cases in which, on the one hand, a wrongdoer potentially caused the damage and, on the other hand, a chance accident or an incident which can be imputed to the injured person also potentially caused the loss (see case 22 and 16). Following up on Wilburg's[20] theory, Bydlinski[21] holds the opinion that in analogy to § 1304 ABGB[22] the injured person may claim compensation for part of the damage.

Other cases of potential causation are those of 'kumulativer oder konkurrierender Kausalität' (cumulative or concurring causality, see case 20): Two (or more) real causes take effect at the same time and each of them could have caused the damage on its own. Therefore, none of them was a conditio sine qua non. Still, common opinion holds that both tortfeasors are jointly and severally liable.[23] This is justified, as both actors are potentially causal.[24] If the second cause is an accident the same is true as in cases of alternative causality, namely, the injured party may claim compensation for part of the loss.

Akin to these cases are those of 'hypothetischer oder überholender Kausalität' (hypothetical or overtaking causality, see 4.a and cases 9, 14): The only difference is that one of the

---

16 For more details *see* F. Bydlinski, [1959] JBl, 10 et seq.; F. Bydlinski, Aktuelle Streitfragen um die alternative Kausalität, *Festschrift-Beitzke* (1979) p. 6; H. Koziol (supra note 4) nos. 3/26 et seq.; OGH in SZ 56/120.

17 I am not so sure that this is the fair solution; *cf.* H. Koziol (supra note 4) no. 14/13; perhaps partial liability would be more reasonable.

18 F. Bydlinski (supra note 16) p. 9.

19 *Cf.* Koziol (supra note 4) nos. 14/16 et seq.

20 W. Wilburg (supra note 9) p. 74.

21 F. Bydlinski, Haftungsgrund und Zufall als alternativ mögliche Schadensursachen, *Festschrift-Frotz* (1993) p. 3. Similar opinion OGH in [1996] JBl, 181; divergent OGH in [1994] JBl, 540 with commentary by R. Bollenberger.

22 It rules that both the tortfeasor and the injured party have to bear the loss in case of contributory negligence.

23 *See* F. Bydlinski (supra note 3) pp. 16–17.

24 F. Bydlinski (supra note 3) pp. 67–68 and 70.

events actually causes the damage and the other one would have done so at a later point in time. As both actors are equally potentially causal, these cases should be solved in the same way as those of alternative or cumulative causality.[25] It has to be stressed that liability of both of the tortfeasors can only be established if the second tortfeasor still acted wrongfully[26] and if, in the concrete situation, he acted dangerously in the highest degree.

However, according to the Supreme Court,[27] only the tortfeasor who actually caused the damage is liable. But this answer is not convincing, as the act of this tortfeasor was not a conditio sine qua non, rather both wrongdoers are merely potentially causal and, therefore, both have to be treated equally, thus explaining why joint and several liability is reasonable.

(c) Other specific legislation
Some special statutes establish rules divergent from §§ 1301, 1302 ABGB, e.g. § 53 sec. 2 Forstgesetz (Forest Act). But the legislators did not give any reasons for these discrepancies and they are thought to be unreasonable.[28] Therefore, it does not seem to be useful to deal with them in depth.

4. The borderline between causation and damage or other factors

First of all, it has to be pointed out that in tort law the decisive question is always, whether the defendant caused a certain damage and, therefore, has to compensate it, thus causality and damage are closely linked.

(a) X poisons a horse in a stable with a slowly working poison. Before the poor animal dies, Y sets the stable afire. The horse perishes in the flames. Who could be sued: X and/or Y and why?

Under Austrian law this case brings up a problem of causality, that of 'Überholender Kausalität' to be precise: X's act was not a conditio sine qua non for the damage incurred by the death of the horse, as it perished in the fire set by Y; but Y's act was not a condition for the loss by the death of the horse either as, otherwise, it would have died from the poison. However, it has to be assumed that according to the opinion of the Supreme Court (see the end of sec. 3.b) only Y would be liable, as he actually caused the death. As mentioned above, the proper answer should be that both X and Y are potentially causal and, therefore, are jointly and severally liable.

(b) X has been exposed to asbestos dust during his work for three subsequent employers (A, B and C). Ten years after retirement he falls seriously ill. Inhaling asbestos dust does not affect a person's health unless the total amount of dust exceeds a certain level. It has to be assumed that the fatal threshold was crossed when X was employed by C. X sues A, as B and C went bankrupt. A argues that he is not liable because the damage was caused by crossing the threshold (in other words: when X was employed by C).

---

25 *See* F. Bydlinski (supra note 3); P. Rummel, *Ersatzansprüche bei summierten Immissionen* (1969).

26 If the first event completely destroyed the property and the second defendant took his action afterwards, the behaviour was no longer wrongful in regard to this property.

27 *Cf.* OGH in SZ 10/272; [1993] JBl, 663 with commentary by W. Kleewein.

28 *Cf.* H. Koziol, *Österreichisches Haftpflichtrecht* II (2nd edn. 1984) pp. 435–436. Uncertain OGH in [1989] JBl, 578.

Even if the threshold was crossed when X was employed by C, X's injury would not have occurred but for his inhaling asbestos dust already during his work for A and B. Therefore, each of the three employers set a conditio sine qua non for the damage and is liable on condition that he acted in fault. As each of the employers was a cause contributing to the whole damage, they are jointly and severally liable and are not only liable for compensating part of the damage.[29]

(c) An attorney (A) makes a mistake by not lodging an appeal timely. His client (C) sues him for damages. A argues that the appeal would have been rejected.
In omitting to lodge the appeal in due time, A did not cause a loss if the appeal would indeed have been rejected: C would have suffered the same damage if the appeal had been lodged in due time.[30] But it has to be stressed that A has to prove that the appeal would have been rejected.[31]

(d) A statute requires a carrier by sea to keep animals in pens. The purpose of this requirement is to prevent the spread of a disease. While P's animals are being carried on deck without pens they are swept overboard in a storm. If they had been penned they would not have been lost. Alternatively, the unpenned animals are lost because the ship sinks in the storm.

If the only purpose of the requirement is to prevent the spread of a disease, one would say that the loss of the animals, which were swept overboard, is beyond the protective purpose of the rule and, therefore, the carrier does not have to compensate the loss even though he caused it. In the case in which the ship sinks in the storm the carrier did not even cause the loss, as the animals would have been drowned in pens as well.

Part II: Cases

Single event occurences

1. D caused the injuries and hence the loss of income of all the attorneys – and their loss is quite adequate. Furthermore, if D violated road traffic law, the damage caused is within the scope of the rule. Therefore, D is undoubtedly liable. But under Austrian law the question is whether D has to indemnify the whole loss in any case: If he behaved slightly negligently, he only has to compensate the 'actual loss', but not the lost profits (§ 1324 ABGB). But common opinion holds that the loss of earnings caused by bodily injury is part of the actual loss. The argument here is that an existing asset, namely the ability to work, has been injured.[32] Furthermore, some scholars think that liability must be restricted if, on the one hand, compensation of the whole loss would ruin the tortfeasor and, on the other hand, the injured party is not dependent on the indemnification.[33]

---

29 *Cf.* OGH in [1989] JBl, 578.

30 *See* M. Karollus (supra note 11) pp. 392–393; OGH in [1994] JBl, 338.

31 OGH in SZ 67/9; *cf.* H. Koziol (supra note 4) no. 16/12.

32 *Cf.* The Austrian Report, in: J. Spier (ed.), *The Limits of Liability* (1996) p. 56.

33 *Cf.* C.-W. Canaris, Verstöße gegen das verfassungsrechtliche Übermaßverbot im Recht der Geschäftsfähigkeit und im Schadensersatzrecht, [1987] *Juristen-Zeitung* (JZ), 995 and 1001–1002.

2. Without a doubt, the wrongdoer D caused the loss of income if the predisposition on its own would not have led to the disablement. Furthermore, the Supreme Court holds that adequacy is given even if the injured party has a predisposition.[34]

3. In this case 'psychological causality' is at stake:[35] O tempted T into using the car by not removing the key from the lock. As the behaviour of O was a conditio sine qua non for the theft of the car and thus for the accident, the prerequisite of causality is given. However, in cases of psychological causation liability very often fails due to lack of wrongfulness. But one has to assume that everyone has a duty of care not to tempt others if a special danger would be provoked as a result.[36] That O violated such a duty is beyond doubt, as § 106 Kraftfahrgesetz (Motor traffic statute) obligates every driver to take care that the car is not driven by an unauthorized person.

4. Under Austrian law causation is beyond doubt, but the subject we are concerned with here is the protective purpose of the rule. I refer to the Answers to the Hypotheticals, case 2.[37]

5. The negligent act of the defendant undoubtedly caused the damage. But if negligence is only established because of mixing unlabeled poison with food, the explosion would not be an adequate consequence of the wrongful behaviour, in addition to which the injury would not be included by the protective purpose of the violated rule. But the defendant would be liable if he also violated the duty of care not to put the poison near a stove.

6. According to the prevailing opinion,[38] D is not liable under tort law as he did not cause the costs of buying and upkeeping the reserve bus; but P is entitled to the costs under the law of negotiorum gestio. However, Christian Huber[39] holds that the injured party has a claim under tort law to compensation for the incurred expenses if it used its own resources to repair the damage.

7. In this case causality[40] is beyond doubt, as A's act was a conditio sine qua non for the railroad accident and thus also for the attempts of C to rescue B. Furthermore, if the tortfeasor, in causing the accident, infringed standards of conduct, common opinion holds that the damage of the rescuer is within the scope of protection of this violated rule.[41] Some scholars are even of the opinion that the tortfeasor violated a separate duty of care towards the rescuers.[42]

Also espoused by F. Bydlinski (supra note 1) p. 226, p. 233; H. Koziol (supra note 4) nos. 7/7 et seq.

34 *Cf.* OGH in [1988] JBl, 649.

35 *Cf.* H. Koziol (supra note 4) no. 3/16.

36 *See* H. Koziol (supra note 4) no. 4/59.

37 *Cf.* The Austrian Report, in: J. Spier (ed.), *The Limits of Expanding Liability* (1998) p. 71.

38 OGH in [1973] JBl, 476 with commentary by H. Koziol; SZ 59/95; SZ 60/65; F.-St. Meissel, *Geschäftsführung ohne Auftrag* (1993) pp. 88–89.

39 Ch. Huber, *Fragen der Schadensberechnung* (2nd edn. 1995) pp. 194 et seq. and 392 et seq.

40 Again psychological causality is at stake, *cf.* case 3.

41 OGH in [1979] JBl, 597; R. Welser, Der OGH und der Rechtswidrigkeitszusammenhang, [1975] *Österreichische Juristenzeitung* (ÖJZ), 6.

42 *Cf.* R. Welser, [1975] ÖJZ, 6; H. Koziol (supra note 4) no. 8/43.

8. In my opinion, the same holds true as in case 7.

Intervening events

(a) a natural event occurs independently of the act of any human being

9. The opinion which probably still prevails holds that a tortfeasor who behaves wrongfully and thus actually causes the harm is liable even if another event later on would have caused the same harm.[43] According to this opinion, D would have to compensate. But Bydlinski[44] rightly stresses that the tortfeasor changes only the real conditions, but does not cause the damage as his behaviour is not a conditio sine qua non. Therefore, both events are merely potentially causal and have to be treated equally. This means that if two tortfeasors are potentially causal, both are jointly and severally liable. Otherwise, if a tortfeasor and an accident by chance are potentially causal, the injured person can only claim part of the damage.

10. D is not liable for the damage due to heavy weather, even though the voyage would not have been made had the collision not occurred. The reason for this is that this damage is not an adequate consequence of the collision and also outside the scope of the rule violated by the act that led to the collision. Therefore, inasmuch as the harm caused by the collision would also have been caused by heavy weather, the same problem is at stake as in case 9.

(b) the event consists of the act or omission of a third party

11. The car accident caused by D was a conditio sine qua non for the second accident caused by X or the avalanche. Therefore, it is beyond doubt that D was also causal for the loss of income over the last two years. Nevertheless, it is doubtful whether the damage can be attributed to D. Former judicial decisions ruled that the causal connection with the act of the defendant is broken if another person takes an independent action which is not an inevitable consequence of the defendant's first act ('Unterbrechung des Kausalzusammenhanges').[45] But it is undeniable that the first act by D is a conditio sine qua non for the damage to P.[46] The only prerequisites that can be called into question are whether adequacy and protective purpose of the violated rule have to be negated. Accordingly, the Supreme Court has recently been examining whether the second act was to be expected.[47] As D did not increase the general risk that P might be involved in a car accident, adequacy has to be negated.[48] Furthermore, the rule violated by D does not have the purpose of avoiding accidents which are part of the 'allgemeinem Lebensrisiko' (general risks of life).[49] The same is true in case the second event was an avalanche.

---

43 OGH in SZ 10/272; [1993] JBl, 663 with commentary by W. Kleewein; A. Ehrenzweig, *System des österreichischen allgemeinen Privatrechts* II/1 (2nd edn. 1928) p. 45; K. Wolff in H. Klang, *Kommentar zum ABGB* VI (2nd edn. 1951) p. 10.

44 F. Bydlinski (supra note 3) p. 26, pp. 32–33 and 65 et seq.

45 OGH in SZ 3/107; [1976] JBl, 650; [1987] ZVR no. 77.

46 *Cf.* R. Reischauer in P. Rummel, *Kommentar zum ABGB* (2nd edn. 1992) § 1295 no. 19; H. Mayrhofer, *Schuldrecht* I*: Allgemeiner Teil* (1986) p. 261.

47 OGH in SZ 55/172; [1989] ZVR no. 130.

48 *Cf.* H. Koziol (supra note 4) no. 8/14.

49 *Cf.* H. Koziol (supra note 4) no. 8/46.

12. Causal connection is clearly established: Without D1's negligent behaviour, P2 and P3 would have suffered no harm; therefore, D1 caused the loss incurred. As explained under case 11 above, the only relevant question is whether adequacy and protective purpose of the violated rule have to be negated. In my view, in the case at stake it is not unlikely that a negligent or reckless driver would run into the broken-down vehicle of D1; therefore, adequacy is given. Furthermore, D1 violated the rule to remove his broken-down car from the highway and this rule undoubtedly has the purpose of avoiding accidents caused by obstacles on the carriageway. Thus, the damage occurred is included by the protective purpose of the violated rule. Therefore, D1 must compensate P2 and P3.

13. Again, psychological causation is at stake (see case 3). As to the question of whether the caused damage can be attributed to D, one has to consider that the thief acted willfully and that adaequacy is only given to a slight degree. Furthermore, it is doubtful whether the loss is covered by the protective purpose of the statute violated by D. Therefore, I feel that D should only be responsible if he behaved in gross negligence (see Part I.2.c).

(c) the event consists of the act or omission of the plaintiff himself or is attributable to a cause which can be imputed to him

14. It goes without saying that D would be liable if the heart attack was a consequence of the car accident. But if the heart attack was solely the result of a disease, D did not have to compensate the whole loss of income: He only caused the loss of income to commence at an earlier date, i.e. exactly the time between the car accident and the heart attack.[50] Bydlinski[51] points out that in such cases the tortfeasor does not even have to compensate part of the loss of income for the time after the second event, as the working capacity of the injured person was time limited. D would only be partly liable if the second event had been a chance accident and the working capacity had only been limited by death (see Part I. 3.b).

15. I refer to my comments on case 6 of the hypotheticals.[52]

Loss of a chance

16. I will leave aside the question which damage the heirs may claim and concentrate on the problem of causation. Under Austrian law one would not argue 'loss of chance', but rather alternative causation: The negligent failure of A and the disease are both potentially causal and, therefore, B's heirs may claim compensation for part of the damage (see Part I. 3. b).

17a. Even if the court arrives at the conclusion that the negligent emissions from D caused the increase of the dangerous illness, it would have to consider that it is uncertain which of the 100 persons were made ill by D and which five persons would have fallen ill at any rate. Therefore, alternative causation is at stake here as well: On the one hand, the illness of each of the claimants could have been caused by the negligent act of D, which was dangerous in

50 *Cf.* OGH in [1956] JBl, 503; [1972] JBl, 368; SZ 38/72 = [1967] JBl, 144; F. Bydlinski, Vergleichsverhandlungen und Verjährung; Anlageschäden und überholende Kausalität, [1967] JBl, 135 et seq.

51 *Cf.* F. Bydlinski (supra note 3) pp. 97 et seq.

52 *Cf.* The Austrian Report, in: J. Spier (supra note 37) p. 78.

a high degree; on the other hand, a chance accident is potentially causal. The prevailing opinion holds that D must compensate 95 per cent of the damage of every claimant.[53] D's liability is all the more reasonable, as he surely caused damage and it is only uncertain to whom.

If the court rules that there is no evidence of D causing the increase of illness, liability of D has to be examined separately for each individual claimant. Liability can only be established if D's negligent act was dangerous with regard to the illness to a very high degree. But if a chance accident was also potentially causal for the illness of the individual claimant, D only has to compensate part of the damage in proportion to the probability in this concrete case.[54]

17b. I think the same is true as under case 17a, first variation.

17c. Again the same is true as under case 17a, first variation, because it is clear that D, in all, caused one third of the harm.

Concurring causes

18. As D1's and D2's behaviour are both a conditio sine qua non, both are jointly and severally liable. If D1 indemnifies P, he has a recourse to D2. That D1 and not P has to bear the risk of D2's insolvency seems reasonable, as D1 acted wrongfully.

19. If each of the hunters fired negligently and each of the shots was dangerous in the highest degree, the acts of D1, D2 and D3 are alternatively causal and, therefore, jointly and severally liable (see Part I.3.b).[55]

It does not make any difference whether or not they go hunting in concert. Only in case they concertedly intended to shoot a walker would they be jointly and severally liable as accomplices (§ 1301 ABGB), even if only one of them fired dangerously.

20. As the same damage would have occurred if one of the two tortfeasors had not discharged poisonous waste, none of them set a conditio sine qua non. But both of them acted potentially causally ('kumulative Kausalität') and, therefore, are jointly and severally liable (see Part I.3.b).

21. Each of the manufacturers is only potentially causal for the harm of every claimant. It is decisive that, on the one hand, each of the producers caused a part of the harm in proportion to his market share and would be liable for the harm caused by his drugs; on the other hand, every injured person would be able to claim damage, provided that he could prove which manufacturer made the drug that caused his injury. Therefore, I espouse the opinion[56] that each injured person has a claim against each manufacturer, but only for such part of his harm which is in proportion to the market share of the manufacturer. In this manner, it is ensured that no manufacturer will have to compensate more harm than was caused by him.

---

53 T. Bodewig, Probleme alternativer Kausalität bei Masseschäden, [1985] AcP 185 at 528–529 and 538 et seq.; P. Jabornegg, Der Schutz der Umwelt durch das Zivilrecht, [1988] *Die Versicherungsrundschau* (VR), 56; H. Koziol (supra note 4) no. 3/40.

54 *See* H. Koziol (supra note 4) no. 3/41.

55 *Cf.* F. Bydlinski, [1959] JBl, 6–7.

56 *See* T. Bodewig, [1985] AcP 185 at 505; J. Koch, *Haftungsprobleme bei Produktspätschäden* (1987) pp. 97 et seq.; K. Otte, *Marktanteilshaftung* (1990); H. Koziol (supra note 4) nos. 3/46 et seq.

22. D's negligent behaviour is only potentially causal for the damage. As the other potential cause is a chance accident, P may claim compensation for only part of the damage (see Part I.3.b).

23. If the information on the case means that the captain of SA did not establish all the causes of the accident, but the crash nevertheless would not have occurred if the captain had acted properly, then the captain set a conditio sine qua non for the entire damage. Therefore, the captain/owner has to compensate the whole damage, unless the caused harm is an inadequate result (see Part I.2.a).

But if, in the case under consideration the captain of SA can prove that only 20 per cent of the damage incurred are caused by his negligence and that his misbehaviour is no conditio sine qua non for the other 80 per cent of the damage, then SB can claim only 20 per cent of the loss.

Miscellaneum

24. As D1's negligent behaviour was a conditio sine qua non for all the damage, adequacy is given and the violated statute also endeavours to avoid such consequences. Therefore, D1 is liable for the entire detrimental consequences. Furthermore, he cannot use the defence that it is impossible to allocate blame to other individual drivers. He has the burden of proof that claimants are to be blamed for contributory negligence and he, therefore, only has to compensate part of the damage. D1 also has to prove joint responsibility of other drivers if he wants to take recourse.

Belgium

Causation under Belgian Law[1]

Herman Cousy and Anja Vanderspikken

1. General Comments on Causation

Questions 1–3

1. As a general rule the Belgian law of extracontractual liability is very favourable toward the victim, insofar as it strictly limits the conditions of liability in tort to the threefold condition of the existence of a fault, a damage and a causal relation between fault and damage. To be qualified as a cause (in this legal sense), an event must fulfill the sole requirement of being a 'conditio sine qua non' for the ensuing damage. Between all the causal events, no distinction is made according to whether they are adequate, or direct, or normal causes: all causes are considered to be *equivalent*.[2] In other words, in principle there is no difference between factual and legal causation. Belgium is one of the few legal systems which radically adhere to the theory of equivalence of causes (or at least which pretends to do so).[3]

2. On several occasions the Cour de Cassation has consistingly underlined that while judging the existence of a causal connection, both the fault[4] and the damage[5] must be appreciated 'in concreto', i.e. as they have actually occurred: 'Attendu qu'il y a relation de cause à effet (si). . ., sans la faute, le dommage tel qu'il se présente in concreto, ne se serait pas réalisé. . ., Qu'en décidant qu'il n'y a pas de relation de cause à effet. . . en se fondant uniquement sur ce que le dommage eût pu se produire sans la faute, mais en s'abstenant de prendre en

---

1 Special thanks to Bart de Temmerman and Ignace Claeys for their useful comments on this text.

2 For references to case law *see*, M. Adams, 'Law is as I've told you before'. Over de zwaartekrachtwerking van rechterlijke ultspraken in Belgie', [1997] *Tijdschrift voor Privaatrecht* (TPR), 1373–1374.

3 M. Adams, [1997] TPR , 1373; H. Bocken, 'Actuele problemen inzake het oorzakelijk verband', in *Recht hallen uit aansprakelijkheid* (Gent, Mys en Breesch, 1993) p. 86; B. de Temmerman, 'Een arrest over de invloed van een foutloos optreden door een derde op het oorzakelijk verband tussen de initiele fout en de schade: aanleiding tot reflectie', annotation of Hof van Cassatie/Cour de Cassation (Supreme Court, Cass.) 20 December 1996, [1998] *Recente Arresten van het Hof van Cassatie*, 174–183; J. Geers, 'Alternative liability under Belgian law: unknown and thus unloved ?', [1994] *European Review of Private Law* (ERPL), 445, nr. 4.

4 Cass. 12 May 1975, [1975] *Pasicrisie* I, 891: 'un lien de causalité entre la faute ainsi commise par le demandeur et le dommage'.

5 Cass. 11 June 1956, [1956] *Pasicrisie* I, 1094.

J. Spier (ed.), Unification of Tort Law: Causation, 23–37.

considération le dommage in concreto, tel qu'il sest produit, à telle date et dans telles circonstances déterminées, le juge du fond a violé l'article 1382 du Code Civil'.[6] As was accurately referred to by M.E. Storme, the Cour de Cassation's insistence upon the necessity of appreciating the damage 'in concreto', tends to give a wider rather than a restricted realm to the concept of causation.[7] Indeed the more the damage is described in vague and general terms, the greater the chances are that it would have occurred anyway, i.e. irrespective of the behaviour of the tortfeasor. The more attention is given to the actual circumstances of the damage, the greater the chance that this very particular damage was due to a particular behaviour of the defendant.

3. One understands that such a radical and broad formulation of the theory of the equivalence of causes must normally lead toward a very liberal (plaintiff-friendly) application of liability rules. From judging published case law, however, it appears that, although lip service is consistently paid to the theory of equivalence of conditions, its application does not really lead to unacceptable results. The Cour de Cassation systematically rejects any reference to all heretical theories which dare to depart from the orthodox equivalence theory such as the theory of the immediate or direct cause (no distinction is made between the immediate and remote cause), the theory that the damage must be the *necessary* consequence (not to be confused with the statement that the fault must be the necessary condition for the damage, which is a somewhat confusing description of the conditio sine qua non-test) or the *normal* consequence of the fault (according to which atypical consequences of the fault would not have to be compensated by the tortfeasor), the theory of the *adequate* cause, or the theory of the *foreseeability of the harm.* Yet somehow the judge will manage to reintroduce most of the limits or limitations which are sought after by these theories, but mostly via other ways than by openly declaring a departure from the official causation theory. Some of these judgements departing from a strict application of the equivalence theory, were submitted to the control of the Cour de Cassation and were upheld on the basis of a favourable interpretation of these judgements.[8] No clear or coherent guiding principles can be deducted from this case law.[9]

4. To our knowledge there are no illustrations of the potentially extreme applications to which a straightforward application of the equivalence theory may lead. This may be due either to the fact that plaintiffs apparently neglect to actually seek compensation from remote tortfeasors or to the fact that in a small country like Belgium there is simply not enough published case law containing many illustrations. Therefore the answer to many a question raised by the hypotheticals does require some speculation as to how courts might actually decide. To establish the causal relation in a particular case, the judge reconstructs the story of events assuming that no fault has been committed. The formulation of this hypothetical legitimate alternative for the actual events is a matter of fact, over which the Cour de Cassa-

---

6 Cass. 11 June 1956, [1956] *Pasicrisie* I, 1094.

7 M. E. Storme, 'Quelques aspects de la causalité en droit des obligations et des assurances', [1990] *Bulletin des Assurances* (Bull. Ass.), 445, with reference to L. Trager, *Der Kausalbegriff im Straf- und Zivilrecht* (Marburg 1904) p. 125; *compare* also M. van Quickenborne, *De oorzakelijkheid in het recht van de burgerlijke aansprakelijkheid* (1972) nr. 12, pp. 13–14.

8 Some examples are given by M. Adams, [1997] TPR, 1378–1379.

9 H. Bocken (supra note 3) pp. 84–85.

tion, judging only the compliance of the judgment with the law and the presence of a motivation for the decision, has no control. Therefore it is not easy and even misleading to draw general principles from the caselaw on causational issues. If such principles can be deducted at all, some of them show a certain incoherence in the law of torts.

5. H. Bocken detects a first flow of caselaw departing from a strict application of the theory of equivalence of causes in cases where a third party's fault can be regarded as an intervening event, in particular in a case where a traffic accident would not have occurred without a foreseeable obstacle on the road caused by another wrongfull action.[10] The Cour de Cassation stated that it does not necessarily follow from the fact that the traffic accident would not have occurred without the unlawfull situation caused by negligence, that this initial negligence actually caused the accident.[11] The Cour de Cassation reached this conclusion in a case concerning a volunteer who wanted to help a victim of a traffic accident caused by the negligence of this victim. In the course of rescuing the victim, the volunteer was hit by a third car and died shortly afterwards.[12] The decision of the appellate judge, upheld in cassation, held that the original tortfeasor could not be held responsable for the death of the volunteer because he could not have foreseen or avoided the second accident. According to the Cour de Cassation, the fact that other drivers could pass the visible and avoidable obstacle caused by the first accident without any problem and the fact that the driver who hit the volunteer was driving too fast, could legitimately lead the appellate judge to decide that no link exists between the cause of this obstacle and the second accident.[13] The Cour de Cassation recently confirmed these judgements.[14] It is important to remember that in other comparable situations the Cour de Cassation found in favour of the liability of a first party who caused an unlawful situation, which was the necessary cause of a second accident caused by a third party.[15] In cases like these, it is very difficult to draw abstract rules to predict their judicial outcome.[16]

6. There is a second flow of divergent case law, i.e. a number of decisions which take into consideration the protective purpose of the violated rule. Such occurred in cases where it seems reasonable to compensate some victims of traffic accidents who committed a fault with regard to the accident itself (e.g. the passenger of a motorbiker who has not yet reached the legally required age to conduct a passenger on a motorbike). A passenger who, knowingly, rides along with a drunk driver. is normally held responsible to a certain degree for his own damage caused by the accident which results from the driver's intoxication. Surpris-

---

10 H. Bocken (supra note 3)pp. 104–106. *See* also B. de Temmerman, [1998] *Recente Arresten van het Hof van Cassatie*, 174–183.

11 Cass. 6 September 1988, [1988–89] *Arresten van het Hof van Cassatie*, 12.

12 Cass. 26 June 1990, [1990] *Arresten van het Hof van Cassatie*, 1382, H. Bocken (supra note 3)pp. 104–1046, nrs. 40–43.

13 For more comments on the causality problems in similar cases concerning damage to volunteers, *see* case 7.

14 Cass. 5 November 1996, [1996] *Arresten van het Hof van Cassatie*, 993; Cass. 5 November 1996,[1996]*Arresten van het Hof van Cassatie*, 997.

15 Cass. 18 February 1981, [1980–81] *Arresten van het Hof van Cassatie*, 698.

16 With regard to situations in which next to the negligence of other parties, the victim himself committed a fault resulting in his own damage, *see* the answer to case 7 (careless volunteer) and to case 8 (voluntary placing an organ at disposal for transplant, suicide).

ingly, some courts decide otherwise if the accident was not at all related to this intoxication (Cass. 16 September 1986, *Verkeersrecht* 1987, 44).[17]

7. A third divergence, or at least lack of clarity, in Belgian case law on causation concerns the acceptance by the Cour de Cassation of the theory that the causal relation is interrupted by the fulfilment of a statutory or contractual obligation by the victim. The case law developments with respect to this issue have not gone unnoticed. In its wellknown 'Walter Kay' decision the Cour de Cassation had (initially) decided that while making costs to fulfill a statutory duty (to salvage a ship which had sunk in the harbor), the city of Antwerp did not suffer damages in any causal relationship with the faulty behaviour of a third person who had caused the sinking of the ship.[18] The statutory (and according to later decisions, also the contractual) duty to salvage or repair damage does constitute a specific legal cause which in itself justifies the obligation to bear the costs of it. In a later decision the Court would confirm its heavily criticised Walter Kay decision, while at the same time introducing an important exception to its earlier holding, stating, that there is no interruption of causation when the statutory (or contractual) obligation is *secondary* to the tortfeasor's primary obligation to repair. While it is not at all clear how to distinguish between the primacy of one obligation to repair over the other one, in some cases statutory provisions in specific cases remove all doubt as to the right of recovery of the public authorities against the tortfeasor. Where no such statutory clarifications exist, the matter remains ambiguous and vague.

8. We can conclude that it is agreed upon, and taught, that the Cour de Cassation and the majority of the lower courts do adhere to the theory of equivalence of causes. Daily law practice however shows the limited role played by this theory. Few judges explicitly swear allegiance to it. Some judges even openly depart from it.[19]
The unpredictability of our case law and the relativity of our answers to the following cases should thus again be emphasized.

Question 4

(a) To assess causation, damage must be taken into account as it presented itself in concreto, in the actual situation and on the actual point in time (see general comments, tir. 2), in casu: the horse dies in the flames or by suffocation. Assuming this damage would also have occurred without X's fault, no causal relation can be established between X's fault and the damage.

(b) If it can be proven that the threshold would not have been crossed without A's negligence, causation between this negligence and the damage is sufficiently established. Indeed, to be qualified as a cause, an event must fulfill the only requirement of being a 'conditio sine qua non' for the ensuing damage. The event does not have to be a sufficient cause. With

17 H. Bocken (supra note 3) pp. 99–102.

18 Cass. 28 April 1978, [1978] *Arresten van het Hof van Cassatie*, 1004.

19 H. Vandenberghe/M. van Qickenborne/L. Wynant, 'Overzicht van rechtspraak aansprakelijkheid uit onrechtmatige daad (1985–1993)', [1995] TPR, 1452–1453. M. Adams quotes a few judgements in which adequacy is taken into account in establishing the scope of causation, *see* M. Adams, [1997] TPR, 1374–1375.

regard to damage caused by the extraction of ground water by several operators, the determining factor is the knowledge whether other possible causes than the extraction by the defendant were sufficient to cause the damage. This requires an examination of the part of each of the relevant causal elements. In the case where damage only occurs after a certain threshold is crossed, it is necessary to establish the chronology and the relative contribution of each of the relevant extractions.[20]

When several (simultaneous or subsequent) negligent actions or omissions cause the damage to its full extent, every liable person or entity will be held to be accountable by the victim for the compensation of the total amount of the damage incurred. With regard to the victim's claim, none of these negligent actions or omissions interrupt their causal relationship with the damage.[21] The ultimate contribution to the total amount of the damage of each of the liable persons or entities, depends upon the weight of each fault in the origin of the damage. The intrinsic severeness of each fault is not taken into account.[22] *I*t goes without saying that this is a very delicate exercise, definitely in the circumstances presented in this case.

(c) In the case of the attorney who did not lodge an appeal in time , the judge will replace the omission by the hypothesis in which the attorney had not been negligent. It will always remain uncertain whether or not the case would have been won in appeal. A causal relation, however, can be established between the negligent omission by the attorney and the loss of the opportunity of successful legal proceedings before an appeal court.[23] More information on the assessment of the value of the loss of a chance or opportunity is given in the answer to question 16.

(d) I Animals swept overboard in a storm.
The carrier was negligent by not keeping the animals on deck in pens because they violated a statute that required them to do so. The violation of the statute in itself implies fault. The main issue is whether the damage would also have occurred without the carrier's fault. Let us assume this would not be the case, as a consequence of which the causal link is established. The fact that the special aim of the violated rule, the prevention of diseases, was not at stake, does not – according to a strict application of the theory of equivalence – result in the interruption of causality. To assess liability, it is not required that the violated rule aims to protect the category of persons to which the victim belongs.[24] As pointed out here above, the Cour de Cassation has indeed in certain cases applied 'de normbestemmingsleer' by

20 H. Bocken, 'Het proces zonder einde: aansprakelijkheid voor schade veroorzaakt door grondwater-winning en bronbemaling', [1995] TPR, 1644–1645.

21 W. van Gerven, *Verbintenissenrecht Boekdeel 2: Verbintenissen uit de Wet* (Leuven, Acco, 1997-98) pp. 323–324.

22 J. L. Fagnart, 'La responsabilité civile. Chronique de jurisprudence 1985–1995', [1997] *Les dossiers du Journal Tribunaux* (J. T.), 36–37.

23 Applications in case law: Gent 26 February 1981, [1982–83] *Rechtskundig Weekblad* (R.W.), 439; Gent 17 March 1983, [1984] Revue Générale des Assurances et des Responsabilités, nr. 10774, E.C. *See* also the point of view of the Cour de Cassation that the victim is not entitled to compensatory interest if the victim was negligent in pursuing his legal demand for compensation (B. de Temmerman, [1998] *Recente Arresten van het Hof van Cassatie*, 174–183 in fine).

24 W. van Gerven (supra note 21) p. 268.

taking the aim of the violated rule into account (see general comments, nr. 6). Although applied in totally different circumstances, this dissident caselaw might influence the judicial outcome of this case.

2 Animals drowned because the ship sunk in the storm.
Only the storm, circumstance beyond the carrier's control, can be upheld as a cause of the damage. It is clear that the damage would have occurred anyway, even if the carrier would not have committed a fault. The carrier will not be held liable.

Part II Cases

Single event occurrences

1. In this case there is no causality problem. D is liable for the total damage. The exceedingly high value of the damage is irrelevant in assessing the causal relationship.

2. It is generally accepted that the predisposition of the victim does not interrupt the causal connection between the wrongful act and the damage.[25] The predisposition does however have an important impact on the estimation of the damage. The main principle is that the tortfeasor must compensate all the damage inflicted on the victim in his present condition. 'The wrongdoer must take the victim as he finds him'.[26] Authoratative doctrinal writings distinguish three situations:[27]

1. the poor condition of the victim already existed before the wrongful act was committed. e.g. A one-handed person had a disability of 30 per cent. If he loses his other hand in a separate accident, the person liable for this accident must compensate for the complementary 70 per cent.
2. before the wrongful act only a predisposition exists.
The victim should be fully compensated if the predisposition did not impede him prior to the accident.
3. before the wrongful act the bad condition was evolving.
In estimating the damage, it will be taken into account that the victim e.a. already had a decreased life expectancy.

The principle that the tortfeasor must carry the consequences of the predisposition of the victim, is often disregarded with regard to the assessment of psychological damage.[28]

3. Despite the control of the Cour de Cassation on the consequent application of the theory of the equivalence of causes, the lower courts have a considerable margin in appreciating the facts. This explains the divergent judgements in typical situations in which a consequent

25 Cass. 13 October 1981, [1982] *Pasicrisie* I, 223.
26 Cass. 21 June 1984, [1984] *Pasicrisie* I, 1283.
27 W. van Gerven (supra note 21) p.320.
28 H. Vandenberghe/M. van Quickenborne/L. Wynant, 'Overzicht van rechtspraak aansprakelijkheid uit onrechtmatige daad (1985–1993)', [1995] TPR, 1488–1490. Some lower courts awarded compensation for psychological damage: H. Vandenberghe/M. van Quickenborne, 'Overzicht van rechtspraak aansprakelijkheid uit onrechtmatige daad (1979–1984), [1987] TPR, 1550–1551.

application of the equivalence theory should lead to liability. This is certainly so for the facts presented in this case.[29] According to ADAMS, in the majority of these so-called 'carkey-cases' it was accepted that the causal relation will be interrupted by the theft and the thief's fault which directly caused the accident. At times the car owner will not be held liable in the light of the fact that the damage is not necessarily the result of his negligence or even that this negligence was not a necessary cause for the damage. In other judgements the causal link between the car owner's negligence and the damage is denied by reason of the independency of the thief's fault or the fact that this fault was the only efficient cause of the damage.[30]

4. See H. Cousy and A. Vanderspikken, 'The Belgian Report (part 1)', in J. Spier (ed.), *The Limits of Expanding Liability*, (The Hague, London, Boston, Kluwer Law International, 1998) pp. 85–86.

5. We reiterate the principles set out in the answer to question 4d. The fact that the special aim of the violated rule was not at stake, does not result in the interruption of causality.

To assess liability, it is not required that the violated rule aims to protect the category of persons to which the victim belongs.

In this case, the defendant violated the rule of article 1382 of the Civil Code because he negligently put rat poison on a shelf full of food. The principle reiterated above, means that to establish the liability of the defendant, it is irrelevant that the harm to the victim was caused by the heat of a stove (of which the defendant should not have any knowledge) and not by the victim consuming the poison. (See also general comment, nr. 6)

We are not happy with the result of the strict application of this principle and speculate that a judge might come to an opposite result on the basis of an other legal reasoning.

As was mentioned above (general comments, nr. 3), the foreseeability of the harm does not have any effect on the issue of causality. The reasonable foreseeability of the harm is however a necessary condition to establish a fault. Thereto, it is sufficient that the harm was foreseeable in the actual circumstances, even if the defendant could not foresee who would actually incur damage. We are inclined to state that in this case, a judge might dismiss the plaintiff's claim on the basis that the defendant did not commit a fault.

6. We would consider this rather as a question of evaluation of damages than as an issue of causation. The judge must decide on the assessment of full compensation. This case raises the issue of the qualification for compensation of utilities companies whose equipment was negligently damaged but repaired by its own employees[31] Even if the company hired these employees for the purpose of repairing damaged equipment – regardless of the cause of damage – the Cour de Cassation holds the tortfeasor liable for all the repair costs, including the employees' wages. Lower courts have reached the same result with regard to the right of these companies if they made use of their spare equipment to recover the damage (deprivation of the damaged bus) from the tortfeasor.

---

29 H. Bocken (supra note 3) p. 92, no. 20. For an overview of the divergent caselaw on this subject, *see* H. Vandenberghe/M. van Quickenborne/L. Wynant, 'Overzicht van rechtspraak aansprakelijkheid uit onrechtmatige daad (1985–1993)', [1995] TPR, 1494–1495.

30 M. Adams, [1997] TPR, 1375–1376.

31 H. Vandenberghe/M. van Quickenborne/L. Wynant, [1995] TPR, 1512–1514.

7. According to the equivalence theory, C will succeed in his lawsuit against A. There is however caselaw (see also general comments, nr. 5) departing from this theory with regard to accidents in which foreseeable obstacles are involved, obstacles caused through negligence (also referred to as an unlawful situation). The judge can consider the unlawful situation as an 'interruption' after which a new story of events develops. He can extract elements from the previous series of events, but he is not obliged to do so. Belgian caselaw diverges on this subject and H. Bocken suggests that it should be possible to classify the different opinions in a more logical way. He refers to the opinion of Van Quickenborne concerning the consequences of the action of a third party following a previous fault of another party with regard to this party's liability. According to Van Quickenborne the action of a third party will not interrupt the causal relation between the first fault and the damage resulting from the act of the third party if this act resulted from the initial fault. If, however, this act can be regarded as totally independent from the first situation, an interruption of the causal relationship can be justified. On the other hand, if someone created a situation so that he can reasonably assume that third parties, through their negligence, would respond to that situation in a way that might harm others, the causal relation will be maintained.[32] The same principle was applied with regard to unprofessional volunteers, who because of their incompetence, sometimes become the victim of a second accident.[33] The person liable for the initial accident will in principle also be held liable for the volunteer's damage. This liability can be reduced by taking the volunteer's fault into account.[34] In the case of an obviously unnecessary action by the volunteer, it was judged that the volunteer has no claim at all for his own damage.[35] According, to the Cour de Cassation, the Court of Appeal could lawfully conclude that there was no causal link between the fault of the 'victim' with regard to the first accident and the injuries of the volunteer who came to his rescue, by assessing that the volunteer violated the traffic code, a violation which he or she easily could have avoided.[36]

8. This case illustrates the problem of the construction of a legitimate alternative (see general comments, nr. 4). It is generally accepted that the judge can (not more than necessarily required) replace the events of the accident by another hypothesis. It seems inaccurate therefore to reason that P would also have given his kidney for transplant one day, notwithstanding D's fault.

In addition, it is generally accepted that the help of a third party cannot reduce the duty of a tortfeasor to compensate the damage. Following this reasoning, P will bring a successful law suit against D.

The application of another principle of Belgian tort law leads to the same conclusion, i.e. the duty of the tortfeasor to compensate the costs incurred by the victim to take all reasonable measures in order to reduce his damage.[37] A would not have survived without the

---

32 H. Bocken (supra note 3) pp.104–106, nos. 40–43.

33 H. Vandenberghe/M. Quickenborne/L. Wynant, [1995] TPR, 1494–1495.

34 Brussel 18 October 1988, [1989] *Verkeersrecht*, 148.

35 Brussel 6 March 1986, [1987] *Revue Générale des Assurances et des Responsabilités* (R. G. A. R.), nr. 11259.

36 Cass. 10 May 1994, [1993–94] *Arresten van het Hof van Cassatie*, 466; B. de Temmerman, [1998] *Recente Arresten van het Hof van Cassatie*, 174–183.

37 Cass. 14 May 1992, [1991–92] *Arresten van het Hof van Cassatie*, 855.

kidney transplant. The costs following the operation will therefore have to be compensated by D.[38]

One could however argue that the damage resulted solely from P's own will. Recently the Cour de Cassation accepted a similar argument in a case of suicide. The Cour de Cassation confirmed the judgement of the Court of Appeal holding that the suicide of the man (who drove the car into the canal) was the occasion but not the cause of death of his beloved (passenger in the same car) because her death was the sole result of her own will to die and consequently, the damage as it actually occurred, would also have occurred without the man's fault.[39] In our opinion, this ruling is not transferable to the facts of case nr. 8 because P did not want the sustained pain and discomfort. P only wanted to help A, unlike the woman who wanted her own death.

Intervening events

(a) Natural event occurs independently of the act of any human being,

9 and **10.** The following principles apply to these cases. Only if circumstances beyond anyone's control (coincidence) exclusively cause the damage, no liability will be incurred, not because of lack of causality but because no fault can be attributed to any one person. If however, besides this coincidence, one or more faults can be proven to have contributed to the occurrence of the damage, the element of coincidence cannot interrupt the causal link.[40]

With regard to question 9, a judge would be inclined to hold D liable for the damage to the extent that this was caused by the fire. We would like to point out two differentiations. First of all, further inquiries seem to be necessary to examine whether the damage caused by the earthquake was aggravated because of the poor state of the building, caused by the fire, in which case the plumber could be held liable for the damage caused by the total destruction of the house (see also the answer to question 14 with regard to the legal effect of events taking place after the wrongful act, having an impact on the damage caused by it).

Secondly, according to the Cour de Cassation, the liability for negligently damaging property will not disappear if it appears that the property was predestined to be damaged. This would e.g. be the case if the devastation by the earthquake would not have had the same impact if P had not negligently omitted to repair his house within a reasonable time. In that case however, it is likely that liability will be reduced, because the owner of a ruin or of defective goods must usually answer for part of the damage caused by that faulty state of the property or the goods.[41]

The facts of question 10 differ from those in question 9 to the extent the the house (of question 9) would have been hit by the earthquake anyway. Had the collision not taken place the ship of question 10 however would not have been damaged in that storm. Applying the

38 A Court of Appeal awarded damages for the loss of the husband's wages who took leave without pay to help his wife in running her business. She was temporarily unfit to work because of a traffic accident (Gent 14 May 1982, [1984–85] R.W., 1464).

39 Cass. 14 June 1996, [1996] *Arresten van het Hof van Cassatie*, 59 1; B. de Temmerman, [1998] *Recente Arresten van het Hof van Cassatie*, 174–183.

40 W. van Gerven (supra note 21) p. 327.

41 Cass. 7 January; 1988, [1987–88] *Arresten van het Hof van Cassatie*, 574.

principles mentioned above, the judge will therefore hold D liable to compensate the damage to its full extent.

(b) The event consists of the act or omission of a third party

11. a. Applying the theory evolved by Van Quickenborne (see case 7), it could be argued that the negligence of the drunken driver is a totally independent action from the initial accident, so that D cannot be held liable for the loss of income of the additional two years. A similar outcome was reached in a case where the medical negligence was considered to have interrupted the causal link between the fault of the person liable for the initial accident and the increase of the damage as a result of the medical malpractice.[42] However, in another case the Court of Appeal of Brussel came to the opposite conclusion holding that the initial medical negligence remained a cause for the victim's death even if another doctor would have been negligent afterwards.[43] This last viewpoint is subscribed to by some doctrine[44] and applied to this case would result in the obligation for D to compensate the loss of income over three years, leaving D with a right of recourse against the drunken driver. See also general comments, nr. 5 and case 7.

11. b. According to the reasoning set out in the answer to the cases 9 and 10, D will also be held liable for the loss of income for the additional two years.

12 and **13.** Case nr. 12 would be an example of the liability of someone who creates a situation so that he can reasonably assume that third parties, through their negligence, would respond to that situation in a way that might harm others. Following the theories set out in case nr. 7, D 1 can be held liable. The rule applied for case 12 is equally useful to solve question nr. 13 but it remains to be seen whether the court will be likely to hold D liable for the theft.

(c) The event consists of the act or omission of the plaintiff or is atributable to a cause which can be imputed to him

14. A question that on many occassions led to extensive case law is whether the judge, in assessing the damage and estimation of the compensation, can take into account circumstances and events which took place after the wrongful act was committed. The Cour de Cassation stated that the situation at the moment of the judgement must be taken into account for the estimation of the amount of damages, but the extent of the damage must be decided at the moment of the wrongful act.[45] There is some uncertainty regarding this principle. Presumably guided by the facts in each case, the court sometimes accepts that events occurring after the wrongful act, having nothing to do with this wrongful act but having an impact on the damage caused by it, will be taken into account.[46] Other

---

42 Police Court Namen (Pol. Namen) 14 March 1986, [1986] *Pasicrisie* 111, 59.

43 Brussel 19 June 1990, [1993] R. G. A. R., nr. 12083.

44 H. Vandenberghe/M. van Quickenborne/L. Wynant, 'Overzicht van rechtspraak aansprakelijkheid uit onrechtmatige daad (1985–1993)', [1995] TPR, 1492, nr. 181.

45 Cass. 22 June 1988, [1987–88] *Arresten van het Hof van Cassatie*, 1397.

46 Cass. 15 December 1981, [1981–82] *Arresten van het Hof van Cassatie*, 526.

case law however, states that these events cannot be taken into consideration.[47]

On the basis of the facts of this case a judge would probably assess D's liability only with regard to the damage caused by the accident. The injuries following the heart attack, i.e. an event occurring after the wrongful act, will not be taken into consideration.

15. We refer to the answer given to this question by T. Vansweevelt, 'The Belgian Report (part 1)', in J. Spier (ed.) *The limits of expanding liability* (The Hague, London, Boston, Kluwer Law International, 1998) pp. 85–86. In addition we would like to point out that the facts of this case would rather lead to the acknowledgment of the events taking, place after the wrongful act, having an impact on the damage caused by it.

One should notice that since the afore mentioned publication, the Belgian Legislation on the prescription of claims has been amended. Since the Act of 10 June 1998: 'Toutes les actions personnelles sont prescrites par dix ans. Toute action en réparation d'un dommage fondée sur une responsabilité extracontractuelle se prescrit par cinq ans à partir du jour qui suit celui où la personne lésée a eu connaissance du dommage ou de son aggravation et de l'identité de la personne responsable. (Ces) actions se prescrivent en tout cas par vingt ans à partir du jour qui suit celui où s'est produit le fait qui a provoqué le dommage. Si une décision passée en force de chose jugée sur une action en réparation d'un dommage admet des réserves, la demande tendant à faire statuer sur leur objet sera recevable pendant vingt ans à partir du prononcé.'

The aggravation of the damage is a starting point for a separate prescription period of five years, irrespective of the fact that the initial damage and the liable party were known to the plaintiff more than five years ago and irrespective of the fact that the victim did or did not claim compensation for this initial damage. According to the preliminary works with regard to the amendment of this Legislation, 'aggravation of the damage' requires an unexpected increase of the damage exceeding the reasonably foreseeable evolution of the initial damage. The compliance with this requirement is a necessary condition in order to prevent the dismissal of the claim on grounds of an earlier ruling on the damage caused by the same facts.

16. The Cour de Cassation has accepted the causal connection between the wrongful act of a physician and the loss of chance of recovery/survival (in a case concerning a potential amputation).[48] It is indeed generally accepted in Belgian case law that the loss of an opportunity gives right to compensation provided that the loss of opportunity is certain and that the opportunity was serious and/or realistic.[49]

Although it is not a simple task, an opportunity is economically assessable. Possible parameters thereof are the probability of the opportunity taking actually place and the advantages the victim would have gained had he not lost the chance. Very often the compensation is set on an equitable basis.[50] It is important to stress that on the basis of loss of opportunity,

47 Cass. 22 June 1988, [1987–88] *Arresten van het Hof van Cassatie*, 1397.

48 Cass. 19 January 1984, [1986] R.G.A.R., nr. 11084, with note T. Vansweevelt. In this case the doctor was held to pay 80 % of the damage because chances for recovery were esteemed 80 %.

49 For an extensive study on the liability for the loss of chance in medical practice, *see* T. Vansweevelt, *De civielrechtelijke aansprakelijkheid van de geneesheer en het ziekenhuis* (Antwerpen, Maklu, Brussel, Ced. Samson, Brussel, Bruylant 1992) pp. 370–400.

50 For a survey of case law on this subject, *see* L. Schuermans/A. van Oevelen/C. Persyn/P. Ernst/

the 'absolute' damage does not have to be compensated (e.g. the loss of a leg). Partial compensation is awarded for the loss of a chance to what could have been gained had the chance been realised. The judge should be careful not to apply medical statistics in a general way. Damage must always be assessed in concreto, taking the individual chances of recovery of the individual patient into account.

According to Belgian doctrine, a patient must have at least 50 per cent chances of recovery/survival in order to be awarded some compensation.[51] Doctor A will not be held liable in this case, unless perhaps for the loss of chance of longer survival (again taking into account all restrictions mentioned above).

17. a. To prove liability, it is not sufficient that the plaintiff shows that the faulty behaviour of the tortfeasor has probably caused the damage, not even when this probability is very high. The link must be legally certain, although it suffices that the damage has to be likely to such an extent that the judge can not seriously consider the unlikelihood of the damage although it remains theoretically possible that the expected damage may never actualize.[52] For example 'future damage' can be compensated if it is the normal result, development, consequence, completion or recurrence of an actual and certain situation. T. Vansweevelt addresses the question which rate of probability of causality has to exist between a fault and the damage in a way that this fault can be considered, in the normal course of events, as the cause of the damage. With regard to medical liability and after having stressed that the judge must decide after examination of the facts of each case, Vansweevelt suggests a limit of 80 per cent. In his opinion rates of 70 per cent or less give no right to full compensation.[53] He refers to certain caselaw subscribing to his point of view.

17. b. and **c**. Vansweevelt states that the statistical proof of the existence of a certain risk (e.g. the risk of 0.05 per cent of a population to contract a serious disease), is not sufficient to prove that a certain damage was due to an unavoidable risk. As a consequence, on the basis of statistical proof only, no person can be held liable with regard to that damage. A judge must always decide on the facts of each case whether the damage was caused by the negligence of someone or not. This might include an examination of whether someone could have avoided the damage.[54] If the number of people who contracted a disease exceeds the normal statistical rate, this judicial scrutiny will most likely be more severe. M. Faure points out some cases where causality was accepted between the consumption of water contaminated with lead and the contraction of certain diseases. He immediately distinguishes these cases from the ones presented in case nr. 17 because in the ' lead in water cases' other causes of the diseases were practically excluded.[55]

[Note 50 continued]
J. L. Schuermans, 'Overzicht van rechtspraak onrechtmatige daad, schade en schade loosstelling (1983–1992)', [1994] TPR, 981–984.

51 T. Vansweevelt (supra note 49) pp.390–391.

52 Bergen 14 November 1990, [1992] *Verkeersrecht*, 77; *See* also applications of this principle with regard to medical liability in: T. Vansweevelt (supra note 49) pp. 401–405.

53 T. Vansweevelt (supra note 49) pp. 388–390.

54 T. Vansweevelt (supra note 49) p. 407, no. 554.

55 M. Faure, *(G)een schijn van kans. Beschouwingen over het statistisch causaliteitsbewijs bij milieugezondheidsschade* (Antwerpen, Maklu, 1993) pp. 26–28.

Concurring causes

18. If the damage is caused by separate wrongful acts by different tortfeasors and if each of these wrongful acts was necessary to cause the damage (i.e. none of these acts could separately have caused the damage), every tortfeasor is 'in solidum' accountable by the aggrieved party for the damage as a whole.[56]

If however, it can be assumed that D1 and D2 collaborated 'knowingly' to conduct their wrongful activity, i.e. if they committed a so called 'faute commune', they are jointly and severally liable toward the victim. This joint and several solidarity is based on a general principle of law.

In either case, P can successfully sue D1 for the entire damage, who in turn must try to recover a part of this sum from D2 according to the weight of his liability in the origin of the damage.

19. In principle, a claim must be declined if the damage is caused by an unidentified member of a well-defined group.[57] Under some circumstances, however, the victim will nevertheless be compensated for his damages if the circumstances of the accident were such that every member of the group participated in the negligent activity, which in turn caused the action that directly resulted in the damage[58] For example, four boys were playing a dangerous game (throwing rocks at each other). Another boy, who did not participate in this game, was hurt and was allowed compensation.[59] Because the hunters all participated (in concert) in the negligent activity, all of them are jointly and severally liable for the damage resulting from their joint action. 'Even a group member who successfully proves that it was not his act which caused the damage, will not be relieved of liability, since it is not the causal relationship between each individual fault and the damage, which is evaluated, but the one between the collective fault and the damage. The plaintiff must prove this causation, but once it is established, a defendant can only be relieved by demonstrating that he was not part of the group. In fact the fault-notion is shifted to an earlier point in time, the point where one takes part in the joint action. This collectivization of the fault by which a whole group is held liable for the act committed by one of its members, is only acceptable if the risk of causing damage was such that it should have restrained the participants of their joint action.'[60]

20. The facts of this case present a special feature, i.e. both A and B commit a wrongful act without acting in concert. Different from the facts of case 18 however, each fault would have been sufficient to cause the damage to its full extent. The strict appliance of the equivalence theory would lead to the paradoxical result that A as well as B could argue that without their fault the damage would have occurred anyway and therefore they would not be held liable. In this case however, a judge will presumably state that the fault of the other party will not impede the other party's liability and will hold both parties liable 'in solidum'. In a similar

56 Cass. 2 April 1936, [1936] *Pasicrisie*, I, 209.

57 Cass. 24 March 1981, [1981–82] R.W., 1980.

58 H. Vandenberghe/M. van Quickenborne, [1987] TPR, 1536–1537, no. 175; J. Geers, [1994] ERPL, 445–446, nos. 5–6.

59 Rb. Turnhout 11 February 1980, [1980] *Pasicrisie*, III, 40.

60 J. Geers, [1994] ERPL, 446.

case the Cour de Cassation upheld a ruling that all tortfeasors are liable if each of them could have caused the damage on his own.[61]

The facts of this case are similar to those presented in question 4a. The reasoning applied to 4a is however not transferable to this case because both the fault and the damage 'in concreto' are the same for A and B in the 'poisonous waste' case.

21. The theory applied in case 19 is not relevant for this case because it is unlikely that the Belgian courts would accept 'concert of action' between the drug manufacturers. Belgian Legislation contains no specific rule of 'alternative liability' similar to Article 99 of Book 6 of the Dutch NBW. Very often this confronts victims of multiple tortfeasors with a 'deadlock', i.e. their claim for compensation against an unidentified tortfeasor will be dismissed. 'If the DES-case or any similar case in which victims of an unidentified drug manufacturer seek for compensation, should be taken to court in Belgium, under the present state of Belgian law, the plaintiffs would be unsuccessful. Even if they could base their claim upon the Product Liability Act, the chance that this would bring them any relief is very minimal. Since the European Product Liability Directive does not define the concept of causation, in Belgium the causal relationship in product liability cases will be evaluated according to the equivalence theory and the claims against unidentified producers will be dismissed'.[62]

Another issue in this case concerns the acceptance of class actions. Apart from certain legal provisions allowing consumer organisations to bring certain legal actions on behalf of their members, no class actions or collective actions are admitted by the Belgian courts.

22. A driver lost control of his motorbike and hit the crash barriers of the highway. Both the driver and his passenger died in that accident. The claim of the heirs of the passenger was denied because it was impossible to determine who, at the moment of the accident, actually drove the motorbike.[63] Following a similar reasoning, D will not be held liable.

23. If damages can be attributed to a defective property (a bad tree) and to a severe storm, the person responsible for that property is liable for the total damage. The occurrence of the natural event will not have any effect on the amount of damages due by that person.[64] The case presented under nr. 23 is similar to the situation described above: the negligence of the captain of ship A and the storm coincide. The captain is liable for the total damage.

Miscellaneum

24. This case reminds us of the horrific traffic accident on 27 February 1996 in Deinze (Belgium). As in this case, liabilities seemed impossible to assess. Because of the severe damage incurred by a large number of people in that accident, the insurers made an agree-

61 Cass. 8 December 1983, [1983–84] *Arresten van het Hof van Cassatie*, 419.

62 J. Geers, [1994] ERPL, 51. This author refers to two rather old judgements where claims of victims of multiple tortfeasors were met. In these cases the number of tortfeasors was very limited and there were reasonable presumptions, pointing at one of them as the responsable party (J. Geers, [1994] ERPL, 448–449). According to R. Q. Dalcq no similar case to the DES-case exists in Belgian case law (R. Q. Dalcq, 'Problèmes actuels en matière de causalité', [1996] R.G.A.R., nr. 12656/6).

63 Antwerpen 1 March 1987, [1987] *Verkeersrecht*, 307.

64 Rb. Charleroi 24 February 1992, [1993] *Revue Régionale de Droit*, 20.

ment to split up the total amount of the damages to be paid, according to each company's share of insured vehicles involved in the accident, so that the victims could be fully compensated for damage to their person and 50 per cent of the damage to their goods. On the basis of this agreement the insurers made a gentlemen's agreement aimed at a quick compensation of the victims, pending the decision on the division of liabilities. It is clear that Dl is liable for the damage to the car in front. With regard to the other cars it can be argued that some of them could avoid the obstacle that was negligently created by D1 so that the judge can legitimately decide that D1 is not liable (or only partially liable) for the damage caused by the other drivers whose negligence can be proven. If it is not possible at all to allocate blame to any of the other drivers, it is our opinion that the court will strictly apply the equivalence theory so that D1 is liable. This outcome is even more likely if D1 is insured.

England

Causation under English Law

W. V. Horton Rogers

Part I.

1. Causation as a requirement?

(a) Causation[1] is a requirement of liability for damage[2] in the English common law. I do not see how a system of *tort* law can operate without some linkage between the plaintiff's loss and some act etc of the defendant from whom damages are claimed. In fact even social security systems (except the minimum for the basic necessities of life) require some causal link, though it may not be the same as that of tort law. For example in the New Zealand Accidents Compensation Scheme there must be a 'personal injury by accident' (as defined in the revised scheme). See also the probably apocryphal story of the Frenchman from Metz who unsuccessfully claimed a war pension when he suffered injury from the bursting of a revolver fired by him in 1919 to celebrate the restoration of Alsace to France. Note that I have said 'some act *etc*' of the defendant. It may be an omission,[3] an act of a person for whom he is responsible or, in suitable cases, it may be a question of damage inflicted by the 'agency' of a thing (e.g. an animal or a defective product) for which he is responsible.

(b) In principle causation is a two stage approach because some test of 'causation in fact' is necessary to eliminate the irrelevant. In practice this is not often adverted to because the issue is generally obvious one way or the other.[4] In so far as the matter is rationalized at all the standard test is that of the *causa sine qua non*, more commonly referred to as the 'but for' test. However, most of the discussion has been about multiple sufficient causes, in respect of which the 'but for' test breaks down. Some of these cases we certainly admit (see below) and justify them by saying that there is causation because the defendant made a 'material contribution' to the plaintiff's injury. Since causation goes to *damage* it is possible that the

1 For a magisterial survey *see* Hart and Honoré, *Causation in the Law* (2nd edn., 1985; 2nd ed. reprint 1994).
2 The same is true in the law of contract. Theoretically, of course, all breaches of contract are actionable per se so that a person can sue without proof of damage. More meaningfully, certain torts like libel and assault are actionable per se.
3 Philosophically there may be difficulty in applying the notion of causation to an omission. But intutively we do ascribe causation when there is a duty to act and the law does likewise.
4 But there may be evidential problems. These are at the root of the 'lost chance' cases (*see* below).

J. Spier (ed.), Unification of Tort Law: Causation, 39–51.

requirement might be satisfied as to one claimed item of loss but not as to another. In the hypotheticals below causation in fact is satisfied unless the contrary is stated.

2. Causation in fact merely eliminates the logically irrelevant. It leaves in many causes which no legal system can accept as effective or adequate. If I cause an accident in 1997 the marriage of my parents in 1943 is in this sense a cause of the accident because without it I would not have been here today to be the immediate cause of it. The distinction between cause in fact and legally effective (or imputable) cause is put in the following way by an Australian judge:[5] 'If a defendant promises to direct me where I should go and, at a cross-roads, directs me to the left road rather than the right road, what happens to me on the left road is, in a sense, the result of what the defendant has done. If I slip on that road, if it collapses under me, or if, because I am there, a car driving down that road and not down the right road strikes me, my loss is, in a sense, the result of the fact that I have been directed to the left road and not the right road. But, in my opinion, it is not everything which is a result in this broad sense which is accepted as a result for this purpose in the law. Thus, if, being on the left road, I slip and fall, the fact alone that it was the defendant's direction . . . which put me there will not, without more, make the defendant liable for my broken leg. I say 'without more': if there be added to the breach the fact that, for example, the left road was known to be dangerous in that respect he may, of course, be liable. But, in relation to losses of that kind, the fact that the breach has initiated one train of events rather than another is not, or at least may not, be sufficient in itself'.[6] It does not matter too much whether you call the next stage 'remoteness' or 'legal cause' or 'proximate cause.' But it is important to remember that although the leading test of remoteness is foreseeability it is not the sole solvent of all stage 2 issues.[7] Where, for example there are intervening acts or events courts still talk in 'causal' language, using metaphors like breaking the chain of causation. Despite the tendency to use mechanical metaphors, such issues are essentially ones of fairness and legal policy and are decided intuitively rather than scientifically. Most of the phrases or concepts found in 2 of the questionnaire could be found in English cases[8] It is debatable whether the last item,

---

5 J. A. Mahoney in *Alexander v Cambridge Credit Corp. Ltd.* [1987] 9 *New South Wales Law Reports* (NSWLR) 310 at 333.

6 On this basis, although an auditor clearly owes a duty of care to the company being audited, he is not liable for losses incurred in continuing to trade even though a proper audit would have brought about a cessation of business: J. A. Mahoney in *Alexander v Cambridge Credit Corp. Ltd.* [1987] 9 NSWLR 310 at 333; *Galoo Ltd v Bright Grahame Murray* [1994] 1 *Weekly Law Reports* (WLR) 1360.

7 There is a tendency in some cases to say that 'legal causation' and remoteness are different issues. *See* e.g. L. J. Staughton in *Wright v Lodge* [1993] 4 *All England Law Reports* (All ER) 299 at 309 and Lord Steyn in *Smith New Court Securities Ltd v Scrimgeour Vickers (Asset Management) Ltd* [1997] Appeal Cases (AC) 254. But in the leading case on remoteness, *The Wagon Mound* [1961] AC 388, the court was concerned with whether the defendants were liable for a harbour fire which (on the evidence) was unforeseeable. The fire was undoubtedly caused in the factual sense by the defendants' dumping oil but the decision that they were not liable because the fire was unforeseeable amounted to a decision that the cause-effect link was not such as to be imputable to them.

8 However, the first, conditio/causa sine qua non is surely relevant only to stage 1. A causa sine qua non is a cause in fact. A causa causans is a legally effective cause for the purposes of liability. Furthermore, despite the American expression 'proximate cause' 'proximity' has become a peculiar term of art in English law.

'protective purpose of the violated rule' (as to which see Part I 4(d) below) is in analytical terms a matter of causation. However, the effect is the same as a second stage rule of causation, to limit the defendant's responsibility.

As to whether the relevant factors are sufficiently clear etc, they do not provide mechanically applicable rules but I do not see how such rules are possible in this context, particularly bearing in mind that different types of conduct may call for different approaches to the limits of responsibility. Lord Wright recognized this in *The Oropesa*:[9]

> 'To break the chain of causation it must be shown that there is something which I will call ultroneous, something unwarrantable, a new cause which disturbs the sequence of events, something which can be described as either unreasonable or extraneous or extrinsic. I doubt whether the law can be stated more precisely than that.'

Lord Hoffmann has pointed out[10] that the meaning of 'cause', like most words, depends on the context in which it is used: if we suppose the theft of a car radio, at the trial of the thief we would unhesitatingly say that his act caused the loss of the radio, but we would not regard the owner's spouse as irrational in saying, by way of complaint, that the owner's negligence in leaving it in the car had caused its loss. Thus it would be surprising if the limits of the responsibility of a fraudster were equivalent to those of the negligent giver of advice and they are not.[11]

3. Specific legislation affecting causation in this area.

I can think of only one example. Under section 187 of the Merchant Shipping Act 1995 (reenacting legislation of 1911), dealing with contributory negligence in collisions at sea, the court is directed to apportion responsibility equally 'if, having regard to all the circumstances of the case, it is not possible to establish different degrees of fault.' However, this is not much of an example because that is probably what a court would do anyway in such a situation under the general Contributory Negligence Act of 1945.[12] The Civil Liability (Contribution) Act 1978 provides a code governing contribution between concurrent tortfeasors, but the Act really leaves the question of *when* defendants are jointly and severally liable to the common law.

4. (a) *The horse*. This seems to me (probably) a case of causation. It is assumed that the acts of X and Y are independent. A logical answer (and perhaps the correct one) is as follows. X

---

9 Lord Wright, *The Oropesa* [1943] *Probate, Divorce and Admiralty Reports* (P) 32 at 39.

10 *Empress Car Co (Abertillerry) Ltd v National Rivers Authority* [1998] 1 All ER 481 (not a tort case).

11 Compare *Smith New Court Securities Ltd. v. Scrimgeour Vickers (Asset Management) Ltd* [1997] AC 254 (fraudster liable for effect of wholly unrelated and unknown matter on value of shares) with *Banque Bruxelles Lambert SA v Eagle Star Insurance Co.* [1997] AC 191 (negligent valuer not liable for consequences of general market fall).

12 Note that while under the Act of 1945 damages are to be reduced having regard to the extent of the plaintiff's contributory negligence, that does not preclude a court finding that while the defendant committed a tort which made some factual contribution to the plaintiff's injury, nevertheless the plaintiff's own blameworthy conduct was the sole effective cause of his injury. The most likely example would be where the defendant had infringed a rule of strict liability and the plaintiff had wilfully disregarded clear safety instructions.

tried to kill the horse and failed (no law of attempted tort).[13] Y did kill the horse, but a much less valuable horse than it would otherwise have been, so he pays very little. Just as it is cheaper to kill a 90 year old than a 30 year old. While this is logical, it is hard on the owner, who a few hours ago had a good horse of which he has certainly been deprived. Contrast the case where X injured P's leg so that it became stiff. Later Y shot P in that leg and it was amputated. Y was liable for shooting off a stiff leg, not a good one. But X's liability extended to cover the difference between a good leg and a stiff leg in the period after the amputation – in other words there was no compensation gap.[14] The rationale was that what Y did did not expunge the effect of what X did, it merely made it worse. I find it difficult to apply this here (even assuming the case to be correct, for it is hard to reconcile with another case about a supervening disease, see below) because the court said that if Y had shot P dead the position would have been different. The court below had held that the loss for which X was liable was terminated by the shooting but one judge suggested that Y would have been liable for depriving P of his full claim against X. Can this be applied here? In any event, how is it to be explained? The act of X is completely unknown to Y and to hold Y liable would be an extension of the thin skull rule, since the damage complained of is not personal injury.[15]

One might (though I doubt it) approach the case differently, via the law of damages – despite a natural anthropomorphism, we are talking about damage to property, not personal injury. Let us assume that there is no effective antidote to the poison, so that the horse is reduced in value from £X to £0. That reduction in value is the prima facie measure of damages for interference with goods and if we were to regard that loss as having crystallized at the moment of the poisoning, subsequent events are irrelevant.[16] Nevertheless, while this may be the law, it does not explain why by this route we can ignore a subsequent independent event which, as we now know, would have had an equally damaging effect. It is true that the measure of damages for the destruction of a thing (which is effectively what X has done here) is generally its value, but 'value' is essentially a shorthand for the ability economically to exploit the thing, by sale or by use. Thus the value of a cargo ship in an economic slump is much less than during a boom. If D wrecks P's ship and, before the claim comes to trial, the shipping market collapses, are we to ignore this in assessing damages?

---

13 Let us assume that there is no antidote to the poison. If the owner shot the horse to put it out of its misery, would anyone deny that X was liable for its death? But in that case the way in which the horse dies is only a variant of what X intended, death as a result of poisoning.

14 *Baker v Willoughby* [1970] AC 467.

15 However, something like this seems to have been the basis of the county court case of *Singh v Aitken* [1998] *Personal Injury and Quantum Reports* (PIQR) Q637. P was injured in an accident by an uninsured driver and had a 'cast-iron claim' against the Motor Insurers' Bureau. P was later treated by D and misdiagnosed, so that he died of a heart attack. P's claim against the MIB was then settled for £20.000, though if he had survived it would have been worth £120,000. P's dependants recovered 75 per cent of the difference against D (the reason for the percentage recovery is that a dependency claim under the Fatal Accidents Act is inevitably smaller than the claim which could have been brought by the deceased, had he survived).

16 *See* e.g. *The Glenfinlas* [1918] P 363 n. and *The London Corporation* [1935] P 70. The point is perhaps more obvious in the tort of deceit. If B buys a horse for ten times its true worth as a result of a fraudulent representation that it is a winner and then it contracts a disease and dies, it seems that is no bar to his recovering from S the difference between what he paid and the true value at the time of the sale: *Twycross v Grant* [1877] 2 *Common Pleas Division* (CPD) 469 at 545.

(b) *Asbestosis*. If A, B and C acted concurrently there is no doubt that each is liable for the full damage, subject to rights of contribution. So also A would be liable in full if his acts combined with those of some contemporaneous 'innocent agent' (such as naturally occurring dust[17] – the defendant need only be *a* cause, not *the* cause. If the injury were truly progressive, like deafness (i.e. it begins with A and is increased by further exposure) and A, B and C act in sequence it is clear that each is liable only for the harm he did.[18] But I doubt if this case is like that. It has been held in England that the development of (currently) non-malignant pleural plaques from exposure to asbestos amounts to damage and presumably some physiological change has been brought about by A's acts. If the problem had been discovered when X left A's employment it seems therefore that A would be liable for damage arising from X's inability to work in the industry. If it is not discovered, A has weakened X, so why should not A be liable for the subsequent onset of disease? There may be some analogy in *Clarkson v Modern Foundries*.[19] P was employed by D and exposed to dust, in breach of duty, over a period of 11 years and developed pneumoconiosis. However, P did not issue a writ until four years after the end of the employment, so that as the law then stood he could only sue in respect of damage incurred during the last two years of the employment. It was held that the disease was indivisible, that the exposure in the last two years had made a material contribution to the disease and, D being unable to prove that any quantifiable part of the harm was caused by the previous nine years' exposure, P could recover in full. This would seem to indicate that if there is no limitation issue,[20] there are two successive employers and it is probable that each made an unquantifiable material contribution, each would be liable on a joint and several basis. Our case illustrates the difficulty of applying the core idea, that of 'the same damage', which underlies joint and several liability. It should be noted that as industrial employers B and C are required to carry liability insurance and in certain circumstances their liquidated companies may be restored to the register for the purposes of the Third Parties (Rights Against Insurers) Act 1930.

(c) *Attorney's negligence*. This is a case of the problem of *proof* of causation. The rule against recovery for loss of a chance[21] does not apply in this type of case, where the occurrence of the loss is dependent upon the action or decision of a third party.[22] Provided there was a realistic chance of success, damages for loss of it are awarded, suitably discounted. Note, however, that this is failure to lodge an appeal, rather than failure to pursue a claim. If the appeal is on an issue of law the court might consider it could determine the hypothetical question definitively.

(d) *The animals lost at sea*. On the main hypothesis this is *Gorris v Scott*[23] the classic illus-

17 *Bonnington Castings v Wardlaw* [1956] AC 613.
18 *Thompson v Smith's Shiprepairers* [1984] *Queens Bench Reports* (QB) 405.
19 *Clarkson v Modern Foundries* [1957] 1 WLR 1210.
20 As, generally, there would now not be, since the present law is based upon a 'discoverability' starting point.
21 *Hotson v E Berks HA* [1987] AC 750. *See* Part II, 16 below.
22 *Allied Maples v Simmins & Simmons* [1995] 1 WLR 602 (defect in lease; loss of opportunity to bargain with head landlord over this).
23 *Gorris v Scott* [1874] *Last Reports* (LR) 9 *Exchequer* (Exch) 125.

tration of the proposition that a claim for breach of statutory duty is confined to damage falling within the risk against which the statute was designed to protect. Of course, that does not preclude a claim based on the theory that it is negligence at common law to carry the animals as deck cargo. But even in that event, if the ship sinks in the storm the negligence would not be causative – the animals would have been lost, penned below or not.

A similar principle has been applied in the context of the tort of negligence in a case which indicates that it is closely connected with causation . In *Banque Bruxelles Lambert SA v Eagle Star Insurance Co*[24] D valued a commercial property for the purpose of a secured loan by P. The valuation was substantially too high, so that P had inadequate security for the loan. However, after the loan was made there was a general fall in property values which substantially increased the inadequacy of the security. The House of Lords, reversing the Court of Appeal, held that D was liable only for the difference between his valuation and the true value at the time of that transaction and the further loss attributable to the market movement had to be carried by P. Similarly, to take an example given by Lord Hoffmann, a doctor who negligently advises a mountaineer, who consults him about his knee, that he may safely undertake an expedition, may be liable for an injury suffered by the mountaineer which is attributable to the problem with his knee, but not for an injury caused by a general risk of mountaineering (say, an avalanche) on which the condition of the knee has no bearing. In both situations the further loss is caused in the purely factual sense by the bad advice (the lender would not have lent or would have required other security and the mountaineer would have stayed at home); in both situations the further loss is foreseeable (market movements are obviously so and avalanches are at least not unlikely); but it is felt that in neither case does that loss fairly fall within the scope of the duty undertaken by the defendant. He is liable for the consequences of the information being wrong, not for all the consequences which follow from its giving.[25]

While the *Gorris v Scott* rule looks very much like a matter of the scope of the proper construction of the statute,[26] it seems legitimate to regard the *Banque Bruxelles* approach as as much a matter of causation as 'duty'.

Part II.

Single event occurrences

1. *The hecatomb of attorneys*. All recover their loss in full. It is a matter of quantification of damage, not legal causation, so foreseeability is irrelevant. Causation is concerned with events or items of damage for which the defendant is responsible, not with the valuation of

---

24 *Banque Bruxelles Lambert SA v Eagle Star Insurance Co* [1997] AC 191.

25 In both cases Lord Hoffmann regards the defendant's function as giving information for the purpose of allowing the plaintiff to decide upon a course of action and he contemplates that liability may be more extensive if the defendant is asked for advice on what course of action he should take. But in the doctor example it is difficult to see how the distinction has much meaning.

26 It is comparable, for example, to those cases which have denied liability for breach of safety legislation to visitors to the factory, on the basis that the legislation was passed for the benefit of 'persons employed'.

the plaintiff's claim. Standard examples involve injury to a 'shabby high-income earner' or to a horse which turns out to be the Derby favourite.[27]

2. *The pre-existing weakness.* P recovers in full. D takes him 'as he finds him.' For an illustration see *Smith v Leech Brain & Co.*[28] (cancer developing at site of burn). Of course the rule cuts both ways: the damages of a predisposed person may be less than those of a normal person for the same injury, because his predisposition rendered him vulnerable from some other cause.

3. *The key in the car.* This was treated by the Court of Appeal in *Topp v London Country Bus*[29] as a matter of duty and liability was denied.[30] Except in very unusual circumstances O would not owe P a duty in this matter. However, in *Lamb v Camden LBC*[31] (damage done to house by squatters after it was rendered uninhabitable by D's negligence, liability again denied) the CA treated the case in terms of causation. However one theorises it, there is a reluctance to hold D liable for the wilfully wrong acts of third parties. Note that if O is not liable the Motor Insurers Bureau pays the damages even though T is not insured.

4. *The cable case.* A full account of this has been given elsewhere.[32] It is not a 'causation' issue. The claims of P2 and P3 are economic loss and inadmissible. P1 recovers for damage to the machine and consequential economic loss.

5. *The rat poison.* This resembles *Larrrimore v American National Insurance*[33] though the claim there was based on breach of a statute and the point was essentially that in Part I 4(d). If a claim is based upon negligence *and if the explosion is not reasonably foreseeable to a person in D's position* I would say the damage was too remote. The accident which occurs is of an entirely different nature[34] from that which could be foreseen. To put it another way, it is not within the risk created by D.

6. *The damaged bus.* P is entitled to damages for loss of use of the bus. Where this does not

---

27 *The Arpad* [1934] P 189 at 202. However, the line between such cases of 'intrinsic' value and cases where thre loss is regarded as a 'consequential event' to which the principles of causation and remoteness are relevant, may be difficult to draw: *see* H. McGregor, *McGregor on Damages* (16th edn.) p. 132. Similarly, judges may disagree about the boundary line between causation and mitigation. In *The Sivand* [1998] 2 *Lloyd's Reports* (Lloyd's Rep) 97 D's tanker damaged P's harbour works and concealed difficulties in the sea-bed disrupted the repair contractors' work and led to their receiving an extra payment under their contract. Although the whole court held that D was liable for this extra cost incurred by P, there was some disagreement as to whether any causation issue was involved.

28 *Smith v Leech Brain & Co* [1962] 2 QB 405.

29 *Topp v London Country Bus* [1993] 1 WLR 976.

30 Though it has to be said that the case involves a rather 'partial' reading of *Smith v Littlewoods* [1987] AC 241.

31 *Lamb v Camden LBC* [1981] QB 625.

32 *See* The British Report in: J. Spier (ed.), *The Limits of Expanding Liability* (1998) p. 95.

33 *Larrrimore v American National Insurance* 89 *Pacific Reporter* 2d 340 (Okl 1939).

34 Not merely different in detail. Compare *Hughes v Lord Advocate* [1963] AC 837 (no practical difference between burns from paraffin lamp and injury caused by explosion of vapour from lamp).

lead to actual lost profits it has been held that he may recover the standing costs of a reserve.[35] Again a matter of quantification rather than causation.

7. *The rescuer.* Where a defendant puts another in danger and a third person is injured in an attempt to rescue or succour the immediate victim it has been accepted for many years that the defendant owes a duty to the third person.[36] Only foolhardy behaviour on his part will break the chain of causation, not merely taking risks. Nor is he met by the defence of assumption of risk. 'Danger invites rescue'.[37]

Intervening events

8. *The kidney donor.* Liability to a person in P's position was found in Canada in *Urbansky v Patel*[38]. There is no difference of principle from case 7.

9. *The plumber and the earthquake.* This is arguably essentially the same as the case of the horse in Part I 4(a) (q.v.). D is probably not liable for the cost of repairs (though he would be liable for loss of use before the earthquake). Compare the case where D injured P's back and before the trial a wholly unconnected disease occurred and disabled P. D was not liable for disability after the onset of the disease.[39] Certainly this is a case of property damage rather than personal injury, but there is no obvious reason why causation should differ on this basis.[40] In this case D has certainly burned P's house but it can be argued that there is no factual causation of P's loss for the period after the earthquake – it would have happened anyway. Of course hindsight must be given some limits. If the earthquake occurs after the plumber has paid the judgment or settled, the matter is res judicata or the subject of a binding compromise and he cannot reopen it. So also (though I know of no case) it seems plain that if the repairs are done before the earthquake, the plumber cannot resist a subsequent claim for their cost.

It may be argued that this case differs from Part I 4(a) above in one vital respect, namely that here there is a tort followed by a natural event, whereas the other case involves two successive torts. Again, it is not clear why this should affect causation, though it is perhaps the only basis upon which the difference between the two leading English cases can be explained.[41]

10. *The collision and heavy weather damage.* This case resembles *Carslogie SS Co v Royal Norwegian Government.*[42] D is not liable for the cost of the repair of the heavy weather damage. The collision was a factual cause of the heavy weather damage (but for the collision the ship would not have encountered the storm). But it is not a legally effective cause. If

35 *See* e.g. *The Mediana* [1900] AC 713.
36 Note that in England this is consistently held to apply to professionals like fire officers.
37 J. Cardozo in *Wagner v International RR* 133 [1921] *North Eastern Reporter* (NE) 437.
38 *Urbansky v Patel* [1978] 84 *Dominion Law Reports* (D.L.R.) (3rd series) 650.
39 *Jobling v Associated Dairies* [1982] AC 794; *Hodgson v General Electric* [1978] 2 Lloyd's Rep 210. But compare *Baker v Willoughby* [1970] AC 467 (above supra note 14).
40 *See*, however, the commentary on Part I 4(a) above.
41 *Jobling v Associated Dairies* and *Baker v Willoughby* (though it is doubtful if this would have been a distinction accepted in the latter case).
42 *Carslogie SS Co v Royal Norwegian Government* [1952] AC 292.

I knock you down and you spend two days in hospital no one would seriously suggest that I was liable for your death when you were hit by a bus on leaving the hospital. He is liable for the cost of repair of the collision damage (other than general dock expenses) but not, according to the *Carslogie* case, for loss of use during the period of repair (except in so far, presumably, as the period of detention caused by the collision damage is longer than that caused by the heavy weather damage). The reason is said to be that it is the storm damage, not the collision damage, which renders the vessel unseaworthy. But if the collision necessitates immediate docking, the defendant responsible for it (and he alone) will be liable for loss of use and docking expenses, nothwithstanding storm damage or further collision damage before docking.[43]

11. *Injury in the ambulance.* Again D's negligence is a factual cause of P's further injury. But (though I know of no cases *directly* in point[44]) both supervening events are mere coincidences, not within the risk created by D's negligence and D is not responsible for them (compare the case where the second injury is attributable to the risk created by D – e.g. rescue from a dangerous place). It seems to me nothing to the point that the avalanche is less 'likely' or 'foreseeable' than the second motor collision. To take a more extreme example, suppose P suffers a slight injury to his left ankle while on D's property, is therefore unable to drive and is given a lift home by X, a normally competent driver who, in a moment of inattention, collides with Y, causing further injury to P. I can see no basis (save post hoc, propter hoc) to impute this to D – had it not been for D's tort, P would have driven home in the normal way and would have been exposed to exactly the same commonplace hazards of motor travel, though we can of course be fairly sure that in that event he would have escaped them. . Hence D is not liable for the extended period of loss, though in one case X of course is.[45] A similar point comes out in one of the contract cases, *Monarch SS Co v Karlshsamns Oljefabriker*.[46] D's delay in breach of contract meant that the ship carrying P's cargo could not reach Sweden before the outbreak of war and the cargo had to be diverted to Glasgow. The costs of this were held recoverable from the D on the basis that the outbreak of war was something which, in the political conditions, could have been anticipated. Lord Porter, however, said that D would not have been liable for loss of the cargo by lightning or in a storm which would have been avoided by sailing on time. 'Either may happen as much at one place or time as another, whereas delay, at a time when war was likely to occur, gives more opportunity for its incidence than a speedy and proper dispatch would give.'

---

43 *The Haversham Grange* [1905] P 307, (as explained in supra note 42).

44 In *Hogan v Bentinck Collieries* [1949] 1 All ER 588 at 601 Lord McDermott was of the view expressed here: 'if [the plaintiff who has been tortiously injured] gets burned because the hospital he has entered goes on fire, or if he is maimed because the ambulance taking him, say, from hospital to a convalescent home is involved in a street accident, I would not link the resulting incapacity with the original injury'. However, the decision in the case, that medical negligence necessarily broke thc chain of causation, is now questionable: *Mahony v Kruschich* (1985) 59 *Australian Law Reports* (ALR) 722.

45 On the basis of the *Carslogie* case (supra note 42) can it be contended that the further accident expunges D's liability for the one year disability? It is thought that the answer is no. The case is more like *The Haversham Grange* (supra note 43) in that the first accident necessitates the first year's treatment.

46 *Monarch SS Co v Karlshsamns Oljefabriker* [1949] AC 196.

12. *Highway obstruction accident.* On similar facts it was held in *Wright v Lodge*[47] that while D1 was liable to P1 (a passenger in her car) she was not liable to P2 and P3. D2's driving was so reckless that it broke the chain of causation. D2 was of course liable to P2 and P3, so the issue was essentially one of contribution. The difference in P1's case was that she was at risk of injury from any sort of collision with the stalled car.

13. *Theft from the accident victim.* In the absence of contract or bailment, wilful wrongdoing by a third party must be 'very likely' to make D liable for it. The classic statement is that of Lord Sumner in *Weld-Blundell v Stephens*:[48] 'In general even though A is in fault, he is not responsible for injury to C which B, a stranger to [A] deliberately chooses to do. Though A may have given the occasion for B's mischievous activity, B then becomes a new and independent cause . . . he insulates A from C.' No liability here.

14. *Car accident followed by heart attack.* It is not clear what is the cause or effect of the heart attack. If it is caused by the initial injury and it kills P, D could be liable for that. If it is caused by the initial injury and has a 'concurrent' effect of disabling him for life, again D could be liable. If it is unconnected with the injury and kills P, then D's liability for loss extends only up to the point of P's death[49] – so much was accepted in *Baker v Willoughby*.[50] If it is unconnected with the injury and has a concurrent disabling effect the case is on all fours with *Jobling v Associated Dairies*[51] and D's liability does not extend beyond the point at which it occurs.

15. *Death of disabled person in fire.* In my report on the original hypothetical[52] I expressed sceptcism as to whether there was an adequate causal link between the initial injury and the death. I am still of that view, even putting aside the procedural[53] and limitation points I raised then.

Loss of a chance

16. *Loss of a chance of recovery.* It was reaffirmed in *Hotson v E Berks HA*[54] that the plaintiff has the burden of proving on a balance of probabilities that the defendant's tort caused his loss. If he does he recovers 100 per cent of his loss. If he falls below the balance of probabilities he recovers nothing. This case falls into the latter category. A shift to a 'loss of a chance' basis would presumably require a discounted approach where the proof was more than 50 per cent. What the overall effect of this would be is impossible to say, since at the moment all the judge has to say is 'P has proved his case on a balance of probabilities'.[55] He

47 Wright v Lodge [1993] 4 All ER 299.
48 Weld-Blundell v Stephens [1920] AC 956 at 986.
49 That is to say, D only has to pay compensation for that period. Of course P (or more accurately his estate) may bring an action for this loss after his death.
50 *See* 4(a) above.
51 *See* 9 above.
52 *See* The British Report in: J. Spier (ed.) (supra note 32) p. 102.
53 I.e. the fact that once the plaintiff has settled or recovered judgment he cannot bring further proceedings arising out of the same act.
54 *Hotson v E Berks HA* [1987] AC 750.
55 *See* the somewhat similar case of *Wilsher v Essex AHA* [1988] AC 1074, in which it was said that

does not have to say whether that is 51 per cent or 65 per cent or 90 per cent or whatever. The consequence of a shift to a loss of a chance approach would therefore be likely to be a significant increase in the complexity of some types of litigation because an assessment would have to be made of what the chance was.

It should be noted that the balance of probabilities requirement applies only to matters of 'history.' If P shows on a balance of probabilities that D caused him a loss but the quantification of that loss is dependent on some future contingency which may or may not occur (e.g. that arthritis will develop at the site of a fracture) the court must do its best to value that chance and award damages accordingly, whether it is less or more than 50 per cent.[56] So also with hypothetical matters which would have affected the 'value' of the plaintiff if he had not been injured (e.g. his chances of promotion in his former job).

17. *Emissions causing cancer.* This is a question of evidence/proof of causation not of causation. Plainly courts do sometimes act on statistical evidence and the line between drawing an inference from observation and drawing an inference from statistics about a defined group is not a sharp one. But as far as I am aware the nature of this evidence has never been fully considered in any appellate case, nor in any reported case at any level here. However, a 'feel' for the nature of such cases can be obtained from *Reay v British Nuclear Fuels Plc*, October 8, 1993, available on LEXIS.[57] What the case does show is that real life disputes are unlikely to present even the scientific (as opposed to individually causative) certainty which we are given in this case. For example, it is likely that in each case there would be competing explanations of particular levels of incidence of disease from one area to another.[58] So it is not very likely that I can give a very decisive answer to this one. For what it is worth I am inclined to say (a) yes (because of the 20 fold increase). The other two seem much more doubtful. Even though (b) looks like a balance of probabilities, is an increase of two (over an undefined period) statistically significant?

Concurring causes

18. *The collapsing wall.* The analogy of cases about 'aggregate nuisances' indicates that each is liable for the whole damage, though the case is perhaps logically more difficult than that of independent sufficient causes, neither act being in itself sufficient.[59] Suppose also that D1 deposited all his rubbish at one time, having no reason to know of the subsequent action of D2? In one of the cases (concerning noise) the judge formulated the principle as follows: 'If

---

[Note 55 continued]
if the trial judge had preferred the expert evidence to the effect that the treatment had on a balance of probabilities made a material contribution to the plaintiff's condition, a decision in the plaintiff's favour would have been 'unassailable'.

56 However, there is now a limited power to award 'provisional damages' if there is a chance of a 'clear and severable event' involving deterioration in the plaintiff's condition.

57 The LEXIS version of the judgment of J. French runs to 97 pages but omits some hundreds of pages of appendices. The case concerns a claim (which failed) for pre-conception parental irradiation.

58 Thus there was evidence in the *Reay* case that clusters of childhood leukaemia, even if attributable to genetic factors, may be caused by genetic 'mixing' associated with population movement, which in its turn is associated with major industrial projects.

59 It is assumed that D1 and D2 do not act in concert.

the acts of two persons, *each being aware of what the other is doing*, amount in the aggregate to what is an actionable wrong, each is amenable to the remedy against the aggregate cause of complaint'.[60]

19. *The three hunters.* This well-known conundrum has never been the subject of a clear decision here. Logically P fails and it should be noted that even on the basis of a reversal of the burden of proof it is statistically less than likely that D1 hit P (as was indeed the position in the famous Canadian case[61] where there were only two hunters). One case in the Court of Appeal gives support to the view that if D1 and D2 cause an aggregate of different injuries the individual causation of which cannot be established each will be liable for the whole but the point was not in issue in the HL.[62] Further, there is no foundation here for the view that the burden of proof of causation can be reversed because D can be shown to be negligent.[63] Joint tortfeasors may be liable for a harm even though only one of them acted, but it seems unlikely that this could be stretched beyond the case where all wilfully fired at P, for example to frighten him.

20. *The concurrent toxic discharges.* There are American cases which support the view that concurrent tortfeasors are liable even though the act of each was sufficient to cause the harm. As far as I am aware there is no English case *precisely* in point (in the sense of categorically stating this to be the law) but I have no doubt that the same view would be taken – indeed the law has probably been assumed to be so on many occasions . If A and B simultaneously shoot P in the head it would be odd if we came to the conclusion that neither had caused his death.

21. *The market share case.* No 'market share' theory has ever been adopted by an English court. As far as I am aware it has never been advanced but if it were it would be inconsistent with the view of causation in *Hotson v E Berks HA* (above).[64] If the plaintiffs sue D1, I doubt if any English court would say that D1's market share of slightly over 50 per cent establishes that D1 caused the harm to any one of them (even though statistically it undoubtedly caused the harm to many of them, and perhaps a majority of them). People with brown eyes outnumber those with blue eyes. But if you were mugged on a dark night I doubt if you would conclude from this that your assailant had brown eyes.

22. *The falling rocks.* This is essentially case 19 but with only one possible tortfeasor. Again, logically P fails, on the assumption that the probability of its being D's rock is no more than 50 per cent.

23. *The collision at sea.* One may interpret this to mean that an identifiable 20 per cent by value of the damage was done by the collision with SA (e.g. damage to the rudder) and then 80 per cent by value by the weather (e.g. damage to the superstructure). In that event SA is

---

60 *Lambton v Mellish* [1894] 3 *Chancery Reports* (Ch) 163.

61 *Cook v Lewis* (1952) 1 D.L.R. 1.

62 *Fitzgerald v Lane* [1989] AC 328. *See* also *Clarkson v Modern Foundries*, above.

63 That would be inconsistent with *Hotson v E Berks HA* [1987] AC 750 (supra note 21).

64 This would be so even in the unlikely event that all possible defendants and all possible plaintiffs were before the court, though in that situation there might be thought to be some analogy to the general rule about the liability of multiple concurrent trotfeasors.

prima facie liable only for the 20 per cent, *save that* if SB is more vulnerable to the storm because of the damage caused by SA, SA might be liable for that. An alternative interpretation is that the damage is indivisible and the collision takes place in a storm, but not one which excuses SA entirely. If so, SA is liable for the whole damage since SA need only be a cause, not the sole cause – it is sufficient if SA's actions make a contribution to the happening of the event. Similarly, if instead of the storm there were another negligent vessel, SC, SA and SC would be jointly and severally liable for the whole damage. The difference is that God is not available for service of contribution proceedings by SA.[65]

Miscellaneum

24. *The motorway pile-up.* In principle, D1 may be liable for damage suffered by other drivers 'down the line.' For an example see *Rouse v Squires*[66] where it was said, that if 'a driver so negligently manages his vehicle as to cause it to obstruct a highway and constitute a danger to other road users, including those who drive too fast or not keeping a proper look out, but not those who deliberately or recklessly drive into the obstruction, then the first driver's negligence may be held to have contributed to the causation of an accident of which the immediate cause was the negligent driving of the vehicle which because of the presence of the obstruction collides with it.' Rather unhelpfully, one cannot say much more in the abstract than that it is a question of degree as to whether the chain of causation is broken.[67] Compare *Knightley v Johns*[68] (collision in tunnel caused by D1's negligence; passage of time; police intervened but failed to close tunnel; P, a police officer, ordered by a senior officer, D2, to ride motor cycle back wrong way down tunnel; collided with X; injury to P too remote a consequence of D1's negligence[69]). In practice most of the property damage would be covered by the loss insurance of the drivers and insurers might not pursue subrogation claims,[70] though there might be litigation by drivers carrying a large 'excess' or by those seeking to preserve no claim discount.[71] However, these factors would not apply to personal injury claims.

The situation would present formidable problems of proof, bearing in mind that the effect of the collision of, say, D9 may have knock on effects back down the line to D1. The burden of proof of contributory negligence on the part of a plaintiff lies on the defendant and a defendant seeking contribution must show that the party against whom he proceeds was also liable to the plaintiff.

---

65 For this reason it is unlikely that a court in real life would attempt to quantify the relative contributions of the storm and SA.

66 *Rouse v Squires* [1973] QB 889.

67 *See* also the remark of Lord Wright, in *The Oropesa*, referred to in Part I 2.

68 *Knightley v Johns* [1982] 1 WLR 349.

69 This of course made no difference to P, who recovered in full from his employers, who were vicariously liable for the fault of D2.

70 I understand that the former 'knock for knock' agreement whereby most insurers agreed inter se not to do so has lapsed.

71 Bonus/malus.

France

Causation under French Law

Suzanne Galand-Carval

Part I: General questions

1. Causation as a requirement

(1) Under French law, causation is one of the three general requirements for establishing liability, the other two being a wrongful act ('fait générateur') and damage. This is so in both areas of civil liability: tortious liability ('responsabilité délictuelle') and contractual liability ('responsabilité contractuelle').

- As far as tortious liability is concerned, the causation requirement is expressed in articles 1382 to 1386 of the Civil Code, which all state that the damage must have been 'caused' by the defendant's fault, or by the act of his animals or things.
- In contract law, article 1151 provides: 'les dommages et intérêts ne doivent comprendre à l'égard de la perte éprouvée par le créancier et du gain dont il a été privé, que ce qui est une suite immédiate et directe de l'inexécution de la convention'. (damages in respect of the actual loss suffered by the creditor and the gain of which he has been deprived should include only the immediate and direct consequence of the non-performance).

As will be seen below, the methods of appreciating causation are not well defined, judges freely applying various criteria. But the rule is clear, there is no liability without causation.

(2) Causation thus plays a prominent role in establishing liability. This is, however, its unique role. In particular, *it is not used as a means of apportioning liability.*

Once causation is proved, the defendant is fully liable. In other words, when damage is caused by several concurrent causes, it does not matter that each would have been insufficient, on its own, to produce the damage.

Provided the defendant's act was *a* necessary cause of the damage, he is liable for its whole extent. According to the Cour de cassation: 'chacun des responsables d'un dommage ayant concouru à le causer en entier doit être condamné envers la victime à en assurer l'entière réparation'. They are jointly and severally liable ('responsables in solidum').

The harshness of the rule may be counterbalanced by the possibility, awarded to the defendant, to recover a contribution from the other authors of the damage. It must be stressed, however, that this possibility is not the justification of the rule. This is well illustrated by the fact that the victim remains entitled to full compensation, even in the cases

J. Spier (ed.), Unification of Tort Law: Causation, 53–61.

where a contribution between co-authors is in fact impossible, for instance because the other tortfeasors are unknown or insolvent. The sole justification of the principle thus appears to be that it clearly benefits the victim, by shifting the risk of one or more tortfeasors being insolvent from the victim onto the defendant.

There is only one exception to the rule of full liability. This occurs when the victim has contributed, by his fault, to his damage. In this event, the defendant is only partly liable, the victim assuming a share of the loss. This exception is usually explained on a causation-basis: the victim contributed to the loss and is therefore answerable to himself for this ('responsable envers elle-même'). But the causation analysis is not fully satisfactory because, as far as the apportionment of liability between the defendant and the victim is concerned, it seems that judges have regard to the respective gravity of the faults (and not to the extent of the causal contribution). Ultimately, it must be noted that the apportionment is limited to the case of a contributory *fault* committed by the victim, which means that, under the present state of the law, a mere contributory act of the victim (eg: not amounting to negligence) is to be disregarded.

NB: in the fifties, the apportionment of liability was also accepted by the Cour de cassation in cases where a natural event played a causal role in the damage. On this solution, which is no longer good law, please refer to case (4,d) below.

2. Relevant factors / reasons / criteria

(i) It must first be pointed out that relevant factors and criteria are not to be found in statute law. Articles 1382 to 1386 of the civil code do not give any definition of the worlds 'cause' or 'causé' which they employ. Article 1151 (relating to contractual liability) is slightly more precise: it states that the damage must be 'the immediate and direct consequence of the non-performance'. However, the Code gives no further information about the meaning of the words 'suite immédiate et directe', thus leaving unresolved the question of how to decide which damage is to be compensated and which is not.

(ii) How is causation understood by French judges ? This is a rather difficult question since cases give very few indications about the different factors taken into account in order to reject or admit causation. Although it is a 'question of law' (question de droit), subject to review by the Cour de cassation, this Court has never given any precise definition of the legal concept of causation. Issues are very often decided in an empirical manner. As Paul Esmein put it: 'c'est par sentiment que les juges décident si la réalisation d'un dommage est une conséquence trop imprévisible d'un acte pour que son auteur en soit responsable'.[1]

All that can be said with confidence is that cases seem equally divided between those applying the elastic but for test ('l'équivalence des conditions') and those which discriminate between the direct causes and the indirect causes of the loss suffered by the plaintiff. When describing the second group of cases, authors usually write that they are inspired by the adequacy doctrine ('la causalité adéquate'). It should be stressed, however, that the Cour de cassation never refers expressly to this theory. Cases admit or reject liability on the ground that causation is 'direct' or 'indirect', 'exists' or 'does not exist', never on the ground that it is 'adequate' or 'inadequate'. It would therefore be quite hazardous to say that the only test

1 "Le nez de Cléopâtre, ou les affres de la causalité", [1964] *Dalloz* (D.), *chroniques* (chr.) 205.

applied in this second category of cases is the 'objective probability' test of the German adequacy doctrine. Other factors are most certainly taken into account by judges, such as the degree of the respective faults.

Two factors used in other countries are, however, broadly rejected by French judges: these are the 'causa proxima' (understood as closeness in time to the damage: 'la proximité temporelle') and the protective purpose rule. The causa proxima doctrine is widely considered as a rough and unfair approach to causation. The protective purpose rule is almost unknown: it has received some application in the very specific area of civil liability incurred by the author of a criminal offence, but even in this field, it seems to be declining.

(iii) Assessment: the opinion is widely shared among French scholars and lawyers that the present state of the law of causation is not satisfactory. Criticism mainly concerns its unpredictibility: as we have seen, judges freely apply two contradictory doctrines (the sine qua non and the adequacy theories), and it is not infrequent to see cases reaching opposite results on very similar facts. (Eg: Com. 28.02.1989, BC IV n°70: a bank which sent a chequebook by ordinary mail is liable for the consequences of its being stolen; Civ. 2, 11.01.1995, BC II n° 21: the owner of a stolen car, who had left it unlocked, is not liable for the accident caused by the thief). In some areas, the Cour de cassation has laid down useful rules: for instance, this Court repeatedly states that the victim's predispositions do not break the causal link between the defendant's act and the loss suffered by the victim, and this rule is usually understood as an application of the 'sine qua non' theory. On many other causation issues, however, the case law is contradictory, making it almost impossible to predict with reasonable certainty the outcome of any given case. It would therefore be useful if more consistent reasoning were adopted by judges and if clearer guidelines were laid down by the Cour de cassation.

Should these guidelines consist in stringent principles, definitely setting aside the but-for test? Although such a proposal might receive some support, from insurers for instance, I do not think it would correspond to the current preoccupation of judges and scholars, whose predominant opinion is that tort law should ensure a comprehensive compensation of damages. Therefore, if there might be a case for clarifying causation, it should not be presented and understood as a case against the establishment of liability, and thus, against compensation.

3. Specific legislation

Several statutes do provide for original solutions on the question of causation.

Some of them relax the burden of proof lying on the victim: in labour law for instance, a worker who suffers an injury at the work place (be it a sudden illness or a heart attack) does not have to prove that the accident originated at work. Article L. 411–1 of the 'code de la sécurité sociale' states that all accidents which take place at work and during worktime are industrial accidents, entitling the victim to specific compensation. The law thus establishes a presumption of causation which can however be rebutted by the employer.

Other statutes direct the judge to adopt a broad approach to causation. For instance, trade unions and consumer associations are entitled by statute to sue the authors of criminal or civil wrongs infringing the collective interests of workers or consumers for damages. And in doing so, they may claim compensation for *direct and indirect damages* suffered therefrom.

Finally, the 'revolutionary' loi Badinter, which has deeply modified the traditional rules of liability in the field of road accidents, must be mentioned. (Loi n° 85–677 du 5.07.1985). Among other innovations, this statute has broken with the previous requirement of an 'active contribution' of the defendant's car to the damage suffered by the victim. The statute now provides that liability is incurred by the owner or the driver of a car 'involved ('impliqué') in the accident in which the victim was injured'. Article 2 adds that the defendants can no longer raise the traditional defence of 'force majeure'.

This new system has two major implications. First of all, there is liability even if the defendant's car was a passive cause of the accident. Thus, the Cour de cassation has repeatedly decided that there is involvement and thus liability, when the victim has collided into a car which was parked, even if this car had no disturbing effect on the traffic. Secondly, in complex accidents, a victim may ask for compensation from the driver of a car which took no part in the injuries suffered by the victim, provided that it took part in the accident in which the victim was injured. Suppose a chain-accident: A collides with B, and two minutes later, C collides with A. B was killed in the first collision. His family may however sue C, whose car was undoubtedly involved in the accident, although it did not contribute to B's death.

4. The borderline between causation and damage or other factors

(a) The horse case: The issue is one of causation.
The proper answer is probably that Y is liable, and not X, since it is Y's wrongful act which caused the damage as it occurred (death by burning).

However, I have doubts as to whether an action against X would actually fail, in the event of Y being insolvent for instance. In such a case, I think it would be possible to argue that before Y's intervention, X's wrongful act had already caused substantial damage, consisting in the diminution of value of the horse. Should this analysis be admitted, X would be liable to that extent.

(b) The asbestos case: the issue is one of causation.
According to the Sine qua non test, A is liable, and it is most likely that, having regard to the nature of the loss, a judge would consider that the damage is a direct consequence of X 's working in A's plant.

A's argument (the fatal threshold was crossed when X was employed by C) is a proximity-based argument, and I have already stressed that closeness in time is not considered by French judges as an appropriate criterion to appreciate directness.

Note that A is liable for the entire loss suffered by X, not withstanding the fact that the exposure to asbestos in A's plant would not have sufficed, on its own, to cause the disease.

(c) The appeal case:
The issue is one of damage.

The concept of 'loss of a chance' could be used here, with good chances of success.

Damage consisting in a loss of a chance is recoverable, as a general principle, provided that the chance lost is certain and material (which means that if the chance is slight, no damages may be awarded).

It appears from the case-law, however, that the liability of attorneys is subject to more stringent principles. In practice, damages are awarded, even if the chance to win the appeal is slight and this is generally thought to be a means of penalizing negligent lawyers.

In any event, when liability is established for loss of a chance, the measure of damages is limited to a portion of what may have been won on appeal.

(d) The carrier case

(i) The unpenned animals are swept overboard:

The issue is one of causation. Under French law, C's liability is beyond doubt, the damage is regarded as the direct consequence of his fault.

The specific purpose of the statute infringed is not a bar to liability as the so-called 'protective purpose theory' is not admitted in French law.

Nor has the storm any exonerating effect. It does not qualify as 'un cas de force majeure', which, in other circumstances could have been an available defence to C, as it appears clearly from the facts of the case that its damaging effects were not *unavoidable* (had C penned the animals, they would not have been swept overboard).

Note that C is liable for the entire loss. Forty years ago, judges might have reached a more lenient result, by holding C liable only to the extent of his contribution to the loss. In the fifties, the Cour de cassation had admitted that such 'proportionate liability' be adopted, when, *out of two concurrent causes, one was a natural event.* In the well-known 'Lamoricière' case,[2] for instance, the owner of a ship which had sunk in the Mediterranean sea, was held liable for one fifth of the loss. In that case, the damage (300 passenger deaths) was found to have been caused, 4/5 by an exceptionally violent storm and 1/5 by the defective quality of the coal used (had the coal been of a good quality, the ship's engine would have been able to resist the storm better).

This case was followed by the 'Houillères' case,[3] in which the Cour de cassation decided that a mining company (les Houillères du Bassin du Nord et du Pas-de-Calais) could only be held liable to the extent of its contribution to the damage. In that case, the damage was due to the conjunction of two factors: the defendant's fault and a violent storm.

These cases, however, remained isolated and by the sixties the Cour de cassation resorted to the previously admitted solution of full liability.

Since then, natural events have always been dealt with on the same basis: either they qualify as 'force majeure' completely exonerating the defendant from liability, and this is so only when they are external, unforeseeable and that their damaging effects are unavoidable (see (ii) below). Or they do not qualify as 'force majeure' and as they have no effect whatsoever on liability, the defendant is fully liable.

(ii) the ship sinks in the storm.

C is clearly not liable: his fault has no causal connection with the damage, as the animals would have perished anyway.

---

2 Cour de cassation, chambre commerciale, (Supreme Court, division specialised in commercial matters), 19.06.1951, [1951] D., 717, note Ripert, [1952] *Sirey* (S.), 1, 89, note Nerson.

3 Cour de cassation, 2eme chambre civile, (Supreme Court, second division for civil matters), 13.03.1957, [1958] D., 73, note Radouant.

Part II: Cases

Single event occurrences

(a) The event causes one damage (cases 1 & 2)

Both cases raise the question of what effect, if any, the exceptional magnitude of the harm has on establishing causation. Under French law, the answer is none, the plaintiffs are entitled to full compensation, whatever the amount of the loss suffered.

1. The causal link is obvious, the extreme magnitude of the loss is not a bar to liability, D is liable for the entire loss.

2. P's predisposition is not a defence for D. P was able to work before the accident, he is entitled to recover damages for loss of income. D must take P as he finds him, just as he had to take P 1/10 as he found them in case 1.

(b) The event causes related damages: ('dommages par ricochet') (Case 4)

4. P1's damage is the direct consequence of D's negligence. As far as P2 and P3 are concerned, their losses are a consequence of P1's damage and thus belong to the so-called category of 'préjudices par ricochet'.

This type of damages are in theory recoverable, they are not indirect as such. Judges do distinguish, however, between the loss suffered by *the family* of the victim as a result of the victim's own damage, and the loss suffered by *other persons*, such as clients, workers and so on.

For loss sustained by the family, damages are widely awarded, the related damage always being regarded as direct.

Loss sustained by suppliers, clients or workers is not so easily compensated. Before they get damages, P2 and P3 will have to convince the judge that their losses are the result of P1's damage (and are not attributable to distinct economic factors). They will also have to show that they had no mean of avoiding the loss, for instance, by contracting with another supplier.

Intervening events

In all the following cases, the question raised is whether the intervening event breaks the causal chain between the defendant's act and the damage.

(a) The intervening act is a natural event (cases 9, 10, 5)

9. In my view, the plumber is fully liable. His wrongful act produced its damaging effect (the destruction of the house) before the earthquake, and P's right to compensation arose at this time. The earthquake is not an intervening event but a subsequent event, which has no effect on causation.

10. The collision damage is recoverable from D. As far as the heavy weather damage is concerned, no definite answer may be given. This damage is due to the collision and the heavy weather. Natural events, as I have already stressed, do not as such have an exonerating effect. The whole issue thus depends on the judge's decision as to the causal effect of the collision. If he applies the but-for test, D will be liable, whereas if he reasons on an adequacy basis, he might well decide that the damage is not the direct consequence of D's act. This case provides a good example of the uncertainty which prevails in the French law of causation.

5. In my view, case 5 may be considered with cases 9 and 10, the heat of the stove amounting to a natural phenomenon. In this case however, causation is much more likely to be established than in case 10. I would even think that in this case, the judicial reasoning would not bear on causation (causation seems obvious) but rather on the issue of negligence.

(b) The intervening event is an act or omission of a third party (cases 3, 11 to 13)

3. Several French cases deal with this factual issue. In most of them, the damage is not considered as the direct consequence of the fault, which means no liability on O.

In the present case however, O has been grossly negligent and the gravity of his fault could justify another result.

11–13: All three cases are about road accidents and are to be solved according to the provisions of the 'loi Badinter'.

Liability is incurred in all of them. In the three cases, the defendant's car was involved in the accident in which the damages were caused (article 1). And, as already mentioned, article 2 prevents the defendants from escaping liability on the ground that the damage was caused by a natural event (case 11) or an act of a third party (cases 12 and 13).

(c) The event is an act of the plaintiff or is attributable to a cause which can be imputed to him (cases 6, 7, 8, 14, 15).

6. Can P recover damages for the costs of the reserve bus? I see no reason why he may not. Cases frequently award damages to compensate the plaintiff for the costs of renting a car while the damaged one is being repaired. It is therefore most likely that P's demand be satisfied, provided that using the reserve bus was necessary.

7. Under the but for test, C's damage is a consequence of A's negligence. Could it be argued that C's wilful intervention has broken the causal chain ? I do not think so. It is most likely that a judge would consider that A's negligence has created a dangerous situation which made it a moral duty for C to intervene. Thus, C's generous act would not be analysed as disrupting the causal chain but as being *a normal consequence of the dangerous situation created by A*.

8. The issue of this case is not as easily predictable as the previous one and I do not think that a definite answer can be given. Under the but for test, causation is established. It could be said, however, that the causal link has been broken by P's conscious acceptance of the damage. The argument is stronger here than in the rescue case because the supervening event is more than a wilful intervention of the victim. It is tantamount to an acceptance of the loss suffered. On the other hand, a fairness argument as well as a policy argument might lead to adopt the opposite solution. If one wants the useful technique of transplants to develop, it is obvious that donors should be encouraged, or at least, not discouraged, and an award of damages may be a means to achieve this general policy.

14. In my view, this case is very close to case 9 and quite different from cases 7 and 8 above since the supervening event is not a wilful act of the plaintiff. The accident has caused a permanent disability. P's right to damages arose on the date the damage was caused. The heart attack has no effect whatsoever on D's liability.

15. A very similar case was decided by the Cour de cassation in 1989 (Civ.2, 8.02.1989, JCP 1990, II, 21546). It was held that there was no causal link between the accident and the death because damages already paid by the defendant included a sum entitling P to be permanently assisted by a nurse. Such assistance should have normally permitted the second accident to be avoided. Save for that circumstance, causation probably would have been admitted, as the lapse of time between the first and the second accident is usually not a decisive factor in assessing causation. In many cases, damages are awarded for loss suffered many years after the wrongful act.

Simultaneous causes (cases 18, 20, 23)

Cases 18, 20 and 23 are all about simultaneous causes of the same damage, the only difference being that in case 20, each of the simultaneous causes was sufficient, on its own, to cause the damage, whereas in cases 18 and 23 the concurrence of both causes was necessary to produce the damage. This does not make any difference however, since there is no need for a cause to be the sole cause of a damage.

18. D1 is fully liable.

20. A is fully liable.

23. SA is fully liable. (for a different solution, see *4d* above, development on the Lamoricière case. But the case is no longer good authority).

Uncertainty of causation (loss of a chance, statistical evidence and other related concepts)

The question of evidence is, of course, very important as well as very delicate. As a principle, the victim can only succeed if he establishes, with reasonable certainty, the existence of a causal link between his damage and the wrongful act committed. Moreover, and this a related question, he must identify the author of the wrongful act. Thus, the Cour de cassation repeatedly states that no damages may be awarded when causation is hypothetical, doubtful, or uncertain.

As a strict application of this principle would frequently result in a very harsh decision for the victim, the case-law reveals that judges have always been willing to mitigate it.

- As far as the link between the damage and the defendant's act is concerned, a frequently used concept is that of loss of a chance. In the field of medical malpractice for instance, it is very frequent that the victim cannot establish with sufficient certainty that the damage would not have occurred, but for the doctor's negligence. In those circumstances, several cases have admitted that a part of the damage suffered could be compensated, on the basis that the doctor's negligence had, at least, deprived the victim of a chance of recovery.
- In relation to the question of the identification of the tortfeasor, a well-established solution consists in resorting to the so-called theory of 'faute commune'. This theory has been frequently applied in cases where the damage was caused by a unidentified member of an

ascertained group of hunters or children.[4] It enables the judge to decide that each member of the group is fully liable toward the victim. The ground for liability is not the fact that the defendant committed one of the individual faults (reckless shooting for the hunters, reckless lightening of matches for the children), since it is not established that this individual fault caused the damage. The ground then is the defendant's taking part in a collective fault, consisting in embarking together on a dangerous activity and encouraging each other to commit dangerous acts.

Still on this topic of the unidentified tortfeasor, it should be added that, in the field of road accidents, the 'loi Badinter' also provides the victim with some convenient solutions: see case 24 below.

16. This is typically the case in which 40 per cent of the loss could be recovered, on the basis of the chance of recovery lost by the victim.
17a–c. All three cases raise the question of the use of statistical evidence in mass-liability. I am unaware of French cases relating to this point.

Under the current state of the law (as stated above), it is very likely that the defendants would escape liability, on the ground of causation not being established with sufficient certainty.

However, this is an area in which the case-law may well adopt new solutions in the near future.

19. The issue depends on whether the hunters acted collectively or not. If they were hunting together, the theory of the 'faute commune' should normally allow P to obtain full compensation from D1. If they were hunting separately, the theory cannot be resorted to: D1 would not be held liable, the causal link between his shots and P's damage not being proved.

21. There is no case-law on the subject. Under the present state of the law, I would say that the problem of identification is a bar to liability.

The solution is unfair, since in this case, it is absolutely certain that all manufacturers caused some damage. The problem thus is only a problem of linking a particular victim to a particular defendant. I have the feeling that the best way to solve this type of problem would consist in a change of the procedural aspect of tort actions. If a group-action could be exercised by the 25000 victims, it then would be possible to decide that each defendant should pay to the group a compensation equal to the loss he has caused: 0.5 per cent if the group sues D20 (hypothetical a), 15 per cent if the group sues D2 (hypothetical b) and so on.

22. Causation is not proved, D is not liable.

24. Again the problem is one of identifying the tortfeasors. As the damages are sustained in a road accident, the 'loi Badinter' must be applied, which provides, in this type of case, a convenient solution to the causation problem. In theory, if the provisions of the statute are applied correctly, it should be considered that one single accident, in which all vehicles were involved, has occurred. Therefore, it is open to the victims to sue any of the drivers involved for damages.

---

4 Cour de cassation, 2ème chambre civile, 12.07.1971, [1972] D., 227 ; 29.11.1978, Bulletin des arrêts de la Cour de cassation, chambres civiles (Bull. civ.) II n° 257.

Germany

Causation in German Tort Law

Ulrich Magnus

Part I: General considerations

1. Causation as a requirement

(a) Requirement and definition of causation

Under German law causation is one of the fundamental elements and necessary prerequisites of liability for damage be it in tort or in contract. In principle nobody can be made liable for another person's damage unless he has caused it by his own act or by some source which can be imputed to him[1] and unless regularly some further elements are present. Despite its evident importance no general statutory definition of causation exists.

Causation is understood as *the judgment that one condition results from another*. It is common understanding that no strict causation definition as used in the natural sciences has to be applied but a specific legal concept.[2] Otherwise an indefinite number of causes had to be taken into account. The requirement of causation thus functions as a filter – not the only one and only a rather rough one – that separates factual consequences which can be imputed to a person from those which can not.

Causation is necessary on two levels which the courts do not always but often distinguish: on the one hand, a causal link must exist between the tortious act or source and the infringement of the victim's right (so-called 'haftungsbegründende Kausalität' – liability establishing causation). On the other hand, the infringed right, e.g. corporal injury, and the ensuing damage, e.g. cost of recovery etc, must be causally linked to each other (so – called 'haftungsausfüllende Kausalität' – liability implementing causation).[3] Sometimes the distinc-

1 J. Esser/E. Schmidt, *Schuldrecht* I *Allgemeiner Teil* 2 (7th ed. 1993) p. 210 ('Grundmoment der Schadenszurechnung'); W. Fikentscher, *Schuldrecht* (9th ed. 1997) no. 475; M. Fuchs, *Deliktsrecht* (2nd ed. 1997) p. 53; H. Kötz, *Deliktsrecht* (7th ed. 1996) no. 142; H. Lange, *Schadensersatz* (2nd ed. 1990) pp. 75–76; H. Heinrich in O. Palandt (Palandt/Heinrichs), *Bürgerliches Gesetzbuch* (57th ed. 1998) Vorbem vor § 249 no. 54.

2 E. Deutsch, *Unerlaubte Handlungen, Schadensersatz und Schmerzensgeld* (3rd ed. 1995) nos. 41 et seq.; J. Esser/E. Schmidt (supra note 1) pp. 210 et seq.; H. Kötz (supra note 1) no. 151; H. Lange (supra note 1) pp. 79 et seq.

3 Compare, e.g., Bundesgerichtshof (German Supreme Court, BGH) in [1998] *Versicherungsrecht* (VersR), 201 (202); *further* H. Lange (supra note 1) pp. 77 et seq.; Palandt/Heinrichs, Vorbem vor § 249 nos. 55–56.

J. Spier (ed.), Unification of Tort Law: Causation, 63–73.

tion is unnecessary or even impossible, if the injury itself is the damage, e.g. the tortfeasor destroys the victim's property with no other consequence than that. But more often than not the infringement and the damage are separate events between which the chain of causation must also be established.[4]

The difference between liability establishing and implementing causation is, however, not a far reaching one and does not concern the basic concept of causation. That remains the same for both kinds of causation. Nevertheless the distinction has its importance: in cases of faultbased liability fault (especially foreseeability) must regularly be related to the causation between act and infringement of right but not necessarily to the ensuing damage.[5] As far as the law of evidence is concerned, the court is allowed to estimate the damage and even whether the damage resulted from the infringement of some right (§ 287 Civil Procedure Code) whereas the fact and causation of the primary infringement normally requires full proof (§ 286 Civil Procedure Code).[6]

(b) One or two step approach to causation

First, it should be stressed that most tort cases are decided without detailed discussion of causation. The judges seem to follow a 'natural' understanding of causation which combines logic, the well-known principles of natural science and some proximity between the respective links in the chain of causation; e.g., in the absence of special facts nobody doubts nor discusses that causation is present if somebody drives either recklessly or negligently or without fault into another person's car thereby damaging it. If, apart from the mere existence of the injured person or damaged thing at that time and at that place, the tortfeasor or a source for which he is responsible solely inflicted the harm causation poses no problem. It is only when other conditions are present (some predisposition of the victim, acts of third persons, intervening events etc) that causation needs discussion. Only the difficult cases with some problematical distance between two conditions generate conceptual considerations. In these cases German courts follow a two or even three-step concept.

As the first necessary but not sufficient step for establishing causation an act or source must be *conditio sine qua non* of the resulting effect: It must be clear that had the act or source in question been absent, the same result would not have occurred.[7] Of this the judge must be fully convinced – 'with a degree of probability next to certainty'[8] Otherwise causation is lacking.

However, the conditio-formula is applied with two restrictions:

---

4 See the examples in *Amtliche Sammlung der Entscheidungen des BGH in Zivilsachen* (BGHZ) 132, 341; BGH [1998] VersR, 200; BGH [1998] VersR, 201: in all three cases a minimal bodily injury led to enormous psychic consequences with following incapacity to work.

5 E. Deutsch (supra note 2) nos. 47–48; H. Lange (supra note 1) p. 79; Palandt/Heinrichs (supra note 1) Vorbem vor § 249 no. 56.

6 BGHZ 58, 48 (53); BGHZ 93, 351 (354); H. Lange (supra note 1) pp. 171 et seq.

7 BGHZ 2, 138 (141); BGHZ 25, 84; *also* H. Lange (supra note 1) pp. 79 et seq.; W. Grunsky in *Münchener Kommentar zum Bürgerlichen Gesetzbuch* (Münch Komm/Grunsky) II (3rd ed. 1994) vor § 249 no. 36; D. Medicus in J. v. Staudinger, *Kommentar zum Bürgerlichen Gesetzbuch und Nebengesetzen* (Staudinger/Medicus) (12th ed. 1980) § 249 no. 29.

8 BGHZ 53, 245 (256); BGHZ 61, 169; BGH in [1993] *Neue Juristische Wochenschrift* (NJW), 935 (937).

- If it has to be decided whether or not a failure to exercise care has caused some injury or damage it need not be nearly certain that the care if taken would have prevented injury or damage; a slightly lower degree of probability suffices.[9]
- If several tortfeasors have contributed to injury or damage in a way that the contribution of each alone would have sufficed to cause the injury or damage (so-called alternative causation) then, as a rule, none of them can excuse himself by saying that, disregarding his contribution, the same injury or damage would have occurred.[10] The same is true if it remains uncertain to what extent a tortfeasor has contributed to the injury or damage (§ 830 para. 1 s. 2 Civil Code).

In a second step the courts normally analyse the adequacy of causation: The chain of causation is established if a fact 'in general and not only under abnormal, completely improbable and in the ordinary course of things neglectable circumstances would have led to the occurrence of the result that happened'.[11] The degree to which the tortfeasor increased the probability of damage is decisive. Causation is lacking if an act results in a very unexpected, unforeseeable consequence that nobody had to reckon with. The standard is set by an objective, optimal or at least experienced observer. That observer for example knows that vaccination damage can happen even if the statistical probability lies under 0.01 per cent.[12] Only very rarely he does not foresee that damage could occur. Thus, causation has been denied, e.g., in a case where the husband of the plaintiff had lost a leg through an accident caused by the tortfeasor and eight years later – in war time – was killed because he could not run away quickly enough together with his family when under fire.[13]

The adequacy-test is much criticised mainly on the ground that it does not enable a precise differentiation between adequate and non-adequate effects of an act or source. The optimal observer would foresee in fact every damage. The adequacy-test it is therefore said, does not fulfill its function and does not operate as a reasonable limitation of liability.[14]

Due to the imprecision of the adequacy-test the courts often apply – as a third step – policy considerations ('wertende Überlegungen' – evaluating considerations). Partly these considerations are connected with the protective purpose of the violated rule (so called 'Schutzzwecklehre' – protective purpose rule).[15] According to that rule causation is only established if the damage in question is of a type against which the infringed provision or

---

9 Compare, e.g., BGHZ 7, 198 (203–204); but for strict proof: Palandt/Heinrichs, Vorbem vor § 249 no. 84.

10 Entscheidungen des Reichsgericht in Zivilsachen (RGZ) 16, 144 et seq.; *see* further H. Lange (supra note 1) pp. 155 et seq.

11 RGZ 133, 126 (127); RGZ 158, 34 (38); BGHZ 7, 198 (204); BGHZ 57, 141; BGH [1995] NJW, 127.

12 BGHZ 18, 286.

13 BGH [1952] NJW, 1010; for further cases *see* E. Deutsch (supra note 2) nos. 55 et seq; H. Lange (supra note 1) pp. 85 et seq.

14 See H. Kötz (supra note 1) nos. 150 et seq.

15 BGHZ 27, 137; BGHZ 95, 199; *see* also H. Kötz (supra note 1) nos. 156 et seq.; H. Lange (supra note 1) pp. 104 et seq; Palandt/Heinrichs, Vorbem vor § 249 nos. 62 et seq.; Staudinger/Medicus, § 249 nos. 40 et seq.; B. S. Markesinis, *The German Law of Torts* (2nd ed. 1990) p. 88 (translates it as the 'scope of the rule' theory).

rule is designed to protect. Furthermore, other considerations – such as apportionment of risk etc – prevail or are combined with protective purpose considerations.

As far as the protective purpose rule is concerned the protective purpose of a statutory provision can be more or less easily revealed in those cases where the provision expressly forbids a certain behaviour that could be detrimental to other persons.[16] The same is true if under a general provision like § 823 para. 1 Civil Code special duties of care have been developed.[17] However, if the provision or rule in question is of a general character it is difficult to detect a specific protective purpose.[18] In these cases the courts more or less openly apply policy considerations which fit to the case at hand.[19]

The courts have developed certain types of cases in which the judges apply specific policy considerations: If, e.g., a policeman is injured when chasing a criminal the latter is deemed to have caused the injury if it happened through some 'increased risk of chasing'.[20] This was held to be the case when a person used a steep staircase in order to escape.[21] On the contrary liability – and causation – was denied where the chased person only crossed a freshly mowed lawn on which the chaser fell down breaking his ankle.[22] The underlying policy is to let the chased person bear the chaser's risk and costs, if any, of a specifically dangerous escape route and thereby make easier the task of prosecution.

Another type of case is that where the victim has some predisposition which increases the effects of an injury and which is unknown to the tortfeasor. Except in cases of extremely improbable and unexpected consequences[23] the courts do not deny causation here since the tortfeasor 'who wrongfully acts against a person with weak health has no right to be treated as if he had injured a healthy person'.[24] The policy consideration behind is to secure participation in society for people with some handicap.

2. Relevant factors/reasons/criteria

In general German courts base their causation judgment on the conditio sine qua non formula and the adequacy-test plus policy considerations among which the protective purpose rule is the most common. But for special groups of cases special factors are taken into account in order to establish or deny causation. These different types of cases and solutions can be grouped in the following way:

---

16 For example the statutory provision that drivers should not leave their cars unsecured, especially unlocked [§ 14 par. 2 sent. 2 Straßenverkehrsordnung (Traffic Ordinance)] also protects those persons who are injured by unauthorised users (e.g. 'joy-riders') of unsecured, esp. unlocked cars; compare BGH [1981] NJW, 113.

17 For detailed discussion *compare* H. Lange (supra note1) pp. 113 et seq.

18 Staudinger/Medicus, § 249 no. 41.

19 *See*, e.g., BGH [1998] VersR, 200 (201): 'Indes hat die Rechtsprechung – Billigkeits- und Zumutbarkeitserwägungen folgend – einer solchen Schadenszurechnung für psychische Folgen stets Grenzen gezogen.'

20 BGHZ 57, 25; BGHZ 63, 189.

21 BGHZ 57, 25; BGHZ 63, 189.

22 BGH [1971] NJW, 1982.

23 An evidently undangerous dog barks at a very nervous woman who falls down and hurts herself: no causation, [1908] *Reichsgericht in Juristische Wochenschrift* (RG JW), 41; similar cases BGH [1976] NJW, 1143; BGHZ 107, 359.

24 RGZ 6, 1; RGZ 169, 117 (120); BGHZ 20, 137 (139).

- Both the act of the tortfeasor (or other source for which he is responsible) and some inherent physical or psychic condition of the victim influenced the impact and/or extent of the tortious act and the damage. In principle the tortfeasor bears the risk of injuring an abnormally weak person.[25] On the other hand, even a weak person must bear the 'normal risk of life': so if, e.g., somebody suffers a heart attack because his dog is bitten by another dog the relevant causation is denied.[26] The relevant aspect is the differentiation between 'daily life' risks attributable either to the tortfeasor or to the victim.
- Both the act of the tortfeasor and some independent act of the victim have contributed to the damage. As a rule causation in law is denied unless the victim was pressed by tortfeasor's act to react as he did. In a leading case a mother was awarded damages who had agreed to the transplantation of one of her kidneys to her child after the defendant doctor had wrongfully extracted the child's only working kidney.[27] The Federal Court held that the mother's decision was prompted by the doctor's failure. Again there is a borderline of reasonable behaviour of the victim. Unreasonable risks – like in some of the chasing cases[28] – are not legally caused by the tortfeasor even if prompted by him. Nevertheless the tortfeasor remains liable if the victim reacted in an unreasonable, but understandable way under the pressure of circumstances in which the tortfeasor had put him.[29] The relevant consideration is that the tortfeasor has to bear the loss if he had put the victim in a risky situation where the latter had no great choice.
- Both the act of the tortfeasor and some independent act of a third person contributed to the damage. In principle, independent acts of third persons 'interrupt the chain of causation', especially where they act against the law. But when the tortfeasor has brought about the danger of the third person's reaction, he is liable.[30]
- Both the act of the tortfeasor and some independent event like fire, flood or other accident were concurrent causes of the damage. Normally the tortfeasor is liable unless a very unusual event contributed to the injury or damage.[31]

Evaluation

It is clear from the above that in German law no single and simple formula exists by which all problems of causation can be solved. The conditio-formula is a helpful starting point for most cases but fixes only the circle of conditions from which a further choice must be made. The choice according to the adequacy test achieves convincing results in simple causation cases only. The more difficult the question of causation appears to be the more intensively policy considerations have to be applied. In the end they decide. Here, there is a clear corre-

---

25 *See* preceding note.

26 Oberlandesgericht (Court Of Appeal, OLG) Karlsruhe in [1993] *Monatsschrift für Deutsches Recht* (MDR), 29; *see* also above (supra note 23).

27 BGHZ 101, 215.

28 Above (supra notes 20–22).

29 H. Lange (supra note 1) pp. 138–139.

30 H. Lange (supra note 1) pp. 144 et seq.; Staudinger/Medicus, § 249 nos. 68 et seq.; a prominent example is BGHZ 58, 162 (The defendant had caused an accident that resulted in a traffic jam. Drivers behind became impatient and passed the traffic jam by driving on to the plaintiff's property, thereby damaging it. The defendant was held liable for the damage.).

31 Palandt/Heinrichs, Vorbem vor § 249 no. 66; Staudinger/Medicus, § 249 no. 51.

lation between the decrease of the subjective fault concept on the one side and the rise of policy considerations in the field of causation on the other. The need is felt to use causation as a more effective filter and limitation of liability than before when the subjective fault concept mainly fulfilled this task.

Among the evaluating considerations the approach of relying on the protective purpose of the infringed rule is widely and rightfully accepted. However, it presupposes an identifiable purpose of the relevant rule. If a clear purpose cannot be revealed the only way seems to the present author to be to apply case-related policy considerations which finally rely on what would be a fair and reasonable apportionment of risks and chances in society. But in order to increase the predictability of results one should not argue from case to case but develop groups or types of similar cases for which the same arguments and solutions are valid.

3. Specific legislation

The German Civil Code contains a provision on causation in case of joint tortfeasors (§ 830). Joint tortfeasors are jointly liable even if it is unclear who caused injury or damage. Their intentional participation in the joint tort suffices to establish the joint liability of all participants for the total damage (§ 830 para. 1 sent 1 Civil Code).[32] The same rule applies if independent tortfeasors have acted and a tort undoubtedly occurred leaving it unclear only which of the tortfeasors and/or to what extent he caused the injury or damage (§ 830 para. 1 s. 2 Civil Code).[33]

In that case of uncertain, but potential causality – whether the question is of the tortfeasor's causative involvement or the extent of his contribution – all potential tortfeasors are jointly liable if each of them – apart from causation – would have been responsible for damage and if each could have caused it.[34] That means that all other ingredients of a tort must be established for each tortfeasor and that other sources of causation – acts of the victim, act of God etc – must be excluded with certainty.[35] If these conditions are not present independent tortfeasors are only jointly liable if the causality and extent of their contribution can be proven (§ 840 Civil Code). Otherwise their liability must be denied.

Some specific provisions on causation are also contained in the Environmental Liability Act of 10 December 1990. The Act introduced liability without fault for damage through emissions of plants but restricts it to cases where the damage has been spread by way of some environmental 'path' like earth, air or water (§§ 1, 3 of the Act). Furthermore the Act establishes a rebuttable presumption of causation 'if a plant under the circumstances of the case appears to be able to have caused the damage that ensued' (§ 6 para. 1 of the Act). In case of several plants able to have caused the damage the presumption also applies. But the presumption does not apply if 'some other fact under the circumstances of the case is able to cause the damage' (§ 7 of the Act). In fact the Act reduces the standard of proof a plaintiff

---

32 E. Deutsch (supra note 2) no. 147; Münch Komm/Mertens, § 830 nos. 7 et seq.; Palandt/Thomas, § 830 no. 1.

33 *See* BGHZ 17, 214 (221); Münch Komm/Mertens, § 830 no. 6; Palandt/Thomas, § 830 no. 1; Staudinger/Belling,Eberl-Borges, § 830 nos. 66 et seq.

34 Münch Komm/Mertens, § 830 nos. 21–22; Staudinger/Belling/Eberl-Borges, § 830 no. 70.

35 BGHZ 60, 177 (181); BGHZ 67, 14 (20); BGHZ 72, 355 (363).

in tort is normally obliged to fulfill: under the Act the proof suffices that the tortfeasor was able to cause the damage unless he proves that he neither did nor could have caused the damage.[36]

4. The borderline between causation and damage

In theory a clear distinctive borderline between the question of causation and that of damage can be drawn: causation means the necessary connection between some act or source and certain negative consequences to the victim's sphere whereas the existence and extent of these negative consequences constitute the damage aspect. Also in practice both questions are normally clearly distinguished. The problem of whether damage can be imputed to some act of the tortfeasor refers to the so called liability implementing causation (see above). But although connected with the damage-complex it remains a question of causation. In rare cases only, causation and the extent of damage are mixed. This is true, e.g., for the costs of preventive measures. They are discussed as a problem of damage instead of causation, because these costs have been incurred before the tortious act happened.[37]

(a) The poisoned horse This is one of the cases where the questions of causation and damage are closely interrelated. The prevailing view is that the question of damage – and not of causation – is involved.[38] The solution seems to be that X is liable for the total loss while Y is only responsible for the loss, if any, that resulted from the earlier death of the horse. But much depends on how certain the effect of the first event and the entry of the second act is. Seen from Y's side it is a case where the victim or his property is already damaged and therefore the already existing damage might be aggravated insofar as it happens earlier.[39] Seen from X's side it can be argued that X also caused only that damage that occurred before the second act became effective. That is the most favoured solution if the victim himself or a natural event was the cause of the second damaging event.[40]

(b) The asbestos case This case would be approached under the heading of cumulative causation. It is common ground that it is no excuse for either tortfeasor that his contribution alone would not have been sufficient to cause the damage.[41] The three employers in the asbestos case therefor would jointly be liable and it is held to be their risk that one of them is unable to pay.[42]

---

36 For further discussion *see* Staudinger/Kohler, Einl zum Umwelthaftungsgesetz (UmwelthaftG) nos. 92 et seq.

37 H. Lange (supra note 1) pp. 293 et seq.; Palandt/Heinrichs, Vorbem vor § 249 no. 43.

38 J. Esser/E Schmidt (supra note 1) pp. 229 et seq.; W. Fikentscher (supra note 1) pp. 343 et seq.; BGH 10, 6 (9); BGH [1986] NJW, 1329 (1332); H. Lange (supra note 1) p. 179; Staudinger/Medicus, § 249 no. 98.

39 *See* the discussion by H. Lange (supra note 1) pp. 188 et seq.

40 RGZ 1, 67; RGZ 68, 353; W. Fikentscher (supra note 1) nos. 557–558; H. Lange (supra note 1) 185 (for cases of permanent injuries when an independant and intervening event caused the same damage at a later stage).

41 RGZ 69, 58; BGH [1964] VersR, 49; BGH [1990] NJW, 2884; *see* also H. Lange (supra note 1) p. 158–159; Palandt/Heinrichs, Vorbem vor § 249 no. 86.

42 For further discussion *see* E. Deutsch (supra note 2) nos. 158–159.

(c) The attorney case If the attorney can prove that the appeal would have been rejected he would not be liable.[43] The argument is that the same damage would have occurred if the attorney (or other tortfeasor) had acted correctly – so-called 'rechtmäßiges Alternativverhalten' (rightful alternative behaviour).[44]

(d) The pens case In the first alternative of that case the loss of the animals is beyond the protective scope of the statute and therefor the courts would deny liability of the carrier. The breach of the statutory duty would not be regarded as the cause of the damage.[45]

In the second alternative the loss of the animals would have occurred anyhow, even had it been the purpose of the statute to protect against being washed over board. Therefore causation is lacking here in any case.

Part II: Cases

Single event occurrences

1. On the assumption that D drove negligently he is liable for the full amount (§ 823 para. 1 in combination with § 252 Civil Code). On the further assumption that D was the car's owner he is liable for a total amount of DM 750.000 even if the collision was not his fault (§ 12 para 1 nr. 2 Straßenverkehrsgesetz – Road Traffic Act).

2. D is liable for P's loss of income. D must take his victim as he finds him (with his predisposition; see above I.2). This solution is even valid if the loss is due to some psychic (over-) reaction of P.[46] It is only if the cause for the psychic reaction was in fact unimportant ('Bagatelle') that the damage cannot be connected with the tortfeasor's act.[47]

3. O is liable for P's damage because it is the purpose of § 14 par 2 Straßenverkehrsordnung (Road Traffic Ordinance) to protect third persons against such risks. The provision obliges the driver/owner to lock his car when leaving it. Combined with § 823 para. 2 Civil Code the provision is the basis for a successful claim.[48]

4. Since P 1 suffered damage to his property (engines) D has to compensate him. But German law does not allow compensation of pure economic loss without the preceding infringement of a protected interest like property.[49] Thus the claims of P2 and P3 would be dismissed.

5. The defendant is liable under § 823 para. 1 Civil Code. It is no defence that some intervening cause – the heat of the stove – contributed to the final damage. German courts would hold that the defendant must have been aware of the fact that placing some chemical in the

43 BGH [1986] NJW, 246 (concerning a notary public).
44 *See* the extensive discussion by H. Lange (supra note 1) pp. 197 et seq.
45 BGHZ 27, 140; BGHZ 35, 315; for further examples compare H. Lange (supra note 1) pp. 113 et seq.; Palandt/Heinrichs, Vorbem vor § 249 nos. 63 et seq.
46 BGHZ 132, 341.
47 BGH in [1998] *Juristenzeitung* (JZ), 680 with note G. Schiemann.
48 BGH [1981] NJW, 113.
49 BGHZ 41, 125; BGH [1968] NJW, 1280.

near of heat could be dangerous. In other words they would approach the question as one of fault and not of causation.

6. A can claim the costs of keeping the reserve bus and also some interest on the sum for buying the bus if under the circumstances it is necessary to have a reserve bus.[50]

7. A is liable if C's attempts were reasonable (not too dangerous for himself).[51]

8. This case has already been discussed (see above N. 27). D is fully liable.

Intervening events

(a) Natural event occurs independently of the act of any human being

9. In general the courts hesitate to recognise a so – called reserve cause. But if its occurrence is certain at the moment of the tortfeasor's act so that the protected interest is predisposed to be certainly damaged then the courts regularly deny full liability of the tortfeasor.[52] In the instant case D would probably not be held liable. But the question is doubtful and despite a discussion since 100 years no firm solution has been developed.[53]

10. D would only be responsible if the first collision had forced the plaintiff's ship to cross the ocean – in order, for example, to have the correct repair in the US. Otherwise the causal nexus between the first collision and the second damaging event would be denied.

(b) The event consists of the act or omission of a third party

11. As a rule the tortfeasor has to bear the risks to which he has exposed the victim by his tort. But since both second accidents are of an extraordinary nature German courts would hold that P is not liable for the increased damage.[54]

12. In principle D 1 is liable. D 2's reckless driving does not interrupt the chain of causation.[55] Safety measures have the very purpose to prevent damage even through reckless or negligent drivers. But if D 1 had taken all necessary measures causation would be denied.[56]

13. D has also caused P's indirect damage because D created the risk that the wallet could be stolen.[57]

(c) The event consists of the act or omission of the plaintiff himself or is attributable to a cause which can be imputed to him.

14. In principle D is liable even if P already had some heart disease before (no matter if

50 BGHZ 32, 280; BGHZ 70, 199. Criticising the solution: H. Lange (supra note 1) pp. 298 et seq.
51 *See*, e.g., OLG Stuttgart [1965] NJW, 112 (a similar case).
52 E.g., BGHZ 20, 280; BGH [1985] NJW, 676; H. Lange (supra note 1) pp. 188 et seq.; Palandt/Heinrichs, Vorbem vor § 249 no. 99; Staudinger/Medicus, § 249 no. 103.
53 *See* E. Deutsch (supra note 2) nos. 70–71; W. Fikentscher (supra note 1) nos. 556 et seq.; H. Lange (supra note 1) pp. 176 et seq.; Palandt/Heinrichs, Vorbem vor § 249 nos. 96 et seq.
54 For similar cases *see* H. Kötz (supra note 1) no. 152; H. Lange (supra note 1) pp. 144 et seq.
55 Compare cases like BGHZ 43, 178 (181); BGH [1972] NJW, 1804.
56 BGH [1969] VersR, 895.
57 Compare BGH [1997] NJW, 865 (things stolen out of the damaged car).

known or unknown to him). This is due to the maxim that the tortfeasor must take the victim as he finds him. But if the disease would very probably have led to the same heart attack then D would be responsible only for that loss which P suffered because he came to hospital days or weeks earlier.[58]

15. In a similar case the German Federal Court has denied causation,[59] whereas the former Imperial Court held that the original tortfeasor was the adequate cause of the injury suffered later.[60]

Loss of a chance

16. It is likely but not certain that the courts would deny causation because there is no sufficient probability that proper treatment would have prevented the damage. To some extent the solution depends on how grave the doctor's negligence was, because in case of severe breach of technical, professional duties causation is presumed.[61]

17 a–c. Under General tort law (§ 823 Civil Code) the mere probability of causation does not suffice. The courts require a degree of probability next to certainty (compare above). But under the regime of the Ecological Liability Act it is not unlikely that the courts in all three cases would assume that D's factory was able to cause the increased cancer or other disease rate. Then according to § 6 of the Act D had to shoulder the burden of proof that his factory did not cause the disease. The greater the increase in the statistical risk, the more likely that the courts would assume D's liability.

Concurring causes

18. D 1 would be liable for the total damage under § 834 par 1 Civil Code.

19. D 1 is liable for the total damage no matter if he acted in concert with D 2 and D 3 (then joint liability under § 830 para. 1 sent. 1 Civil Code) or independently (then § 830 para. 1 sent. 2 Civil Code).[62]

20. Same solution as in case 19.[63]

21. So far no judgment of the highest German civil court exists accepting a market share liability in tort law. But the Federal Court may develop this concept in future. For the moment liability would be denied because the victims cannot establish the necessary concrete causal link between their injury and the drug production of each single producer. As a rule the courts are also reluctant to help in these cases through measures of evidence like prima facie evidence or a shift of burden of proof.[64]

---

58 *See* for similar cases: RGZ 156, 191; BGHZ 20, 280; BGH [1985] NJW, 676; H. Lange (supra note 1) pp. 188 et seq.; Palandt/Heinrichs, Vorbem vor § 249 no. 99.

59 BGH [1952] NJW, 1010; *see* also (supra note 13).

60 RGZ 119, 204.

61 BGH [1968] NJW, 1185; BGH [1988] NJW, 2948.

62 *See* for a like case RG Recht 1911 no. 1551.

63 For a like case RGZ 16, 144.

64 For further discussion *see* Staudinger/Kohler, Einl zum Umwelthaftungsrecht (UmweltHR) nos.

22. It is an excuse that an event for which the potential tortfeasor is not responsible could also have caused the victim's injury. In these cases the conditio formula leads to the denial of a potential tortfeasor's liability because it is not certain that the injury or damage would not have happened if the tortfeasor had not acted.

23. If the impact of different causes on the injury or damage can clearly be measured and percentagewise attributed to each cause each tortfeasor is only responsible for his proportion of the damage.[65] So the captain in the example has to answer for 20 per cent of the damage.

Miscellaneum

24. In collision cases of this kind the first negligent driver (here D 1) is deemed to have caused all following collisions.[66]

[Note 64 continued]
129 et seq.

65 The same is true in case of several tortfeasors if their respective contribution can be separated and attributed to each tortfeasor. Only if they act jointly together or if their contribution or the extent of it is uncertain each tortfeasor is liable for the total damage and can claim redress, as the case may be, from his co-tortfeasors.

66 BGH [1959] VersR, 194; BGHZ 43, 178 (accident in fog); H. Lange (supra note 1) pp. 144–145; Staudinger/Medicus, § 249 no. 72.

Greece

Causation under Greek Law

Konstantinos D. Kerameus

Part I

1. Causation as a requirement

a. Under Greek law liability for compensation presupposes a causal relation between the legal grounds for liability, *i.e.* breach of contract, and the damage caused.

b. Greek tort law, as indeed Greek contract law, has adopted since the 1920's rather a uniform approach to causation as a requirement of both, delictual and contractual liability. Under this approach, the adequate cause of the loss is always searched, in an effort to link to the prejudicial behaviour those effects, and those effects only, which in the regular course of events seem to a reasonable person to be regarded *ex ante* as a normal consequence of the act or omission under consideration [see Ligeropoulos in ErmAK, vol. II, 1949, Introduction to Arts. 297–300, nos. 44–46; Stathopoulos, *Law of Obligations* (3rd ed. 1998, in Greek) pp. 179–180].

2. The question whether the concept of causal relation is governed only by the rules of causation, as these are determined by reason, or whether it is a legal concept whose meaning is determined by the legislator has not been given by doctrine a single answer. Three theories have been advanced: the *conditio sine qua non*; the "*causa adequata*"; and the theory of the purpose of the rule. The second theory prevails in Greece (see *inter alia* AP (Full Beyck) 23/1988, HellDni 1989. 1180–1181; 1286/1976, NoB 1977.906; 854/1974, NoB 1975.479) but it is also held that the last two theories can be used in combination as well [Stathopoulos, *Law of Obligations* (3rd ed. 1998, in Greek), pp. 184 – 185]. In accordance with the above the Greek Supreme Court by its decision 302/1979, NoB 1979.1293 determined that the *conditio sine qua non* is a necessary but not a sufficient prerequisite for liability.

3. Plurality of parties to an obligation is provided for in the Greek Civil Code (C.C) in two instances: where the plurality arises from a contract or where it is born *ex lege* (see *i.e.* Arts. 926, 927 C.C for a delict committed by several persons). The C.C regulates these instances by non-mandatory rules to be found in Articles 480 et seq. C.C In case of doubt the obligation is divisible: in other words, it is divided among creditors or debtors, respectively, in equal shares. Additionally, if it can be concluded that each of the debtors has an obligation as against the creditor to effect the whole performance, the creditor is entitled to ask for such

J. Spier (ed.), Unification of Tort Law: Causation, 75–78.

performance only once, from whichever debtor he chooses and *vice versa* for creditors (joint and several liability). If no solution can be deduced from the respective relations of creditors and debtors, the parties' liability is regarded to be, as far as their internal relationship is concerned, in equal shares. Finally, if the injured party has contributed by his own conduct to the occurrence or the extent of the damage sustained, then according to the Greek Civil Code (Art. 300) the judge may, as an alternative to awarding full compensation, either not award compensation at all or reduce its amount.

4. (a) Y is liable for the damage caused by the fire, including the death of the animal. If of course Y can prove that the animal would have died irrespectively of the fire, he would not be considered liable for that part of the damage.

(b) In this case all three employers could be held liable. If one can not pay the other two will have to pay his part of damages (C.C 926, 927, 481).

(c) A can be held liable for the damage caused by the untimely lodging of the appeal, since the outcome of the appeal cannot be predicted; damage is conceived here as a loss of chance.

(d) It is important to note that the answer to this hypothetical is not a clear-cut one: if the statute expressly refers to the purpose of preventing disease, it is obvious that, according to the theory of the purpose of the rule, P can not ask for compensation for the damage caused by the loss of animals. The answer will be different in case of application of the *causa adequata* theory.

Part II: Cases

Single event occurrences

1. P (1/10) have the right to sue D if they can prove that D is liable for the collision (C.C 929, 298). However, *causa adequata* would limit the amount of damages to the median income, unless the special character of the coach passengers was clearly indicated to D.

2. The claim of P against D in accordance with the *causa adequata* theory is not valid except to a very limited extent (the corresponding number of weeks), since the inability of P to work has not to do with the accident but relates to his predisposition, which is an unusual circumstance.

3. Pursuant to Article 300 C.C on concurrent fault both 0 and T are liable towards P; however, 0 to a lesser degree since stealing a car does not necessarily imply injuring other people.

4. In Greek law indirect damage of this nature is not compensated except in exceptional circumstances or in cases provided by statute (C.C 932); see Athens Court of Appeal 3839/1978, no. 6 [see 'The Greek Report', in: J. Spier (ed.), *The Limits of Expanding Liability* (1998) p. 130].

5. No liability. The explosion does not seem to be a foreseeable event; the vicinity to the stove, however, creates a dangerous environment.

6. P can claim the costs from D, if P regularly used the bus.

7. No liability; there is no *causa adequata*, unless it is adequate, if not required, to try to help other people in dangerous situations.

8. P can claim from D the damages for the pain and discomfort associated with the surgery; but P's consent was his own prerogative and will.

Intervening events

9. The earthquake is neither a usual nor a foreseeable event, so that D's argument is not valid.

10. D can only be sued for the specific damage and not for the entire damage; no *causa adequata* to the heavy weather.

11. The answer is in the affirmative with respect to the damage and loss of earnings caused by the initial injury. For the next two years only X may be held liable.

12. There is, in principle, *causa adequata*; however interrupted through D2's recklessness. In any case if Dl pays, he can ask from D2 to pay his part (concurrent fault).

13. No liability.

14. The answer is in the affirmative since the first accident was an adequate cause of the inability to work.

15. There is adequate causation because, since the death is related to a condition of the victim produced by the prior event, the chain of causation is not severed; see also Athens Court of Appeal 491/1988, HellDni 1989, 1191 [see The Greek Report, in: J. Spier (ed.), *The Limits of Expanding Liability* (1998) p. 134] under no. 6.

Loss of a chance

16. B's heir can sue Doctor A: the mere, yet reasonable, chance is already an asset.

17a. This case is a matter of proof.

17b. This is also a matter of proof, but mere statistics do not allow the identification of causally connected victims.

17c. Idem.

Concurring causes

18. This is a typical case of joint and several liability, *cf.* Art. C.C 80 mentioned above (under I 1 3).

19. It is important whether the parties act in concert. Assuming no concert, Dl's liability requires proof that he fired the shot.

20. Joint and several liability.

21. To affirm liability here would amount to adopting something like a class action on defendants' side.

22. No claim if it can not be proved which rock hit P.

23. Presumably no claim at all, since the standard of proof is not met.

Miscellaneous

24. Dl is in principle liable for the whole damage if there was heavy traffic on the highway; additional liability may burden other careless drivers.

Italy

Causation under Italian Law

Francesco D. Busnelli and Giovanni Comandé

Part I General framework

Causation is a requirement under Italian tort law. It consists of a two step approach.[1] Better: it concerns two different facts; the damaging event and the reparable damages.[2]

In the first step a material connection should be established between human behaviour and event. At the same time we investigate whether or not there are concurrent causes, arising from natural facts or from the conduct of somebody different from the wrongdoer since in the second hypothesis the extent of the wrongdoer's responsibility (quantum respondeatur) may be limited while in the first hypothesis such limitation is admitted only by some scholars.[3]

The second step looks for a legal connection between the fact and its negative consequences. It also sets the borders for reparable damages: only ordinary and regular losses can be compensated, but losses that would have occurred anyway cannot. Indeed it is similar to the proximity test in common law.

The first step: cause in fact

Judges unanimously say that the same criteria governing causality under criminal law (article 40 and 41 of the criminal code) must be used also for the first step in tort.[4] In fact, decisions

1 Contra G. Valcavi, Intorno al rapporto di causalità nel torto civile, in [1995] *Rivista di diritto civile* (Riv. dir. civ.) II, 481 et seq. and especially 487.

2 For general references *see* P. Barcellona, Scopo della norma violata, interpretazione teleologica e tecniche di attribuzione della tutela aquiliana, in [1973] Riv. dir. civ. I, 311; P. Forchielli, *Il rapporto di causalità nell'illecito civile* (Padova, 1960); P. Trimarchi, *Causalità e danno* (Milano, 1967); F. D. Busnelli, *La lesione del credito da parte di terzi* (Milano, 1964) pp. 116 et seq.; F. Realmonte, *Il problema del rapporto di causalità nel risarcimento del danno*, (Milano , 1967).

3 *See* infra pp. 2–3 and expecially (note 13).

4 *See* Corte di Cassazione, 24 maggio 1968, n. 1599, in [1969] *Responsabilità Civile e Previdenza* (Resp. Civ. Prev.), 68; Corte di Cassazione Sezioni Unite (S. U.), 26 Gennaio 1971, n. 174. Note that several Corte di Cassazione decisions find a substantial analogy between art. 40–41 codice penale (c. p.), on one hand, and art 1218 art 2043 c.c. (c. c.), on the other hand in containing the applicable rules for material causation. *See* Corte di Cassazione, 27 maggio 1995, n. 5923 in [1996] *Danno e Responsabilità*, 1, 126.

J. Spier (ed.), Unification of Tort Law: Causation, 79–92.

given in criminal trial are beyond recall in civil trials for damages in so far material causation is concerned (artt. 442 and 651 criminal procedure code),[5] but this judgment does not have any effect on civil trials when the issue is about reparable damages.

Scholars interpreted these rules under two quite different theories. Under the first theory (conditio sine qua non) the wrongdoer's behaviour is the cause in fact if, ex post, it is established that the event would not have happened without his conduct on the basis of the best science and experience of the moment. On the contrary, under the suitable causality theory there is material causation only when wrongdoer's behaviour would be a sufficient cause of the event under an ex ante evaluation.

Neither theory is accepted in its pure from by judges. In fact, they mix them in a default rule with a qualification. Under the general rule everything without which the result would not have followed is a sufficient cause of it. However – and this is the qualification – judges exclude causation when an anomalous deviation from the normally expected chain of causal events follows the behaviour.[6] This helps to limit the chain of reparable consequences.[7]

Usually scholars argue that article 2055 of the civil code, which provides for joint and several liability, expresses the general principle that concurrent causes are irrelevant or – to put it another way – that all concurring causes are equivalent in causing damages[8] (article 1227 section 1 of the civil code, that reduces the amount to be paid according to the contributory fault of the injured, would be an exception to this rule). Several cases establish this. For example the negligent issuing of documents by a public authority was deemed a concurrent cause of a fraud practised by means of these certificates. Hence, liability was found.[9] Analogously, the principle of the equivalence of causes was established when competitors distributed photocopies of a newspaper containing incorrect information (on the soft wheat composition of a brand of pasta). Again joint and several liability was found on the basis of art. 2055 c.c. explaining that different levels of concurring fault are relevant only to the (internal) apportionment of damages among wrongdoers.[10]

However, a more satisfactory interpretation may be given. Between the tort of the wrongdoer and the final damage an event occurs. If this can be considered a consequence of wrongdoer's original tort (according to a principle of causal regularity), liability also extends to the final damage. Once causality is determined, liability results even if the tort just contributes to causing the damage. If another party is also responsible for the event that intervenes in the causality link then there is a joint and several liability between him and the person liable for the initial damage (Art. 2055 c.c.). The Courts state that the two liable

5 Decisions are pretty uniform on this point. *See* Corte di Cassazione, 27 maggio 1992, n. 6334, in *Foro italiano* (Foro it.), Repertorio, 1992, voce Giudizio (rapporto), n. 18.

6 *See* Corte di Cassazione, 5 Febbraio 1971, n. 279, in [1971] Resp. Civ. Prev., 541.

7 *See* Corte di Cassazione, 11 Febbraio 1988, n.1473, in [1989] *Giustizia Civile* (Giust. civ.) I, 196.

8 Corte di Cassazione, 2 dicembre 1969, n. 3859, in [1973] *Archivio Giuridico della Circolazione* (Arc. giur. circ.) 67.

9 Corte di Cassazione, 10 febbraio 1996, n. 1030, in [1996] *Danno e Responsabilità* 171 with comment of V. Carbone.

10 Corte di Cassazione, 24 aprile 1997, n. 3596, in [1997] *Danno e Responsabilità* 438 with comment of V. Carbone, Concorso di cause o causa da sola sufficiente?; *See* also Corte di Cassazione, 15 gennaio 1996, n. 268, in [1996] *Danno e Responsabilità* 521; Corte di Cassazione, 16 febbraio 1996, n. 1199, in [1996] *Gius* 11, 1397.

persons do not pay compensation in proportion to the amount of damages caused by their respective torts: only between them is the liability load distributed according to the seriousness of their faults.[11] This does not exclude that both can concur in causing the damaging event. According to that, concurring causes which do not break the chain of causation still play a role in damages reduction (art. 2055 section 2 c.c.). Of course section 1 of art. 2055 for joint and several liability grants an easier and more certain compensation to the victim. On the other hand, when the foreign element inserted between the initial act of the person and the final damage either cannot be considered a normal and regular consequence of the original event or it is per se sufficient to cause the result, the causality link is broken.[12]

Hence, the joint and several liability rule of article 2055 c.c. and the comparative fault rule of art. 1227 section 1 are both actual manifestations of the general relevance of concurring human causes.[13] It is not entirely clear whether or not this principle of general relevance of human concurring causes might be extended to natural concurring causes as well.[14] Note that this reading of the rules may lead to different solutions in several cases.

The second step: legal cause

There should not be just a de facto causality link but a juridical causality link as well between event and damage. In other words, it is not enough for the tort to be the necessary condition for the damaging event, because the liability is not extended to all consequences. These are selected according to juridical criteria and the most significant one is that according to which the victim cannot be guaranteed against all the risks that he may have been exposed to even if the original tort had not taken place. In fact, the second step is governed by the general principle of art. 1223 c.c. and art. 1227 section 2.

Art. 1223 of the Civil Code (which applies to liability for breach of contract, but also to liability for torts, according to Art. 2056) allows compensation for those damages that are 'immediate and direct consequences' of the tort.[15] Art. 1223 gives a very strict definition of the damages that can be compensated but it is normally interpreted more broadly. In fact, the Courts go beyond the strict sense of 'immediate and direct consequences' to include those damages that can be considered consequences of the tort according to an evaluation of the relationship between cause and effect carried out on the basis of the so-called suitable causality criterion. It is also said that a fact is the cause of an event if it satisfies a statistical regularity criterion. That is: in an ex ante valuation it can be said the event is a foreseeable and avoidable consequence of the fact.[16]

---

11 *See* Corte di Cassazione, 25 settembre 1987, n. 3641, in [1988] *Giustizia Civile* (Giust. civ.) I, c. 362.

12 Corte di Cassazione, 19 settembre 1996, n. 8348, in [1996] *Gius* 24, 3643.

13 For a fuller explanation *see* F. D. Busnelli, *L'obbligazione soggettivamente complessa. Profili sistematici* (Milano, 1974) pp. 136 et seq.

14 F. D. Busnelli (supra note 13) pp. 137 et seq.; F. D. Busnelli, *Nuove frontiere della responsabilità civile*, [1976] 23 *Jus*, 41, 51 et seq.

15 For the argument that art. 1223 c.c. presupposes other rules for causation *see* G. Gorla, Sulla c.d. causalità giuridica: 'fatto dannoso e conseguenze', in [1951] *Rivista di diritto commerciale* (Riv. Dir. Comm.) I, 450, 409; G. Visintini, *Trattato breve della responsabilità civile* (Padova, 1996) p. 557.

16 F. Galgano, *Diritto privato* (Padova, 1992) p. 346.

Decisions usually affirm that the legislator in art. 1223 c.c. wanted only to set a limit to 'remote or considerably indirect consequences'.[17] A clear application of the rule is expressed by art. 1227 section 2, according to which damages that the victim could have avoided with ordinary due diligence cannot be compensated.[18]

In synthesis: the two steps are distinct moment of a sole process of valuation. The first one looks for causality between fact and event actually determining liability. The second one looks for juridical connections between the event and its consequences. In the end it turns to a matter of reparable damages fixing the extension of liability.

Relevant factors

As we said before, the criterion of conditio sine qua non is used in establishing the scope of causation (cause in fact), but it is tempered by an investigation on the adequacy of the cause and its foreseeability. Actually, under contract law (art. 1225 c.c.) compensation is limited to those foreseeable damages at the time the obligation arose, but under tort law it is not because art. 2056 c.c. does not adopt this rule. However, in the second step foreseeability plays a role as it is understood as regularity of the consequences coming from the caused event, turning to an evaluation of remoteness of damages. In this, common sense and policy arguments certainly play a role, but usually in a cryptic way.

Temporal proximity may play a role but it is not decisive. Take for example the case of a traffic accident with personal injuries; during transportation toward the hospital the ambulance has another accident in which the injured is killed. The first wrongdoer is liable only for personal injuries, he is not liable for the death: his behaviour did not cause the death it was only an occasion for it.[19] Anyway, Courts sometimes refer to a lengthy interval between two events as an additional reason, in order to confirm the interruption of causality link previously excluded on the basis of causal regularity.[20] Alternatively consider the case in which a cancer arises in causal connection to the shock suffered in an accident occurred 40 years before. The court said the length of time did not break the causation link.[21]

It is really a difficult task to find out workable criteria (factors) to be taken into account in establishing the scope of causation. The leading guide should be certainty, but real cases often do not fit in the regular consequences paradigm. Hence, uncertainty clearly follows. However, in defining factors to set causation requirements it should not be forgotten that some room for flexibility is necessary. Therefore, what it is needed is to work out principles clear enough to guide judges in actual cases without entirely fixing ex ante the path they should follow.

---

17 Thus the Corte di Cassazione, 10 ottobre 1967, n. 2397, in [1968] Foro it. I, c. 1311.

18 *See* Corte di Cassazione, 20 novembre 1991, n. 12439, in [1993] Foro it. I, c. 1223. Note that in this case the damaged person's behaviour is not concurring to cause the damaging event, but it comes after it weighing on the consequences. But *see* on the contrary P. Forchielli, *Il rapporto di causalità nell'illecito civile* (Padova, 1960) 58 who thinks art. 1227 section 2 contains only a 'pleonastic cross-reference' to article 1223 c.c.

19 *See* The Italian Report, in: J. Spier (ed.), *The Limits of Expanding Liability* (1998), case 6.

20 *See* Corte di Appello Roma (Court of Appeal of Rome), 1 febbraio 1993, in [1993] Resp. Civ. Prev., 462 et seq.

21 Tribunale di Cassino (Court of Cassino) , January 14th 1994, in [1994] *Archivio Giuridico della Circulazione e dei trasporti* (Arch. giur. circol. trasp.) 225.

Often scholars are unsatisfied with the legal framework for causation.[22] saying it is a too poor one. In fact, as we will see discussing the cases, it may lead to unacceptable results.

The protective purpose of the violated rule plays a role in establishing causation in the sense that the mere violation of a rule does not imply automatically causation.[23] The plaintiff should prove it. Most examples come from violations of the traffic code leading to an accident. Driving without a driving license or transporting more persons than permitted (hence violating specific rules) have no influence on causation[24] if the violated rule is not intended to prevent the event which occurs.

Part II Cases

(a) Here the issue is one of material causation. Under the case only Y can be sued for damages. His act (setting the stable afire) clearly stops the chain of consequences started by X.

Courts acknowledge one out of several facts attributable to different persons as the sole sufficient cause of an event either if it cuts the chain of events driving the original causal link or it is by itself able to cause the event so that the other facts are not concurring causes but merely occasions.[25] This is the case as described under the stated facts.[26]

Under tort law, if a second chain of events causes the result independently from the first one, this is the sole cause of the result. In the case, there are two different acts (poisoning and setting afire) both able to produce the fatal result for the horse but the second one does so before the first.

Indeed, tort law does not look to the wrongdoer but to the victim to be compensated, and the attempt to kill the horse cannot lead to compensation for damages otherwise caused by another person's behaviour. Note that the case is different from the 'plumber case'. Please see under case 9 for more details.

(b) The general framework, especially the normative framework, has been given elsewhere[27] Once again here the issue is material causation. We have three different courses of conduct (employing X for a dangerous job) that can be imputed to three different persons. According to the principle of equivalence of all concurring causes A's conduct is a conditio sine qua X

22 P. Trimarchi, *Causalità e danno*, p. 25; F. Realmonte(supra note 2) pp. 174 et seq.

23 The mere violation of a legal rule does not lead to liability if it is not demonstrated it caused the accident. *See* Corte di Cassazione, 10 novembre 1967, in [1969] Resp. Civ. Prev., 608.

24 *See* Appello Napoli (Court of Appeal of Napoli) 2 aprile 1986, in [1986] *Archivio Giuridico della Circulazione Stradale* (Arch. giur. circ. strad.), 710; Corte di Cassazione, 9 agosto 1973, n. 2319, in [1974] Riv. giur. circ. trasp., 383.

25 Corte di Cassazione, 19 settembre 1996, n. 8348, in [1996] *Gius* 24, 3643.

26 It is worth to remember that, under contract law, art. 1221 c.c. lets the debtor to free himself from liability proving that the thing would have perished anyway (that is the damages would have resulted independently from his behaviour). The same hypothetical reasoning applies under tort law. Note, however, that art. 2056 c.c. does not recall art. 1221 c.c. P. Trimarchi, Condizione sine qua non, causalità alternativa ipotetica e danno, in [1964] *Rivista trimestrale di diritto e procedura civile* (Riv. trim. dir. proc. civ.), 1431, 1435 refers this hypothetical evaluation to damages instead of referring it to causation.

27 *See* The Italian Report, in: J. Spier (ed.) (supra note 19) case 7 (cancer case).

would have not been injured, because without his exposure during his work time at A's plant he would have not passed the fatal threshold.[28] However, if A fulfilled his legal duty to adopt the necessary security measures to protect workers' physical and psychological integrity (ex art. 2087 of the Civil Code) and had reason to believe that X would take into account he was already exposed, it would be more difficult to find him liable. Nevertheless, a judge may covertly use a policy argument to load liability on the shoulder of the only available defendant. In this case art. 2055 c.c. on joint and several liability would apply giving to A the – theoretical – possibility to seek reimbursement from B and C.

Moreover, since asbestos is a so called 'increasing dangerous factor', even under criminal law, A would be liable.

(c) We would approach the case from a causation perspective. Lawyers' liability is governed by a specific provision in article 2236 c.c. according to which, if the solution of specially difficult technical problems is involved, he is liable only if he acted with intent or if was grossly negligent. Note that the rule applies only for services requiring the solution of specially difficult technical problems.[29] In any event, his duty of diligence must be evaluated, according to the principle laid down in article 1176 section 2 c.c., comparing it with the circumstances and the required services.[30]

Clearly enough to lodge an appeal in time is not a difficult service even for an inexperienced lawyer. However, in order to obtain damages from A, C may not limit himself to a complaint that a timely filled appeal would have presumably led to a favourable decision's reform. C must show either that the decision to be appealed is wrong or that there are new documents or evidence according to which he would have won the appeal.[31] Note, however, that in a case in which the lawyer lost the client's bills of exchange causation was presumed. The court said it rested upon the lawyer to show their execution would not have reached a positive outcome.[32]

A carrier by land is liable for losing what he agreed to transport unless he demonstrates the loss is due to chance, or to the nature/the flaws of the transported goods, to their packing or to the act of the sender or of the consignee. There is a presumption of liability. However, artt. 423 and 952 of the Navigation Laws for carriage by sea do not prescribe such a presumption. Indeed, carriage by sea has a quite different regime. The Navigation Code distinguishes between nautical fault – which refers to captain's or crew members' negligence, unskilfulness or carelessness in managing or maintaining the ship – and commercial fault – which refers to captain's or crew members' negligence, unskilfulness or carelessness in using the ship for transportation. The carrier is liable for nautical fault if it occurred before the voyage started and for commercial fault during the voyage. Moreover art. 422 of the

28 For a recent application of the rule *see* Corte di Cassazione, 19 settembre 1996, n. 8348, in [1996] *Gius* 24, 3643.

29 Corte di Cassazione, 7 maggio 1988, n. 3389, in [1988] Foro it., Repertorio, voce Professioni intellettulali, n. 74 and 96.

30 Corte di Cassazione, 21 giugno 1988, n. 4245, in [1988] *Giurisprudenza agraria italiana* (Giur. agr. it.) 665.

31 Corte di Cassazione, 5 aprile 1984, n. 2222, in [1992] Foro it., Repertorio, voce Professioni intellettulali, n. 59.

32 Corte di Cassazione, 16 ottobre 1980, n. 5557, in [1980] *Repertorio Giurisprudenza Civile* (Rep. Giur. civ.), voce Avvocato e procuratore, n. 124.

navigation code lists several dangers that exonerate the carrier from liability (so called excused dangers). Storms are among them. Nevertheless, the carrier might still be liable if his contractual counterpart demonstrates his negligence (art. 422 section 2 navigation code).

Leaving the animals on the deck without enclosing them in pens as prescribed by a specific statute clearly shows the crews commercial fault. Hence, if animals are swept away during the storm the carrier is liable, but the damaged person must prove both that animals were not enclosed and that they were lost for this reason. On the contrary, if animals' loss is due to the sinking the carrier is not liable even though they were not in pens because the sinking by itself caused the loss and it is an act of God expressly provided for in the code (please see also above on protective purpose of the violated norm).

Single event occurrences

1. It seems from the facts that causation is clear: D's collision with the coach caused lawyers' personal injuries. Article 1223 c.c. allows compensation for 'immediate and direct consequences' of D's tort. Lawyers' loss of income are among them.

P1/10 can recover from D no matter how large the amount of damages is. Clearly enough, here the issue is one of damages. As explained before, Italian law sets limits for the kind of compensable consequences, but it does not generally set limits according to the amount. In fact, art. 2058 c.c. allows the judge only to exclude specific redress because it is too burdensome for the tortfeasor, but he cannot limit the amount of damages because of their size. Nevertheless, loss of income should be awarded by the judge taking into account all the circumstances of the case (art. 2056 c.c.) and he might probably use this power to reduce the amount of damages. In reality, however, since the hypothetical is a traffic accident and D must have compulsory insurance it must surely be inevitable that the court will condemn the insurance company for an amount greater than the premium.

2. Again this is a matter of damages and D is liable regardless of P's predisposition.
The third paragraph of art. 2054 c.c. makes the owner, the purchaser by instalments, the holder of an usufructuary right over the vehicle, jointly and severally liable with the driver for a crash, unless he proves the circulation of his/her car was against his/her will. It is usually said that the law presumes culpa in vigilando on the owner. Courts established that to escape liability an actual precaution to enforce the denial of permission should be satisfied.[33]

In one case in which a thief had stolen a car, causing with it an accident, the owner went free of liability having proved that he locked the car and activated antitheft devices.[34] This showed that the car was being driven against his will. On the contrary, in our case O behaved negligently, leaving the key in the lock in an area where several cars are usually stolen. The car's theft and its subsequent circulation causing damages is a foreseeable consequence of his conduct. The theft by itself does not cut the causal link between his behaviour and the event causing damages.

---

33 Corte di Cassazione, 12 aprile 1990, n. 3138, in [1990] Foro it., Repertorio, voce Circolazione stradale, n. 185. But *see* contra Corte di Cassazione, 29 ottobre 1971, n. 3072, in [1971] Foro it., Repertorio, voce Circolazione stradale, n. 336.

34 Corte di Cassazione, 10 luglio 1973, n. 2003, in [1973] Foro it., Repertorio, voce Circolazione stradale, n. 68 and 273.

3. Please see hypothetical number 2.

4. The legal framework for this case has been dealt with elsewhere.[35]

5. Following the legal rules we set forth above, liability is clear in this case according to art. 2043 c.c.. So far as cause in fact is concerned the defendant's negligent behaviour unequivocally caused the explosion – the mere fact that the poison happened to be near the stove does not make it a fortuitous case.

The personal injuries damages we suppose follow the blast are the (regular) immediate and direct consequences of such an event.

6. Here the only problem appears to be whether or not costs of buying and maintaining a reserve bus can be compensated.

Courts constantly award what is called under Italian law 'danno da fermo tecnico': the out of pocket expenses of renting a vehicle during the damaged one's repair period. However, in the proposed case P is trying to get reimbursed for the costs of 'buying and maintaining ' his reserve bus. But these costs are not the direct consequence of D's tort. He did not cause P to buy a reserve bus – he bought for his own convenience. Probably some courts could award P with the same amount of money he would have paid to rent a reserve bus for the needed period of time. Nevertheless, this controversial outcome has nothing to do with the causation problem we are asked to discuss. So far legal causation is concerned buying and upkeeping costs in the hypothetical are not a direct and immediate consequence of D's tort.

7. There are decisions interpreting the criterion of regular causality in a way for which it is enough the tort created a situation without which damages would have not occurred.[36] Accordingly, C might seek compensation from A especially if A himself left B in his dangerous position. In this case would be regularly foreseeable that someone would have tried to rescue B. But the solution is not entirely clear; some courts may think the railroad accident is a mere occasion for C's damages.

8. P cannot recover from D. P's pain ad discomfort are not immediate and direct consequences of D's tort. Even though D could foresee that A would need a kidney transplant he cannot be made liable for P's suffering. Indeed, P's 'damages' come from his voluntary undergoing the surgical operation. From a naturalistic standpoint D's tort is an essential antecedent for P' damages but there is not legal causation.

Intervening events

9. From a naturalistic standpoint the earthquake would have destroyed the house anyway. Nevertheless, D's tort has given to P a right to compensation. The earthquake did not break the causal link between the plumber negligent behaviour and the damaging fire. Indeed, the whole chain of consequences of D's conduct was already completed before the earthquake destroyed the house. What if the house had been already repaired? Would D claim back his money?

---

35 *See* The Italian Report, in: H. Koziol (ed.), *Unification of Tort Law: Wrongfulness* (1998), cable case.

36 Corte di Cassazione, 11 gennaio 1989 n. 65, in [1989] Foro it., Repertorio, voce Responsabilità civile, n. 81.

Compare also the case with the horse poisoning one. If the horse perished because of the poison would X be free of liability because the horse would have died anyway because of the fire? Of course the answer is no.

10. The hypothetical is built in a way that the original collision looks like the material cause of the extensive damages suffered because of heavy weather. Nevertheless, as explained before, art. 1227 section 2, precludes compensation for damages that the victim could have avoided with ordinary due diligence. It seems to be the case, since weather conditions are known quite in advance.

The mere fact that the ship would not have made the voyage, had the collision not occurred, does not make the collision the cause of the heavy weather damages. The result would be different if the heavy weather conditions had appeared after the collision but before any possibility of permanent repair had occurred. It is not a matter of time proximity. Extensive damages would be an immediate and direct consequence of the collision under these different circumstances. On the contrary, the wrongdoer cannot be forced to pay for the ship taking the chance to have only temporary repairs. In the end, it was the bad weather condition to cause damages: the collision was just an occasion.

11. Please see above under relevant factors for the general framework. To summarize: here D is liable only for one year loss of income. Sub variant-case a) the drunk driver is liable for the two more years of lost income. Under sub-case b) the two more years loss of income rests on P.

12. In this case we have to assume that D1 was negligent. Either he did not leave his car in the proper emergency lane or he just left it there for quite a while. Note, parenthetically, that the police are supposed to patrol turnpikes and there might be liability even on them, but we leave aside this issue.

According to the general framework we find joint and several liability for D1 and D2. Hence, P2 and P3 may seek compensation from D1. He might recover part of his payment for damages from D2 according to the general rules of concurring fault (see art. 2055 c.c.).

Alternatively if D1's failing to take steps to remove his car from the highway does not amount to negligence – say he left the car on the proper emergency lane and rushed to call a breakdown lorry – he is not liable for damages occurred to P2 and P3. Of course D1's car was a necessary antecedent for damage to have occurred, but from a legal standpoint it was only an occasion.

Courts plainly say that several simultaneous or subsequent facts imputable to different persons have the same causal suitability unless one of them breaks the causal link.[37]

13. Please see the general framework above for this case. Clearly enough the theft is not a regular, direct and immediate consequence of an accident. In a similar case in which the damaged car was stolen the court said these kinds of losses 'are not normal results of the event.[38]

---

37 Corte di Cassazione, III Sezione Civile (Division for Civil matters, Sez. Civ.), 19 settembre 1996, n. 8348, in [1996] *Giustizia Civile Massimario* (Mass.).

38 Corte di Cassazione, 20 luglio 1984, n. 4661, in [1985] Arch. giur. circ. strad., 108.

14. Here the result is the same as we found in case number 9. P's right to compensation is not removed by the heart attack. Think about a variant of the case: the heart attack happens during the trial for compensation or right after. Would it make any difference? We think it does not.

15. Please see the answer under hypothetical n. 6. However, it is worth mentioning here a couple of cases.[39] In the first one the driver of a car was deemed liable for the suicide of the customs officer injured in the caused accident. In fact, right after the accident the victim, understanding the seriousness of his injury (his left leg was completely smashed), pulled out his weapon and shot himself. Our Corte di Cassazione said that the anomalous behaviour of the customs officer did not break the causal link. In another personal injury case leading to the victim's death it was said that medical doctors' gross negligence at the hospital did not break the causality link[40] with the accident.

16. Here the problem is whether or not loss of a chance is an item that can be compensated. There are several cases involving wrong (or more specifically, omitted) diagnosis or late therapy that contributes to the death of the patient. They are decided by reference to loss of survival chance.[41] In the latest cases an increase of the risk ranging around 30 per cent is sufficient to bring about liability.[42] Indeed, the original understanding according to which the plaintiff must demonstrate there was more than a 50 per cent of probability of the defendant's conduct having caused the damage is not any longer followed. Nowadays it is enough to show defendant's behaviour certainly increased the risk to damage a given plaintiff. Moreover, in a very recent case[43] the court explained that, when the omitted diagnosis is due to (clear) negligence, the plaintiff is not required to scientifically prove the causal link since it is possible to use criteria of verisimilitude and common experiences. In other words, when negligence is extremely clear (almost self-evident) valuation on causality is surrogated by the fault evaluation.[44] Sometimes a different technique is used to skip causation uncertainty problems when negligence is clear: the burden to proof of either chance or due diligence is

---

39 Corte di Cassazione, 7 febbraio 1996, n. 969, in [1996] Foro it. I, 2482.

40 Corte di Cassazione, I Sezione Penale (Criminal Division, Sez. Penale) 31 ottobre 1995, in [1996] *Studium Iuris*, 494.

41 *See* Tribunale Torino (Court of Torino), 11 marzo 1985, in [1986] *Giurisprudenza italiana* (Giur. it.) I, 2, 681; Corte di Cassazione, Sez. Penale, 17 gennaio 1992, in [1992] *Nuova giurisprudenza civile e commentata*, 358 with comment of V. Zeno Zencovich, Questioni in tema di responsabilità per colpa professionale sanitaria; and [1992] *Responsabilità Civile e Previdenza* (Resp. Civ. Prev.), 552 with comment of G. Ponzanelli, Tanto rumore per nulla: a proposito di gazzette e di responsabilità medica.

42 *See* Corte di Cassazione, IV Sez. Penale, 17 gennaio 1992, n. 371, in [1992] Nuova giur. civ. comm., 358 with comment of Z. Zencovich, Questioni in tema di responsabilità per colpa professionale sanitaria.

43 Corte di Appello di Genova (Court of Appeal of Genua), 10 marzo 1997, in [1997] *Danno e Responsabilità* , 470 with comment of R. de Matteis, Colpa omissiva, nesso di causalità e perdita di chances. A similar case was decided by Tribunale Torino, 11 marzo 1985, in [1986] Giur. it. I, 681.

44 For a less recent case *see* Corte di Cassazione, 13 ottobre 1972, n. 3044, in [1973] Foro it., I, 1170.

imposed on the defendant using a res ipsa loquitur argument.[45] Note, however, that all cases refer to medical malpractice and they concern cases of fault by omission.

17. All three cases actually do not concern loss of a chance. In the hypotheticals actual victims are suing, not potential ones. In other words, people who got the cancer are seeking compensation. All the others, just exposed to an increased risk, are not. Hence, the problem is just one of cause in fact and not of reparable loss (loss of a chance).

(a) In the last years the concept of causation has moved toward a more probabilistic approach. Please see case 16. Accordingly this case would likely be decided against D. Of course, this will be the answer if defendant's behaviour 'certainly' increased the risk. Therefore, if there are doubts that the statistically increased rate of ill persons is still due to coincidence, this means there is not enough scientific evidence D caused the increased rate.

Note that if scientific evidence is contradictory (i.e. some experts say yes some others say no) it will rest upon the judge to decide. Probably, even cryptically, policy arguments would come into the picture and a compensation oriented tort system might still say D is liable even though there is not scientific certainty his emissions increased the risk.

In the end, here the only problem is one of cause in fact and the general trend seems to dilute more and more the probabilistic requirements to find causation. Yet, it is difficult to set precisely the statistical relevance of defendant's contribution to the harm judges would consider enough to find liability.

(a) Please see discussion of the foregoing case and the general remarks.
Consequently D is liable for damages occurred to all three victims. Of course, medical science tells us several concurring factors give rise to cancer and almost no one may be the sole cause of it. According to our jurisprudence increasing the risk of cancer leads to the wrongdoer's liability (obviously when the risk does materialize).

As the Court said in the aforementioned medical doctor case[46] (mutatis mutandis), there is liability even though the damaging outcome (death in that case and cancer in this one) might have resulted independently of the defendant's wrongful behaviour, but the wrongdoer's act or omission increased the risk of it.

Note also that only from a statistical standpoint it may be said that one out of three damaged persons is not a defendant's victim. Statistics is a science that does admit errors; and in any event D actually increased the risk for all the victims leading his conduct to be a concurring cause of their illness.

(a) Once again the decision of this case rests on what we said under a and b.
Here, D's negligence is not an important issue. What the plaintiff must show is that D's emissions (more likely than not) increased the risk for him. That is: D's quality and quantity of emitted pollutants are carcinogenic for the kind of cancer the victim incurred and the victim was exposed to them.

---

45 *See* for example Corte di Cassazione, 15 dicecmbre 1972, n. 3616, in [1972] Foro it., I, 1474.

46 Corte di Cassazione, IV Sez. Penale, 17 gennaio 1992, n. 371, in [1992] Nuova giur. civ. comm., 358 with comment of Z. Zencovich, Questioni in tema di responsabilità per colpa professionale sanitaria.

Once again scientific evidence may not be uncontroversial leaving the per cent amount of certainty to find liability to the judge.

Concurring causes

18. D1 and D2 are jointly and severally liable for the wall collapse.
According to article 2055 c.c. P may sue D1 recovering the entire damage, but D1 may still seek reimbursement from D2 recovering from him the portion of damages he created piling rubbish.

19. In 1992 our Constitutional Court examined a similar case.[47] Two hunters injured a third one. The latter sued for compensation under art. 2050 c.c., since hunting is constantly deemed a dangerous activity and fault is presumed. Nevertheless, the plaintiff should still demonstrate causation and, as in the hypothetical, it was impossible to establish from whose shotgun he was injured. The question of constitutionality was raised to seek to extend the liability rule of art. 2050 in order to presume also the causal link in cases as the one under examination. The Constitutional Court rejected the case. Hence, under tort law P should still prove causation and will probably lose his case (note that the law 11 February 1992, n. 157 provides for a special compensation fund).

In reality, there are 33.3 per cent chances that D1 actually caused the damage. It is still widely open to debate whether a judge would find D1 jointly and severally liable together with D2 and D3. We did not find cases on the point.

20. We found the same result as case 18 above. Note, however, that the rubbish case was plainly governed by art. 2055 section 1. Both D1 and D2 were concurring in causing the wall collapse, since the sole conduct of neither of them would have created the collapse by itself. On the contrary, in this case both acts are sufficient to cause damage. That means both wrongdoers are individuated and each own individual behaviour could be said the exclusive cause of fish killing.

P may also sue only one of them disregarding altogether the other one. Of course the defendant may seek reimbursement from the other one according to his concurring liability.

The easy singling out the actual wrongdoers as defendants greatly differentiates the hypothetical both from the hunters case and the following one in which there are potential defendants who did something that it is not possible to demonstrate reached the actual plaintiff, but it is wrong anyway.

21. Preliminary remarks: Here the problem is to pin liability on one of the producers. That is the product actually manufactured by Dx injured Px (where x is a specific producer or a specific victim).

In the hypothetical it seems possible to assume there is enough scientific evidence to say the drug caused the injury.

Note that all D1/D20 did something wrong (negligently manufacture a dangerous drug), as in the hunters case (negligently shooting), but all of them caused damage (probably they

---

47 Corte Costituzionale (Constitutional Court), 4 marzo 1992, n. 79, in [1992] Foro it., I, 1348 with comment of G. Ponzanelli, 'Pallino anonimo', ovvero attività pericolosa con responsabile ignoto e problemi di welfare state.

injured the percentage of victims corresponding to their own market share). This last point is different from the hunters case where only one of them has caused damages. However, it is not possible to establish who produced the drug in each of the 25000 cases. Indeed, we can show the drug caused the harm but we cannot demonstrate who exactly produced it in each case. Put it another way, we know each D damaged a certain amount of Ps but we cannot say who precisely they are. Even though we have all the persons who caused injury and the victims there is no way to put together the right ones. Of course we are assuming all the producers sold their product in the same place at the same time – otherwise some of them would be clearly out of reach.

Therefore, prima facie, under the conventional scholars' wisdom of Italian causation law the result would be for D1/D20.[48]

Nevertheless, we may argue for different results. Putting aside variant c, it may be argued that all the producers together caused the whole damages (the entire damage caused to P1/25000) applying joint and several liability to them all (this means that no matter how big Dx's market share he may be forced to pay the whole damage leaving to him to seek reimbursement from the other producers according to their own market share/concurring liability). Alternatively, if we assume that art. 2055 c.c. is an actual manifestation of the general relevance of concurring human causes, we might say cause in fact is established, limiting damages to the loss imputable to the actual Dx on trial. However, this line of reasoning requires each victim to sue all producers to recover his whole damage. Analogously, if we think about the duty to compensate these victims as an obligation that can be severally paid, each producer is liable for his own market share.

In any event, tort law does not give a final clear cut solution for these cases. At least because in Italy we lack instruments like class actions that may help to solve the problem deeming all the producers liable for their market share and pooling the resources to be collected and distributed.

1) see above
2) see above
3) This last hypothetical looks more controversial because the fact that D1 dominated more than 50 per cent of the market makes it appear more likely than not he did cause damage to the actual plaintiff. Nevertheless, this reasoning would be followed in all 25000 cases leading the dominant producer to pay all damages.

22. On several occasions our Corte di Cassazione expressed the idea according to which evaluation of concurring natural causes (not imputable to anybody) and imputable human causes may well reach either the result of excluding liability or of imposing it on the defendant if the causal link still remains despite the natural cause.[49] However, the hypothetical under examination is more similar to 21 c, because we have a 50 per cent chance that D's behaviour caused the injury. Yet, it is different from 21 c, because here we have only one person potentially liable. Therefore, the case might be easier than the hunters one. In fact, it may be argued that D's negligence increased the risk of injury by a falling rock leading

---

48 *See* C. Salvi, voce Responsabilità extracontrattuale (diritto vigente), in *Enciclopedia del Diritto* (vol. XXXIX, Milano 1988), 1186, 154 note 462.

49 For more details *see* G. Alpa/G. Bessone/V. Zeno Zencovich, I fatti illeciti, in *Trattato di diritto privato* (Tratt. dir. Priv.), coordinated by P. Rescigno, (Torino, 1995), XIV, 64.

him to be liable for the actual injury (as in the doctor case). Of course the burden of proof is still on the plaintiff to show causation, but a diluted probabilistic causation link may satisfy today's jurisprudence.

23. SB can plainly sue the Captain of SA. According to the general principle that concurrent causes are irrelevant, the SA's Captain did cause the collision and he is liable for the entire damage. Alternatively, if we interpret art. 2055 c.c. as an actual manifestation of the general relevance of concurring human (and natural) causes, we might still say the Captain is liable, but he will be charged only for what he contributed to the collision (i.e. 20 per cent pf the total damage).

Miscellaneum

24. We suppose the question here is: would D1 be liable for all damages? Under the given facts he is not. Art. 2054 c.c., first paragraph, sets the obligation to redress damages upon drivers of vehicles (other than those on rails), unless they prove they did everything possible to avoid damage. The driver may rebut this presumption showing he behaved according to all the rules provided for traffic using the needed diligence according to the circumstances.[50] Those drivers who can demonstrate this and, nevertheless, were hit by other cars may seek compensation (from them) and are not liable. However, the case says it is not possible to 'allocate blame to individual drivers'. Hence, the presumption of equal fault provided for by article 2054, paragraph 2, applies. Clearly enough D1 is liable for damages caused to the vehicle he crashed in.

50 *See* Corte Costituzionale, 17 febbraio 1987, n. 1724.

South Africa

Element of Causation in South African Law of Delict

Johann Neethling

Part I

1. Causation as a requirement

The *causing* of damage through conduct, or, put differently, a *causal nexus* between conduct and damage, is required for a delict in South African law. A person can thus not be liable if he has not *caused* any damage.[1]

Various criteria for causation have been developed over time. It is, however, noteworthy that not all of them are applied on the same level. This is apparent from the fact that the *conditio sine qua non* test is generally accepted as a point of departure or the first step in order to determine whether a *factual* causal nexus exists between the act and the harmful consequence; if so, so-called *factual causation* is present. Such a factual causal nexus may, however, extend very far – in fact *ad infinitum* – because a single act can in principle give rise to an endless chain of harmful events. Because no legal system can, on the ground of fairness, allow unlimited liability merely based on causation, the next step is to ascertain for which of the harmful events flowing from his conduct a defendant should be liable. All the other criteria for causation attempt to solve this problem of so-called *legal causation*.

The element of causation is therefore divided into a two-step approach: factual and legal causation.

Factual causation

Apparently, most writers as well as the South African Appellate Division are in favour of the *conditio sine qua non* test, also known as the 'but for' test, for factual causation.[2] According

1 *See* J. Neethling/J. M. Potgieter/P. J. Visser, *Law of Delict* (1994) pp. 159 et seq.; N. J. van der Merwe/P. J. J. Olivier, *Die Onregmatige Daad in die Suid Afrikaanse Reg* (1989) pp. 197 et seq.; P. Q. R. Boberg, *The Law of Delict: Vol I Aquilian Liability* (1984) pp. 380 et seq.; J. C. van der Walt, *Delict: Principles and Cases* (1979) pp. 94 et seq.; J. M. Burchell, *Principles of Delict* (1993) pp. 32–34 and pp. 114 et seq.

2 *See* e.g. P. Q. R. Boberg (supra note 1) pp. 380 et seq.; N. J. van der Merwe/P. J. J. Olivier (supra note 1) pp. 197 et seq.; J. C. van der Walt (supra note 1) pp. 95 et seq.; *contra* J. Neethling/J. M. Potgieter/P. J. Visser (supra note 1) pp. 162–169; C. R. Snyman, *Strafreg* (1992) pp. 80–83; A. D. J. van Rensburg, *Juridiese Kousaliteit en Aspekte van Aanspreeklikheidsbegrensing in die*

J. Spier (ed.), Unification of Tort Law: Causation, 93–103.

to this test one should, in order to determine whether X was a cause of Y, eliminate X mentally (in your mind) and consider whether Y still appears or not. If Y falls away when X is eliminated, X is a cause of Y. If Y still appears even when X is eliminated, Y has not been caused by X.

The general view is that the *conditio sine qua non* test may also be applied to determine whether an *omission* caused a certain damaging consequence by inserting positive conduct – the steps the reasonable man would have taken to prevent the damage – in the place of the omission.[3] This is, however, not a true application of *conditio sine qua non* because this test requires one to eliminate something in the mind and not to 'add' (or insert) something to the given facts.

Although *conditio sine qua non* has been widely accepted, A. D. J. Van Rensburg[4] has, after a thorough examination, subjected it to convincing criticism.[5] According to him[6] a causal nexus exists where *one fact arises out of another*. To determine such factual causation, no magical formula exists, but human knowledge and experience are required and the outcome will of course be dependent on the facts of a particular case and the evidence produced in court.[7]

Legal causation

As said, legal causation is about determining for which harmful consequences factually caused by the wrongdoer's wrongful, culpable act he should be held liable; in other words,

---

[Note 2 continued]
Privaatreg (1970) ch. 1. *See e.g.* also the following cases: *Minister of Police v Skosana* 1977 1 SA 31 (A); *Siman and Co (Pty) Ltd v Barclays National Bank Ltd* 1984 2 SA 888 (A); *S v Mokgethi* 1990 1 SA 32 (A); *International Shipping Co (Pty) Ltd v Bentley* 1990 1 SA 680 (A); *Standard Chartered Bank of Canada v Nedperm Bank Ltd* 1994 4 SA 747 (A).

3 *See Minister of Police v Skosana* 1977 1 SA 31 (A); J. Neethling/J. M. Potgieter/P. J. Visser (supra note 1) pp. 166–167.

4 A. D. J. van Rensburg (supra note 2) pp. 3–65.

5 It is not necessary to deal here with all the points of criticism in detail and only the following will be mentioned [*see* J. Neethling/J. M. Potgieter/P. J. Visser (supra note 1) pp. 162–166]: (i) The *conditio sine qua non* test is based on a clumsy, indirect process of thought that results in circular logic; (ii) the *conditio sine qua non* test fails completely in cases of so-called *cumulative causation*. Here we deal with cases where more than one act actually cause a particular consequence, *e.g.* where X and Y simultaneously, but independently of each other, fire a fatal shot at Z's head. If one eliminates X's shot, Z's death does not fall away; on account of this one may conclude that X did not cause Z's death. Subsequently, when Y's act is eliminated, the same result is achieved, namely that Z's death does not fall away. The application of the *conditio sine qua non* test thus permits one to come to the absurd conclusion that neither X nor Y has in fact caused Z's death. The solution to this problem lies in the common-sense approach of the man in the street, as it was put in *Portwood v Swamvur* 1970 4 SA 8 (RA) 15: 'I think it would be quite profitless to expect C, the injured bystander, to have to try and prove what might or might not have happened if one or other of A or B had not been negligent [the judge means 'had not acted']. The proper approach surely is the direct common sense approach of the man in the street and, in the example given, he would, without doubt, simply say: 'Of course they are both to blame.' This is how I propose to approach the facts of this case"; (iii) the *conditio sine qua non* test is in fact not a test of causation because it is merely an *ex post facto* way of expressing a predetermined causal nexus.

6 *Cf.* A. D. J. van Rensburg (supra note 2) pp. 141–152.

7 *See* J. Neethling/J. M. Potgieter/P. J. Visser (supra note 1) pp. 167–169.

which consequences should be *imputed* to him. In general terms the wrongdoer is not liable for harm which is 'too remote' – hence the term 'remoteness of damage' for legal causation or the problem of imputability of harm.

Different criteria have in the past been applied in South African law to determine legal causation (*adequate causation, direct consequences, fault* and *reasonable foreseeability*), but the latter criterion was preferred by the courts.[8] However, the Appellate Division has now expressed itself in favour of a *flexible approach, taking into account policy considerations based on reasonableness, fairness and justice.*

(i) *Flexible approach.* In *S v Mokgethi*[9] the Appellate Division held that there is no single and general criterion for legal causation which is applicable in all instances. A flexible approach is accordingly suggested. The basic question is whether there is a sufficiently close relationship between the wrongdoer's conduct and its consequence that such consequence may be imputed to the wrongdoer in view of policy considerations based on reasonableness, fairness and justice. However, the criteria for legal causation which already exist (such as adequate causation, direct consequences and reasonable foreseeability), may play a subsidiary role in determining legal causation within the framework of this elastic approach.[10]

(ii) *Adequate causation.* According to this criterion, only so-called 'adequate' consequences are imputed to the wrongdoer, that is, consequences which, according to human experience, in the normal course of events the wrongdoer's act has the tendency to bring about. In order to determine such a tendency, the following questions are, for example, asked: was the damage the reasonably-to-be-expected consequence of the act; did the damage fall within the expected field of protection envisaged by the legal norm that was infringed; were the consequences 'juridically relevant' with reference to the cause? Although this criterion, especially as it was formulated originally, has been subjected to sharp criticism, it nevertheless enjoys the support of certain writers and it has also been recognised in decisions in the field of criminal law.[11]

(iii) *Direct consequences.* According to this criterion, which stems from English law, an actor is liable for all the 'direct consequences' of his negligent conduct. In other words, liability is not necessarily limited to the foreseeable consequences of this conduct. In South

8 *See* in general J. Neethling/J. M. Potgieter/P. J. Visser (supra note 1) p. 169; N. J. van der Merwe /P. J. J. Olivier (supra note 1) pp. 196 et seq.; P. Q. R. Boberg (supra note 1) pp. 439 et seq.; J. C. van der Walt (supra note 1) pp. 94 et seq.; J. M. Burchell (supra note 1) pp. 119 et seq.; A. D. J. van Rensburg (supra note 2) pp. 154 et seq.

9 1990 1 SA 32 (A) 40–41, confirmed in *e.g. International Shipping Co (Pty) Ltd v Bentley* 1990 1 SA 680 (A) 700 et seq.; *Standard Chartered Bank of Canada v Nedperm Bank Ltd* 1994 4 SA 747 (A) 764 et seq.; *Smit v Abrahams* 1994 4 SA 1 (A) 14 et seq.; *Napier v Collett* 1995 3 SA 140 (A) 143 et seq.

10 *See* J. Neethling/J. M. Potgieter/P. J. Visser (supra note 1) pp. 191–193.

11 *See* e.g. C. R. Snyman (supra note 2) pp. 86–91; *S v Daniëls* 1983 3 SA 275 (A) 332; *see* in general J. Neethling/J. M. Potgieter/P. J. Visser (supra note 1) pp. 172–174; N. J. van der Merwe/P. J. J. Olivier (supra note 1) pp. 202 et seq.; P. Q. R. Boberg (supra note 1) pp. 440–442; J. C. van der Walt (supra note 1) pp. 98–99; J. M. Burchell (supra note 1) p. 119; A. D. J. van Rensburg (supra note 2) pp. 216–224.

African law this criterion was recognised in *Frenkel & Co v Cadle*[12] but, particularly because of its mechanical nature, it has been subjected to severe criticism.[13] Be that as it may, J. C. van der Walt[14] opines that the direct consequences criterion should be applied to establish legal causation in regard to personal injuries where the wrongdoer is held liable even for those consequences which were not reasonably foreseeable, for example, in the so-called egg-skull cases.[15]

(iv) *Fault.* According to this approach, the wrongdoer is liable only for those consequences in respect of which he had fault (intent or negligence).[16] However, both intent and negligence fail to serve satisfactorily as criteria for legal causation.[17] As far as *intent* is concerned, it is traditionally accepted that 'intended consequences . . . can never be too remote'.[18] This approach is however too simplistic in a situation where a foreseen consequence occurs in a totally unexpected manner and intent fails to keep liability within acceptable limits. On the other hand, in certain circumstances[19] intent as a criterion for legal causation may exclude liability for consequences which should reasonably be imputed to the wrongdoer.[20] With regard to *negligence* (test of reasonable foreseeability and preventability of harm) the main objection is that it is pointless, once it has been established that a reasonable man in the wrongdoer's position would have foreseen and prevented damage, to ask again whether the wrongdoer should have refrained from acting because the specific remote consequence could ensue. In other words, in the event of further consequences it is unnecessary once again to apply the second leg of the negligence test (whether the wrongdoer should have acted differently).[21]

(v) *Reasonable foreseeability.* An examination of the South African case law clearly indicates that in many cases the courts apply a foreseeability criterion in determining imputability of harm.[22] However, the case law does not offer a clear picture of the content of the reasonableness criterion. Normally the foreseeability test is not exactly defined, the decision simply being that a specific result was foreseeable or not and that is the end of the matter.

---

12 1915 NPD 173; *see* too *Thandani v Minister of Law and Order* 1991 1 SA 702 (E) 705.

13 *See* A. D. J. van Rensburg (supra note 2) pp. 222–223; J. Neethling/J. M. Potgieter/P. J. Visser (supra note 1) pp. 174–176.

14 J. C. van der Walt (supra note 1) pp. 102–104.

15 These cases arise where the plaintiff, because of one or other physical, psychological or financial weakness, suffers more injury or loss than would have been the case if the plaintiff did not have such weakness. In such a case the wrongdoer is liable also for the harm which may be ascribed to the weakness, in other words, the wrongdoer must take his victim as he finds him (*talem qualem* rule) [*see* J. Neethling/J. M. Potgieter/P. J. Visser (supra note 1) pp. 189–191].

16 *See* N. J. van der Merwe/P. J. J. Olivier (supra note 1) pp. 198 and 206 et seq.

17 *See* J. Neethling/J. M. Potgieter/P. J. Visser (supra note 1) pp. 176 et seq.

18 *See* P. Q. R. Boberg (supra note 1) p. 440.

19 E.g., in instances of assault resulting in unintended personal injuries (*cf. Brown v Hoffman* 1977 2 SA 556 (NC) 557–560).

20 *See* J. Neethling/J. M. Potgieter/P. J. Visser (supra note 1) pp. 178–181.

21 *See* J. Neethling/J. M. Potgieter/P. J. Visser (supra note 1) pp. 182–185 for detail.

22 *See* e.g. *Bester v Commercial Union Versekeringsmpy van SA Bpk* 1973 1 SA 769 (A); *Mafesa v Parity Versekeringsmpy Bpk* 1968 2 SA 603 (O) 605; *Kruger v Van der Merwe* 1966 2 SA 266 (A) 272; *Brown v Hoffman* 1977 2 SA 556 (NC).

There is no clarity on the question as to what should be foreseeable to found liability.[23]

Conclusion

The flexible approach of the South African Appellate Division to the question of legal causation, that is whether a consequence may reasonably be imputed to the wrongdoer, is commendable because a court is not bound beforehand to any specific criterion or criteria, but has the freedom to apply the criterion or criteria which serve reasonableness and justice best in the light of the circumstances and taking into account considerations of policy.

2. Specific legislation

The position of joint wrongdoers is regulated by the Apportionment of Damages Act 34 of 1956 (section 2).[24] The Act abolishes the common law distinction between joint and concurrent wrongdoers. Joint wrongdoers are defined as persons who are jointly or severally liable in delict for the same damage. A person may thus be sued as a joint wrongdoer only if he was indeed delictually liable as against the plaintiff.[25]

3. The borderline between causation and other factors

(a) X cannot be sued for damages based on the *death* of the horse, simply because he did not cause (*conditio sine qua non*) its death. Factual causation in this respect is thus absent. Y on the other hand did cause the horse's death and is therefore in principle liable. However, this conclusion does not mean that X goes out scot-free. A clear distinction must be made between the damage to the horse caused by the poison before its death by fire, reducing its value quite substantially, and the damage caused by its death (killing of a much less valuable horse than it would otherwise have been). Therefore, X should be liable for the damage he caused (diminution of the value of the horse) and Y for its (diminished) value at the time of its death.

(b) In South African law the general principle is that if the defendant's conduct in any way contributed to the plaintiff's loss or harm, factual causation is present.[26] This is indeed the position as regards A, B and C's contribution to X's illness, applying the *conditio sine qua non* or 'but for' test. A, B and C therefore caused X's illness. However, it is doubtful whether A will be liable for the damage because of absence of legal causation.[27] The damage was probably not reasonably forseeable when X left A's employment – being too remote – and since the fatal threshold was in any case crossed only when X was employed by C, it

---

23 *See* in general J. Neethling/J. M. Potgieter/P. J. Visser (supra note 1) pp. 185–187; P. Q. R. Boberg (supra note 1) pp. 445–447; J. C. van der Walt (supra note 1) p. 98.

24 The principles of this Act were extended to spouses married in community of property and deceased and injured breadwinners (Apportionment of Damages Amendment Act 58 of 1971). *See* J. Neethling/J. M. Potgieter/P. J. Visser (supra note 1) pp. 259–263.

25 *See* in general J. Neethling/J. M. Potgieter/P. J. Visser (supra note 1) pp. 257–258.

26 *Cf.* J. Neethling/J. M. Potgieter/P. J. Visser (supra note 1) p. 291 no. 172.

27 And probably also wrongfulness (voluntary assumption of risk by X through his exposure to asbestos over such a long period) and negligence (reasonable foreseeability and preventability of damage).

does not seem reasonable and fair to impute the damage to A.
(c) If A can prove that the appeal would have failed and as a result C did not suffer any damage, he will go out free because factually he did not cause any damage (*conditio sine qua non*) through his omission. This he can do by demonstrating that the replacement of his omission by positive conduct would not have made any difference.[28] Furthermore, one may argue that wrongfulness is also absent, because there was no damaging result (a necessary requirement for wrongfulness).
(d) Although there is a factual causal nexus between the loss of the sheep and the defendant's omission (see (c) above), there was probably no wrongfulness on P's part – the loss was not in breach of a statutory duty because the nature of the harm and the manner in which it occurred were not such as was contemplated by the statute.[29] However, if the sheep would in any case have drowned because the ship sunk in the storm, there is no causal nexus between the damage and the defendant's omission; factual causation is then absent.

Part II Cases

Single event occurrences

1. Because this is not a case of pure economic loss, but financial loss resulting from bodily injuries, D is in principle liable for all the damage of P 1/10 (loss of income). As far as causation is concerned, factual causation presents no problems (*conditio sine qua non*). Legal causation is in principle also present – unlike in instances of pure economic loss,[30] the fact that liability in this case results in a multiplicity of actions creating an overwhelming potential liability, would not lead to the conclusion that legal causation is absent because it would be not be fair and reasonable to impute the damage to D.[31]

2. This is a classic so-called egg-shell case.[32] As said,[33] such a case arises where the plaintiff, because of one or other physical weakness or predisposition as in the case of P, suffers more injury or loss than would have been the case if he did not have the predisposition. In such a case D is liable also for the harm which may be ascribed to the predisposition ('the wrongdoer must take his victim as he finds him') – *in casu* the loss of income as a result of P's inability to work.

3. If wrongfulness (that is, a legal duty according to the *boni mores* to remove the key and

28 *See* supra under par 1 (note 3).
29 J. C. van der Walt (supra note 1) p. 39 explains this with reference to the English case *Gorris v Scott* (1874) LR 9 Ex 125, where the court held that the defandant was not liable, because the purpose of the statute was not to avoid occurrences such as the one complained of, but to prevent the spread of contagious diseases among animals. *See* also J. Neethling/J. M. Potgieter/P. J. Visser (supra note 1) p. 65 no. 176.
30 *See* J. Neethling/J. M. Potgieter/P. J. Visser (supra note 1) pp. 285–286; A. van Aswegen, 'Policy considerations in the law of delict', [1993] THRHR 192–193.
31 *Cf.* A. van Aswegen, [1993] THRHR 192–193.
32 *See* J. Neethling/J. M. Potgieter/P. J. Visser (supra note 1) pp. 189–191; J. C. van der Walt (supra note 1) pp. 99–100; N. J. van der Merwe/P. J. J. Olivier (supra note 1) pp. 211 et seq.
33 *See* (supra note 15).

prevent the damage) and negligence (reasonable foreseeability and preventability of harm) can be established on the part of O, the remaining question is whether the damage caused by T can be attributed to O (legal causation). Despite the fact that the theft was reasonably foreseeable, the imputation of P's harm to O – caused by a thief – would seem to be unreasonable and unfair.

4. Since P1 suffered physical damage through the negligent act of D, it may in principle claim for the damage to its engines as well as for consequential losses (for example, loss of production), provided that such damage was reasonably foreseeable (not too remote)[34] and legal causation is therefore present. However, as far as the other two groups of plaintiffs (P2 and P3) are concerned, they merely suffered pure economic loss. Therefore, before the question of legal causation can be considered, it must first of all be ascertained whether D acted wrongfully as against them. Here it must be determined whether there was a legal duty on D to prevent the financial loss to P2 and P3. *In casu* such a duty will probably be absent because – according to *Coronation Brick (Pty) Ltd v Strachan Construction Co (Pty) Ltd*,[35] where the defendant also damaged the electrical cables to the plaintiff's factory – (i) the plaintiffs were subjectively not foreseeable and D therefore did not know about them and (ii) the situation is fraught with an overwhelming potential (indeterminate) liability.[36]

5. There is factual causation between defendant's negligent act and the plaintiff's personal injuries (*conditio sine qua non*). The question is whether the injuries can be imputed to him (legal causation). Applying the direct consequences criterion as supplementary yardstick to the flexible approach,[37] the plaintiff will probably be held liable despite the fact that the explosion and resultant injuries were not reasonably foreseeable.

6. In South African law the present problem is dealt with from the perspective of damage and the question of mitigation of loss.[38] The general principle is that where the deprivation of the use of a damaged *res* occurs in circumstances which make it reasonable for the owner of the *res* to make use of a temporary substitute and he suffers patrimonial loss as a consequence, the defendant who negligently damaged the *res* is in principle liable for the loss.[39] Usually a plaintiff claims for the reasonable rent of a substitute *res* (here the bus). In principle, however, there seems to be no reason why P should not succeed in claiming part of the cost of buying and upkeeping the reserve bus provided that he acted reasonably in mitigating his damage.

---

34 *See* supra par 1 (notes 22–23) in regard to this criterion for legal causation.

35 1982 4 SA 371 (D) 383–384, 386–387.

36 *See* J. Neethling/J. M. Potgieter/P. J. Visser (supra note 1) pp. 283–284 and 285–286. A. van Aswegen, [1993] THRHR 192–193 convincingly argues that the present factor is not really relevant with regard to wrongfulness, but should rather be utilised in connection with legal causation which is directly concerned with the *extent of liability*.

37 *See* supra par 1 (notes 12–15).

38 *See* J. Neethling/J. M. Potgieter/P. J. Visser (supra note 1) pp. 222–223; P. J. Visser/J. M. Potgieter, 'Skadevergoeding vir gebruiksverlies: 'n Welkome nuwe ontwikkeling' [1994] THRHR 312 et seq.

39 *See Kellerman v South African Transport Services* 1993 4 SA 872 (C); *Shrog v Valentine* 1949 3 SA 1228 (T).

7. This is a typical so-called rescue case.[40] The question whether A should be liable for the injuries of C (the rescuer), was recently identified in South African case law as a question of legal causation.[41] Applying the reasonable forseeability test as a supplementary test to the flexible approach, it is probably reasonably foreseeable that people (like C) may try to rescue the injured in a railway accident, and that they themselves may be injured in the process. Provided that C acted as a reasonable person in his rescue attempt, his conduct will probably not be considered to be a *novus actus interveniens*.[42] A will therefore be liable.

8. As in the previous case, the question of factual causation presents no problem (*conditio sine qua non*). The question as to legal causation is also similar to that in the previous case, but *in casu* it will probably not be regarded as reasonably forseeable that a person (like P) will permit the transplant of his kidney to A. A's conduct seems to be a *novus actus* and his consequential pain and discomfort should therefore not be inputed to D.

Intervening events

(a) Natural event occurs independently of the act of any human being

9. According to current authority the date of the commission of a delict is generally the decisive moment for the assessment of damage; and the date of the commission of a delict is the earliest date on which all the elements of a delict are present.[43] In this case D committed a delict when he caused the fire and he is therefore in principle liable for the damage caused by his action. The fact that the house was later destroyed by an earthquake, is completely irrelevant (*res inter alios acta*) as far as P's claim against D is concerned.

10. A *novus actus interveniens* may be brought about by the (culpable) conduct of the plaintiff himself or a third party, or by natural factors such as wind and rain.[44] In South African law an event will generally qualify as a *novus actus* if the event was not reasonably foreseeable.[45] *In casu* factual causation is present since the voyage to the USA would not have been made but for the defendant's collision. As far as legal causation is concerned, it is questionable whether the damage caused by the bad weather on the way to the USA was reasonably foreseeable. But even if a case can be made out for such foreseeability, according to the flexible approach it nevertheless seems that it would be unfair and unreasonable to impute the damage concerned to D because it was indeed caused by a *novus actus* (albeit reasonably foreseeable).

(b) The event consists of the act or omission of a third party[46]

11. As in the previous case, the question is whether the further damage caused by X or the avalanche can be imputed to D (legal causation). Again the primary enquiry is whether the

---

40 *See* J. Neethling/J. M. Potgieter/P. J. Visser (supra note 1) 157–158.
41 *Gibson v Berkowitz* 1996 4 SA 1024 (W) 1052 (J. Neethling/J. M. Potgieter [1997] THRHR 552).
42 *See* J. Neethling/J. M. Potgieter/P. J. Visser (supra note 1) pp. 187–189.
43 *See* J. Neethling/J. M. Potgieter/P. J. Visser (supra note 1) pp. 210; P. J. Visser/J. M. Potgieter, *Law of Damages* (1993) pp. 75–76.
44 *See* J. Neethling/J. M. Potgieter/P. J. Visser (supra note 1) pp. 188–189.
45 *See* also cases 7 and 8 *supra*.
46 *See* also supra under case 10.

further damage was reasonably forseeable. Since the chances of an ambulance being hit by a drunk driver or by an avalanche are probably not very high (perhaps slightly higher in the case of X), the further damage was probably not reasonably foreseeable and X's conduct and the avalanche will therefore be regarded as new intervening causes. D will thus not be liable for the further damage.

12. Once again the question is whether the sequence of events leading to P1 and P2 colliding with D2, can be imputed to D1 because of his negligent omission to remove his car from the highway. The answer is probably no, not only because the sequence of events was improbable and therefore not reasonably foreseeable, but also because, according to the flexible approach, it would be unfair and unreasonable to impute damage caused by a reckless driver to D1. D2's conduct thus constitutes a *novus actus intervenience*.

13. Similar to case 12 – the theft was probably not reasonably foreseeable, and it will likewise be unfair and unreasonable to impute damage caused by a thief to D.

(c) The event consists of the act or omission of the plaintiff himself or is attributable to a cause which can be imputed to him[47]

14. Similar to case 9 – the damage caused by the heart attack is irrelevant (*res inter alios acta*) as far as D's delict is concerned.

15. The question is whether P's death by fire can be imputed to D because of his negligent conduct with regard to the accident. Applying the reasonable foreseeablity test, as well as the flexible approach to legal causation, damage seems to be too remote. P's death by fire thus constitutes a *novus actus intervenience* and D is not liable to P's widow for loss of support.[48]

Loss of a chance

16. In South African law heirs have no claim for damages on the ground that the premature death of the deceased had probably prevented his estate from being larger.[49] However, dependants may have a claim for loss of support if on a preponderance of probability, A's negligent diagnosis factually caused B's death. This does not seem to be the case since the substitution of the failure to diagnose cancer by a reasonable (correct) diagnosis, would probably not (40 per cent chance) have prevented his untimely death.[50]

17. All three cases (a, b and c) are concerned with the question of quantum and onus proof of factual causation. The plaintiff(s) must prove on a preponderance of probability that the defendant's emissions caused their illness or cancer. This means that it must be more probable than not that the emissions caused the illness. To this end, the plaintiff must at least establish a *prima facie* case, that is *prima facie* evidence that the emissions caused the illness. If so, the burden is then on the defendant (D) to rebut this inference by showing what

47 *See* also supra under case 10.

48 *Cf. Mafesa v Parity Versekeringsmaatskappy Bpk* 1968 2 SA 603 (0).

49 *See Lochat's Estate v North British and Mercantile Insurance Co Ltd* 1959 3 SA 295 (A); J. Neethling/J. M. Potgieter/P. J. Visser (supra note 1) p. 268.

50 *See* supra par 1 (note 3) as regards causation in the case of an omission.

the true facts were. If D cannot do this, the plaintiffs will succeed. Because of the extremely high percentage of people falling ill in case (a), it seems that the plaintiffs (P1/100) will be able at least to establish a *prima facie* case that the emissions caused their illness. Also in case (b) the statistics indicate that it is more probable than not that D's emissions caused all three plaintiffs' cancer. In both cases the evidentiary burden is then on D to produce contradictory evidence. However, in case (c) the position seems to be different since the preponderance of probability is not in favour of the three plaintiffs.

Concurring causes

18. Similar to case (b) (par 3) above. As said, the general principle is that if the defendant's conduct in any way contributed to the plaintiff's loss or harm, factual causation is present. This is indeed the position as regards D1 and D2's contribution to collapsing the wall, applying the 'but for' test. D1 and D2 therefore caused the damage. If all the other requirements for delictual liability are also present, D1 will be liable as joint wrongdoer. He may then claim recourse from D2.[51]

19. If it cannot on a preponderance of probability (perhaps by ballistic experts) be proved who (D1, D2 or D3) fired the negligent shot that injured P, P will not succeed against D1.

20. As said,[52] the *conditio sine qua non* test fails completely in cases of so-called *cumulative causation*, such as in the present case, because according to this test neither A nor B caused the death of the fishes. However, if one applies the common sense approach of the man in the street, as one should, A and B are, of course, both to blame and are in principle liable as joint wrongdoers as against P.[53]

21. It will be very difficult to prove factual causation since after ten years the plaintiffs can no longer identify the manufacturer of the drugs bought by them. The preponderance of probability definitely favours D20 and D2 because of their small market share, while it is slightly against D1 because of his market share of 50.01 per cent. It therefore seems that D20 and D2 should escape liability for lack of proof of factual causation, while D1 may be held liable. On the assumption that the total harm can be attributed to D1/D20, it may perhaps be argued that they are then joint wrongdoers with regard to the total harm and that each of them may in principle be sued for the whole amount of damages, but that the one who paid, has a right of recourse against the others. This argument is however not likely to succeed since the damage was done to individual plaintiffs who each has to prove that a particular defendant(s) caused him/her harm.

22. Since it cannot be proved on a preponderance of probability that D's negligent conduct caused P's injuries, P's action will fail.

23. In South African law, SA will be vicariously liable, because of the captain's negligence, for the full damage unless it can be proved which specific damage can be attributed to his negligence. An apportionment or reduction of damages only comes into the picture where

51 *See* J. Neethling/J. M. Potgieter/P. J. Visser (supra note 1) pp. 257–258.
52 *See* supra note 5.
53 *See* again *Portwood v Swamvur* 1970 4 SA 8 (RA) 15 (supra note 5).

there was contributory negligence on the part of the plaintiff or in the case of joint wrongdoers, but not where factors such as the weather conditions contributed to the plaintiff's damage.

Miscellaneum

24. There is no doubt that D1's delict factually caused the entire damage. He will therefore be liable unless absence of legal causation can be established (for example, liability may be excluded on the ground of the policy consideration that liability will extend too wide). However, this does not seem likely because damage to property and personal injuries (which were reasonably foreseeable) are involved.

Switzerland

Causation under Swiss Law

Pierre Widmer

Part I

1. Causation as a requirement

a. Causation is a prerequisite to the creation of the obligation to compensate a loss. There has to be a causal link between the infringement which generates the loss and the act or fact on which liability is based ('Anknüpfungstatbestand/fait de rattachement').

The general clause of Art.41 para. 1 of the Swiss Code of obligations (SCO) which establishes a general responsibility for fault and is considered to be the basic norm of the entire law of torts states that:

A. Liability in general I. *Requirements* of liability	**Art.41**	[1]*Whoever* ***causes*** *damage to another person in an unlawful way, be it wilfully or be it by negligence, is liable for compensation.*

And the draft General part of tort law (DGP) which is intended to replace the current articles 41 et seq. SCO in the framework of a comprehensive revision of Swiss tort law, lays down in an even more explicit way that:

III. Causal link 1. Principle	**Art.15**	*A person is liable for compensation only to the extent that the fact imputable to him is related to the damage by a link of legally relevant causality.*

This draft provision makes clear that – for the purposes of tort law – causation is not a merely physical phenomenon but has to be 'legally relevant'. This rather vague expression is used deliberately in order to show that the statute does not endorse a determinate theory, and certainly not the theory of 'adequate causation', even if, or just because, this theory corresponds to the current – at least apparently prevailing – opinion in Swiss literature and jurisprudence.[1]

---

1 K. Oftinger/E. W. Stark, *Schweizerisches Haftpflichtrecht* I (5th ed. Zurich 1995) § 3, nos. 14 et seq., pp. 109 et seq.; A. Keller, *Haftpflicht im Privatrecht* I (5th ed. Bern 1993) pp. 65 et seq.; H. Honsell, *Schweizerisches Haftpflichtrecht* (2nd ed. Zurich 1996) § 3, nos. 6 et seq., pp. 27 et seq.; H. Rey, *Ausservertragliches Haftpflichtrecht* (2nd ed. Zurich 1998) § 5, nos. 522 et seq.,

J. Spier (ed.), Unification of Tort Law: Causation, 105–122.

b. The wording of article 15 DGP ('to the extent') shows also that no conceptual distinction is to be made between causation as a prerequisite of liability as such ('haftungsbegründende Kausalität') on the one hand, and as a measure allowing determination of the amount of compensation ('haftungsausfüllende Kausalität') on the other hand. This conception of an 'integrated (legal) causality' is controversial,[2] but it seems correct to admit that it corresponds to the actual structure of tort law. In our opinion, this is clearly demonstrated by the fact that Art.44 SCO (under the heading 'reduction of compensation') allows the judge to adjudicate compensation ('reduce or refuse') between 100 and 0 per cent, according to the circumstances, i.e. to proportion the amount of the compensation to the volume or measure of ('legally relevant') causal involvement imputable to the tortfeasor.[3] If the judge admits in a first step that a certain person is responsible under a certain head of liability, but then, in a second step, reduces the compensation down to zero, considering that other causes (a fortuitous event, or the act or fact of a third party or of the victim himself) override the link of responsibility previously established, he does – in the last analysis – nothing else than to negate the previously established causal link and, consequently, to completely negate responsibility that was initially assumed, at all; the apparent 'two step approach' comes finally to the same result that would be reached by a 'one step approach'. We then are in precisely the same situation as that contemplated by article 16 DGP which states

---

[Note 1 continued]
pp. 117 et seq.; H.Deschenaux/P. Tercier, *La responsabilité civile* (2nd ed. Bern 1982) § 4, nos. 30 et seq., pp. 57 et seq.; P. Engel, *Traité des obligations en droit suisse* (2nd ed. Bern 1997) ch. 28, nos. 114 et seq., pp. 484 et seq.; R. Brehm, *Berner Kommentar zum schweizerischen Privatrecht* (Bd. VI/1/3, Bern 1986–1990) nos. 120 et seq. ad art. 41 SCO; A. K. Schnyder, *Basler Kommentar zum Schweizerischen Privatrecht, Obligationenrecht* I (2nd ed. Basel/Frankfurt a.M. 1996) nos. 15 et seq. ad art. 41 SCO.

2 In the sense supported here: R. Brehm (supra note 1) nos. 53–54 ad art. 43 SCO; probably also: A. Keller (supra note 1) pp. 83–84; K. Oftinger/E. W. Stark (supra note 1) § 3, no. 20, p. 114, in contradiction with nos. 25/26, p. 116f.; H. Deschenaux/P. Tercier (supra note 1) § 28, nos. 15/16, p. 244.

3 Art. 44 SCO reads as follows:

IV. Reduction of compensation	**Art. 44**	*The court may reduce or refuse compensation where the injured person has assented to the injury, or where circumstances for which he is responsible have contributed to the occurrence or to the aggravation of the loss or have otherwise prejudiced the position of the person liable.*

See The Swiss Report, in: J. Spier (ed.) *The Limits of Liability* (The Hague/London/Boston 1996) pp.137 et seq. (Détermination et réduction de la réparation en droit suisse), nos. 3, 5 and 6. *See* also Art.25, para.1 of the Draft General Part of Tort Law (DGP):

E. Assessment of compensation I. Extent of compensation	**Art. 25**	[1]*In assessing compensation the court shall consider all the circumstances; in particular it shall take into account the gravity of fault and the intensity of the characteristic risk imputable respectively to the person held liable and the injured person, as well as the measures taken by the injured person in order to prevent or mitigate the loss.*

[III. Causal link] **Art.16** *A person is exonerated from any liability, if a fact not*
2. Exoneration *imputable to him has contributed to the occurrence of the damage or to its aggravation in a way that is manifestly preponderant, in particular an event of force majeure or a behaviour or characteristic risk imputable to a third person or the injured person himself.*[4]

From this perspective, it is not even certain, that 'natural' or 'factual' causality is a reliable 'preliminary filter', because this filter works – if at all – in a very rough way, excluding only the most exorbitant facts, which actually should never have come into the picture. This is particularly true in systems based on the doctrine of 'equivalence of causes (*conditio* sine qua non)'; but the situation is not very different where 'natural causality' is said to be 'refined' by the doctrine of 'adequacy ('Adäquanz')'.[5] Moreover, this approach is unable to explain how law can construe a causal link between a loss and an omission: from nothing, nothing can emerge. An omission can be a liability-generating 'cause' only because the law has previously established a duty to act. In such a case, 'causation' is always purely hypothetical.

2. Relevant factors/reasons/criteria

As already mentioned, Swiss tort law is officially governed by the doctrine of 'adequate causality'. The constant formula, created and repeated over almost one hundred years by the Swiss Federal Court,[6] sounds as follows:

> The Federal Court considers an established natural causal link to be adequate, if, according to the ordinary course of things and the general experience of life, the contemplated cause was apt to entail a result of the kind of that which has effectively occurred, in such a way that the occurrence of this result appears to be generally favoured by the cause referred to.

Applied to the concrete case of a postman having been bitten by the dog of one of his clients, this formula leads to the very impressive finding that *'there is a link of adequate causality between the bite of the dog and the loss suffered by the postman because, according to the normal course of things and the general experience of life, the keeping of dogs is apt to entail ripped trousers, particularly of postmen, in such a way that the rip in the postman's trousers appears to be generally favoured by the keeping of a dog'*.[7]

---

4 In such a case, one is not only 'in der Nähe der Unterbrechung des Kausalzusammenhangs' as A. Keller (supra note 1) p. 127 admits somewhat timidly in his comments to art. 44 SCO, but there simply remains no legally relevant causal link.

5 *See below* point 2.

6 Last example: *Decisions of the Federal Court* (DFC) 123 [1997] III 110 et seq. (c.3a, 112 with references to numerous precedents).

7 *See* also DFC 123 [1997] III 306 et seq. (c.5b, 313–314) treating a case where a swimmer had hurt himself jumping from a spring-board at a place where the lake was not deep enough: 'En effet, d'après le cours ordinaire des choses et l'expérience de la vie, l'absence d'une profondeur suffisante de l'eau autour d'un plongeoir est en soi de nature à occasionner un dommage du genre de celui qu'a subi le défendeur'.

Some authors[8] are of the opinion that this kind of statement is a bare truism, vicious circle or *petito principi*, and that it in no way achieves the expected purpose of limiting liability, the more because – always according to the Federal Court and the prevailing doctrine – the aptitude of a cause to generate a loss of the kind of that which has concretely occurred, has to be judged on the basis of a test of objective foreseeability which takes place at the time of the assessment of liability, the so-called OBJECTIVE RETROSPECTIVE PROGNOSIS.[9] Quite apart from the fact that only a jurist is able to invent a 'retrospective prognosis', this method appears to be some kind of 'scientific' consecration of the famous saying: 'after the event even a fool is wise'; hence, a judge, who is by definition a wise man, will be even wiser than the fool and there will practically remain no event whatsoever that cannot be considered – retrospectively – as being generally apt to generate the precise result that is at stake.[10] This may also be the reason why the Federal Court itself has come to the conclusion, that a cause can also be considered as 'adequate' when it generates a very uncommon result;[11] afterwards, and overlooking the whole causal development, you can indeed always say that there must have been a certain aptitude of a certain fact to cause even a quite unusual loss.

The doctrine of adequacy which has been developed on the basis of a theory of probability,[12] mixes together and combines elements of almost all the criteria enumerated in point 2 of the questionnaire (foreseeability; remoteness; proximity; purpose of the violated rule, probability; common sense and reasonableness). However, it has very recently been expressly recognised by the Federal Court,[13] that the essential aspect is a political one and one of COMMON SENSE AND EQUITY, and that adequacy is – properly speaking – not a question of causality but rather one of imputation ('Zurechnung/imputation') based on a value judgment. The aim is to limit liability to a reasonable extent. In the same decision, the Federal Court also says explicitly that the theory of adequacy is very close to the German 'Normzwecktheorie' in that both of them try to determine the extent of liability in accordance with the aim of the applicable norm.

This means, in other words, that, in the field of liability for fault (or negligence), one has to assess the liability according to the degree of this concrete fault; it may be 'inadequate' to oblige a person to provide full compensation of a very important harm if this person's

8 Among them the author of this article.

9 DFC 119 [1993] lb 334 et seq. (c.5b, 345). The notion of 'objective subsequent prognosis' seems to go back to M. Rümelin, *Der Zufall im Recht* (1896). *See* also: H. Rey (supra note 1) § 5, nos. 538/539, p.109; and, for a critical view: P. Widmer, Standortbestimmung im Haftpflichtrecht, in [1974] *Zeitschrift des Bernischen Juristenvereins* (ZBJV), 110 pp. 289 et seq. (pp. 320–321 and fn. 77 ibidem with further references).

10 K. Oftinger/E. W. Stark (supra note 1) § 3 no. 22 and fn. 26, p. 115.

11 DFC 93 [1967] II 329 et seq. (c.4, 337–338), 87 [1961] II 117 et seq. (c.6b, 127); H. Rey (supra note 1) § 5, nos. 535 et seq.; H. Deschenaux/P. Tercier (supra note 1) § 4, nos. 33–34, p. 58; R. Brehm (supra note 1)no. 124 ad art.43 SCO.

12 It goes back to a German physiologist called Von Kries, *see* H. Weitnauer, Zur Lehre vom adäquaten Kausalzusammenhang – Versuch einer Ehrenrettung, in: Revolution der Technik – Evolutionen des Rechts, *Festgabe-K. Oftinger* (Zurich 1969) pp. 321 et seq. (pp. 326 et seq.).

13 DFC 123 [1997] III 110 et seq. (c.3, 11 et seq.): '. . .*dass es sich bei der Adäquanztheorie nicht um eine rein logische Kausalitätstheorie, sondern um eine wertende Zurechnungstheorie* handelt'. *See* also: R. Brehm (supra note 1) nos. 150 et seq. ad art.43 SCO.

fault is very slight and/or if the dimensions of the loss were not reasonably foreseeable for this very person. That shows, by the way, that the test of 'objective foreseeability' is entirely useless where the final imputation based on fault has to be based on the strength of subjective foreseeability.[14] Instead, adequate causation, correctly understood as an attempt to bring compensation into line with the policy goals of a norm founding liability, is useful in the field of strict liability, where sometimes the concrete physical causality as it appears at first sight has to be relativized or even set aside at second sight: it may, indeed, turn out that the person hit by a car or a train was dead drunk so that this drunkenness has to be regarded as the prevailing or at least as a concurrent 'cause' of the accident. Seen in the light of the policy goals of the norm, this means that one considers that the characteristic risk of a motor vehicle or of a train does not include (or does not fully include) damage to persons who expose themselves to danger in an unreasonable way; it means on the other hand that this kind of accident is considered to belong (fully or partially) to the personal sphere of risk of the injured person. Here we have a classical 'two step-approach', but in the end the result will again be a determination of the borderline between two spheres of risk: that of the tortfeasor on the one hand, and that of the victim on the other hand. If liability for fault is at stake, one can speak of a 'link of fault' ('Verschuldenszusammenhang/lien de faute'); if one has to do with a liability for risk, the problem is the 'link of risk' ('Risikozusammenhang/lien de risque'). Summing up, one can therefore state that the legally relevant causal link is the link between the loss and the basis (reason) or principle of liability.

Thus, even admitting that the factors and criteria which in Swiss law are used in order to determine the legally relevant causal link, i.e. the proper and reasonable link of imputation, are not satisfying 'scientifically', it seems very difficult, if not impossible, to find additional and more specific criteria which could improve predictability. One has therefore to accept that the judge has quite a large margin of discretion; and it is certainly better to recognise frankly that this is the situation than to disguise it with pseudo-scientific tricks like 'adequacy', passed off for a kind of sophisticated measuring technique which would enable lawyers to solve their problems of imputation in terms of mechanical causation.

3. Specific legislation

a. At present, there is no specific legislation in Swiss law dealing with causation. We would, in particular, not consider the rules on joint and several liability to be established according to this special concept. On the contrary, the concept of 'solidarity' – as it is partly understood in literature and jurisprudence, namely giving rise to an undifferentiated full liability of each of several tortfeasors vis-à-vis the victim – is clearly in opposition as much to a theory of natural causality (or equivalence of causes), which should logically lead to an equal per head-partition of liability and of the corresponding compensation, as to the doctrine of adequacy which would require a differentiated imputation to each tortfeasor in proportion to his part of the total responsibility, determined in consideration of all relevant circumstances.[15] This is precisely what article 29 DGP aims at, when it states:

---

14 K. Oftinger/E. W. Stark (supra note 1) § 3 no. 31, p.120; K. Oftinger/E. W. Stark (supra note 1) § 5 nos. 16 et seq., pp.193 et seq.

15 K. Oftinger/E. W. Stark (supra note 1) § 3 nos. 83 et seq. (no. 88, p.138); K. Oftinger/E. W. Stark (supra note 1) § 10, nos.10 et seq., pp. 490 et seq.

III. Concurrent liabilities 1. External relations	**Art.29**	[1]*Where several persons are answerable for the harm sustained by a third party, they are jointly and severally liable for compensation.* [2.]*For each person thus answerable, the maximum extent of such joint and several liability is the amount this person would have owed if he would have been liable alone.*

Para 2 of this provision tries to limit the part of each liable person to such share of the damage as is attributable to him in accordance with the heads of liability under which he is responsible; it may well be that this responsibility comes up to 100 per cent for more than one of the codefendants (e.g. in the case of a concerted criminal action or that of an accident caused by several motorcars of the same power); but it can also be less for some of them, due to special circumstances like e.g. a very minor fault or a contributory negligence of the injured person or any other external cause. In the last hypothesis, it is only up to this borderline that the single defendant should have to pay for his fellow debtors and to bear the risk of their insolvency. Still, this solution has nothing whatsoever to do with causation; it is derived from a value oriented weighing of the different principles of liability involved.

b. One might mention as specific legislation regarding causation those provisions which deal with the burden of proof in this field. In Swiss law as it currently stands, there are no such rules; there is however something like a de facto-presumption of causation developed by jurisprudence particularly in the context of medical and environmental liability.[16] The reform project DGP goes in the same direction; its article 49 reads as follows:

2. Burden of proof and prima facie-evidence	**Art.49**	[1]*A person claiming for compensation has to prove the damage and the existence of a causal link.* [2]*If a conclusive proof is not possible or if it cannot be reasonably required from the person bearing the burden of proof to provide such a proof, the court may be satisfied with a convincing probability; the court may also assess compensation according to the degree of probability.* [3]. . .

This provision is intended, on the one hand, to legalize the practice of the courts, which are ready to diminish the strictness of proof in the field of causation, and on the other hand – and that is the real novelty – to allow the judge to determine the amount of compensation as a function of the probability of the alleged causal link. The wording is deliberately vague so as to permit also the granting of partial compensation in cases of the so called 'loss of a chance'.[17]

---

16 DFC 108 [1982] II 63/64; 109 [1983] II 304 et seq. (Fluor-Case). *See*: H. Rey (supra note 1) § 5, nos. 655 et seq.

17 E. W. Stark, La perte d'une chance im schweizerischen Recht, in: *Colloque – Développements récents du droit de la responsabilité civile* (Zurich 1991) pp. 101 et seq; T. Weir, Loss of chance – compensable in tort? Common Law, in: *Colloque – Développements récents du droit de la responsabilité civile* (Zurich 1991) pp. 111 et seq. and F. Chabas, La perte d'une chance en droit

c. The draft provision just mentioned should also allow the judge to establish differentiated solutions in other cases of 'hypothetical causation', in particular:

- in cases of 'alternative causation' where it is certain that one out of a determined number of possible tortfeasors has caused the loss (e.g. one of three car drivers who passed during the critical period over the road where a pedestrian is found dead after having been run over), but it cannot be proven who it was who inflicted the decisive injury. At present, the majority position in Switzerland would probably be that for lack of evidence – none of the potential tortfeasors would be liable. There are however some recent authors who opt for joint and several liability or for an apportionment of liability between the potential tortfeasors, based on the probable quota of causation of each of them.[18]

  Another solution, which could be adopted in the framework of the draft provision, is that of a 'rnarket-share-liability' as it has been applied in the United States and in the Netherlands in cases of product liability where several producers had sold a drug while it was impossible to establish which of the different preparations had caused the particular loss. Up to now, there are no decisions in Switzerland going in that direction.

  Furthermore, the above mentioned provision could also be a basis for partial compensation in cases where there is statistical evidence that a certain disease (e.g. cancer) is more frequent in the neighbourhood of a particular plant (e.g. a nuclear power station) than elsewhere, but where, in an individual case, it cannot be proven that the disease of precisely this patient is caused by the emanations of the plant under consideration.
- in cases of 'cumulative causation', where two or more tortfeasors have contributed to the loss and where the contribution of each of them would have been sufficient to cause the whole loss. In such cases, it is generally accepted that the tortfeasors involved are jointly and severally liable for the loss as a whole[19]
- in cases of 'overtaking causality' where one causal development which would have led to a determinate loss is so to say overtaken by another development which actually causes the loss in question (see the horse-case mentioned below). In such cases, the conditio sine qua non-test fails for both original causes, because there is always the other cause that would have led to the loss anyway. The problem has been acknowledged by the Federal Court, but the judges have not taken a clear standpoint yet.[20]

Also controversial is the extent to which the so-called 'constitutional predisposition' of the injured person, i.e. the fact that this person was particularly prone to certain injuries or diseases, should be taken into consideration. The Federal Court has repeatedly stated that the tortfeasor has no right to be treated as if he had injured a normally healthy person, however,

---

Note 17 continued]
français, in: *Colloque – Développements récents du droit de la responsabilité civile* (Zurich 1991) pp. 131 et seq.; *See* also: P. Engel (supra note 1) ch. 27 i.f., pp. 479 et seq.; P. Loser, Schadenersatz für wahrscheinliche Kausalität, in *Allgemeine Juristische Praxis* (AJP) 1994, 954 et seq.

18 H. Rey (supra note 1) § 5, nos. 621 et seq.

19 H. Rey (supra note 1) § 5, nos. 614 et seq.

20 DFC 115 (1989) II 442 et seq. (c. 4). *See* also H. Rey (supra note 1) § 5, nos. 584 et seq. and nos. 604 et seq.

a preexistent disease can be regarded as a circumstance which may lead to an adequate reduction of compensation.[21]

In this context, one may also mention a relatively new concept which seems quite close to these types of hypothetical causation: the 'alternative lawful behaviour (rechtmässiges Alternativverhalten)'. It means that, where liability is based on a breach of a duty of care, a potential tortfeasor could be (totally or partially) exonerated by proving that the loss would have occurred anyway, even if he had (hypothetically) observed all his duties.[22] This view shows again how closely the problem of causation is linked with that of wrongfulness[23]

4. The borderline between causation and other factors

As has already been indicated in relation to the quite close connection between (adequate) causation and 'Normzwecklehre' (supra point 2), it is certainly correct to say that the borderline between causation and the other requirements of liability – not only damage, but also unlawfulness and fault – is fluid. This is necessarily the case because 'adequacy' is somewhat like the bracket around the whole question of imputation.

As for the examples:
(a) Death of a horse. The case can be considered under both concepts: damage and/or causation. One could say that, because damage is defined as the difference between the state of the injured person's fortune as it is after the loss and as it would – hypothetically – have been if the loss had not ocurred, X was not able to cause any damage, as the horse would have perished anyway in the fire set by Y. On the other hand, this is an example of so-called 'overtaking causality' ('überholende Kausalität').[24] In a recent decision – DFC 115 [1989] II 440 et seq. – the Federal Court seems, in principle, inclined to take into account hypothetical causal developments, and it refers to former decisions where it had already taken the same approach. From the point of view of 'adequacy', this appears to be a rather 'causalistic' conception, especially in cases – as the one presently under discussion – where intentional injury comes into play. One could well argue that the 'causal' link, and thus the liability deriving from a wilful act is (and remains) always 'adequate' – particularly where the overtaking cause is not imputable to any third party. Instead, if there is a second or even more persons involved, I would not hesitate to admit (joint and several) liability upon all of them. Causation (in the natural, mechanical sense) is only a crutch for imputation, certainly not a condition, nor a constraint.

(b) Asbestos-case This situation where each of several persons has contributed a partial cause for the harm that occurred is sometimes dealt with applying the concept of 'cumulative causation'. In reality, if the causal contribution of each presumed tortfeasor can be proven,

---

21 DFC 113 (1987) II 86 et seq. (c. la, 90).

22 DFC 122 (1996) III 229 et seq. (c.5, 232 et seq.). *See* also below under point 4 c): case of the 'shipwrecked sheep'.

23 The Swiss Report, in: H. Koziol (ed.) *Unification of Tort Law: Wrongfulness* (The Hague/London/Boston 1998) pp. 115 et seq. (p. 123).

24 H. Rey (supra note 1) § 5, nos. 604 et seq., pp. 122–123.

we have a simple situation of concurrent, and that means also joint and several, liabilities. The adequate solution seems to be to render A, B and C fully liable for the damage suffered by X, because the fact that the fatal threshold was crossed when X was employed by C is purely accidental. Thus, A has also to support the risk of insolvency of his co-debtors (see above point 3). If the causal contribution of each employer cannot be determined with sufficient precision, one could perhaps have recourse to so-called 'market share-liability'[25] or an analogous procedure. Up to now, there is however no example of such a decision in Swiss jurisprudence.[26]

(c) Delayed appeal In DFC 87 (1981) II 366 et seq (c.2, 372 et seq), the Federal Court held that – in principle – the attorney had to pay compensation for his mistake only if there were a sufficient probability that the suit would have been successful; in the concrete case this probability was found to have existed. If the attorney had been able to show that the outcome of the trial was in any case very uncertain or that it was even likely to be lost, he could also have argued on the basis of his 'alternative lawful behaviour' (see above point 3c).

(d) Shipwrecked animals Outwardly, the problem is that of the 'link of unlawfulness (Rechtswidrigkeitszusammenhang)': it can be argued that because the statute violated did not aim at the security of the animals in the eventuality of a storm (but was intended to prevent the spreading of diseases), the violation of this norm is irrelevant for this particular accident. This means nothing else than to say that P's unlawful behiaviour was not (adequately) 'causal' for the accident due to the fact that the animals have been swept over board. In terms of fault this leads to the conclusion that the loss that has effectively occurred has no 'link of fault' with P's negligence.

However, the conclusion that liability would have to be completely negated in this case seems rather unsatisfactory. So it would certainly not be inconceivable to construe liability by admitting a general duty of care, derived from common sense and experience of life, according to which animals carried on the deck of a ship should be protected against the risk of being swept overboard by adequate security measures like locking them in pens or at least chaining them up at a fix installation. If the storm is so violent that the whole ship sinks anyway, it seems likely that no liability at all will attach to P., either because the storm will be considered as an event of force majeure or because we are again confronted with a case of 'alternative lawful behaviour' ('rechtmässiges Alternativverhalten'). In a brand-new decision – DFC 122 [1996] III 229 et seq. (c.5, p.232 et seq.) – the Swiss Federal Court has held that the Canton of Vaud was not liable, as an owner of embankments of a river which had broken down in a very violent thunderstorm, for the losses suffered by the owners of flooded properties in the neighbourhood, because the embankments had been correctly designed in order to resist thunderstorms of a degree of violence which happens once in thirty years, while the two tempests that had provoked the damage in question were of a power that occurs only once or at most twice a century.

---

25 H. Rey (supra note 1) § 5, no. 624, p. 125.

26 *See* above under point 3c.

Part II Cases

Single event occurrences

1. Attorney hecatomb
D (assuming that he is the holder of the car under Swiss law) will be liable to all ten attorneys, i.e. his (mandatory) liability insurance will pay the 250'000'000 $; in the eventuality of gross negligence or even intention (including the case of 'dolus eventualis') on the part of D, the insurer will try to take recourse action against him for at least a part of the damages paid.

Assuming that D is not insured (and disregarding the fact that in such a case the damages will be covered by a pool of the Swiss motorcar and liability insurers), article 44, para 2. SCO could be applied if no serious fault can be attributed to him:

[IV. Reduction of compensation]	**Art.44**	[2]*Where enforcement of the compensation would cause economic distress to the party liable, the court may equitably reduce the compensation, provided the damage was not caused wilfully, or by gross negligence or imprudence.*

In the opposite sense, article 62, para 2. of the Swiss Road Traffic Act (RTA = Strassenverkehrsgesetz[27]) states that:

[Compensation and satisfaction in case of pain and suffering]	**Art.44**	[2]*Where the person killed or injured drew an exceptionally high income, the judge may equitably reduce the compensation taking into account all circumstances.*

And article 25, para. 2 of the DGP, merging both approaches, provides:

E. Assessment of compensation 1.Extent of compensation	**Art.44**	[2]*Exceptionally, the court may also take into account the economic positions of the parties, in particular the presence or absence of insurance cover.*

2. Predisposition
Predisposition can be taken into account as a kind of concurrent cause and thus as 'a circumstance for which he (i.e. the injured person) is responsible' (art.44, para 1 SCO), i.e. a 'contributory factor'. The impact of predisposition on liability is controversial, and it is often emphasized that its importance is not the same within (private) tort law on the one hand, and in the context of social security on the other hand.[28] The tendency seems rather to go in the direction of diminishing the influence of predisposition. In its decision DFC 113 [1987] 1186 (c.1c, 90), the Federal Court declared: 'Whoever hurts unlawfully a person who was already of weak health, can not pretend to be treated as if he had caused damage to a healthy victim'.[29]

---

27 Systematic Digest of Swiss Federal Legislation (RS/SR) 741.01.

28 K. Oftinger/E. W. Stark (supra note 1) § 3 nos. 95–96, pp. 141 et seq.; *see* also: DFC 123 [1997] III 110 et seq.

29 *See* above under point 3 c.

3. *Stolen car*
This hypothesis is explicitly considered in article 75 of the already mentioned Road Traffic Act. This provision disposes of the case as follows:

Vehicles used without authorisation	**Art.75**	[1]*Whoever steals a vehicle with the intent to use it, bears the liability of a holder. The driver is jointly and severally liable, if he knew or ought to have known, had he acted with all the attention required by the circumstances, from the beginning of the ride, that the vehicle was stolen. The holder is also liable, except towards those who have used the vehicle and who knew, from the beginning of the ride, that the vehicle was stolen or could have known it, had they acted with all the attention required by the circumstances.*

Para. 2 of the provision then establishes a right of recourse of the holder and/or his insurer against the persons involved in the theft, a right which normally will not be of great value. Important for the holder is para. 3 of article 75 RTA which excludes the possibility for the insurer, in this particular situation, to charge the holder with a 'malus' (punitive supplement on the insurance premium), except where the holder has negligently contributed to rendering the theft possible, e.g. by omitting to remove the key.

4. Cable-case
The solution of this kind of case under Swiss law was already explained in our answer to the Tilburg Hypothetical No.2.[30]

There are no new developments, but it may be worthwhile to quote an excerpt from DTF 102 [1976] II 85 et seq. (c.6c, 90) where the Federal Court, after having approved the claim of a factory which had suffered (pure economic) loss in consequence of the rupture of an electric cable caused by a building company, declared literally. '*The rupture of the cable having infringed the claimants' interest [i.e. the interest in being supplied with electricity, protected by article 239 of the Swiss Criminal Code], they are direct victims of an unlawful act and thus entitled to claim compensation, by the defendant, of the loss suffered. This conclusion suggests itself, no matter if one examines the question of the protective aim of the legal duty violated by reference to the concept of adequate causation or that of the link of unlawfulness ('Rechtswidrigkeitszusammenhang')*'.[31]

5. Exploding rat poison
It is almost certain that the causal link between the behaviour of the defendant and the explosion and accordingly also with the damage resulting therefrom for the plaintiff, would be regarded as adequate, even if the development of events seems quite uncommon. The reason

30 The Swiss Report, in: J. Spier (ed.), *The Limits of Expanding Liability, Eight Fundamental Cases in a Comparative Perspective* (The Hague/London/Boston 1998) pp. 197 et seq (pp. 200–201). *See* also: The Swiss Report, in J. Spier (supra note 30) no. 23, p.23.

31 Emphasis added by the author.

lies not only in the fact that the jurisprudence (and particularly the Federal Court) – thanks to the 'objective retrospective prognosis' – considers even extraordinary causal developments to be adequate (see above point 2), but primarily in the 'objectivized' notion of fault which is 'infected' by the concept of objective foreseeability used in the assessment of adequacy. In this respect, the conception of the prevailing Swiss literature and jurisprudence, even if it seems inappropriate under the aspect of fault as a necessarily subjective condition, can be qualified as coherent: the 'extent' or range of fault must inevitably coincide with adequacy.

6. 'Chômage'

The question raised by this hypothetical is normally not dealt with in the framework of causation, but as a problem of definition of damage. In this context, it is generally accepted that a loss suffered as a result of damage caused to property and of the impossibility of using that property ('Nutzungsausfall/Chômage') must be compensated, at least where the damaged object is used for professional and/or commercial purposes. From the point of view of causation, this means that compensation is owed also for mediate/indirect consequences of the wrong as long as these consequences (and thus their compensation) seem adequate.[32]

To this end, article 9 para. 3 DGP – summing up a consistent jurisprudence – proposes the following wording:

[Damage to property]	**Art.9**	[3]*Where an object was necessary or useful for the injured person, in particular for the exercise of a professional activity, the compensable damage includes also the rental cost of an equivalent object, or the earnings lost during the time for repair or replacement of the damaged object.*

7. 'Rescue-damage'

The extension of liability arising for a primary accident to the damage suffered by persons who intervene in a rescue operation, is explicitlv envisaged in the context of road traffic accidents. Art.58. para. 3 RTA[33] reads as follows:

[Liability of the holder of a motor vehicle]	**Art.9**	[3]*The holder* [*of a motor vehicle*] *is equally liable, to an extent to be determined by the judge, for compensation of the damage resulting from assistance rendered on the occasion of an accident in which his vehicle was involved, provided that the accident is imputable to him or that the assistance was rendered to him personally or to passengers of his vehicle.*[34]

32 K. Oftinger/E. W. Stark (supra note 1) § 6 nos. 371 et seq., pp. 370 et seq.; H. Rey (supra note 1) § 4, nos. 312 et seq., pp. 64–65: R. Brehm (supra note 1) nos. 80 et seq. ad art.41 SCO; H. Deschenaux/P. Tercier (supra note 1) § 24, nos. 10–11, p.224.

33 *See* above (supra note 20).

34 K. Oftinger/E. W. Stark, *Schweizerisches Haftpflichtrecht* II/2 (Zürich 1989) § 25 nos. 401 et seq., pp. 175 et seq; A. Keller (supra note 1) pp. 271–272.

The idea underlying this provision could be extended to other areas on the basis of the general provisions governing the 'negotiorum gestio' ('Geschäftsführung ohne Auftrag/gestion d'affaires').

According to article 422 SCO:

II. Rights and duties of the principal 1. Acting in the interest of the principal	**Art.422**	[1]*Where the principal's interest required an action to be undertaken, he has to indemnify the agent for all expenses plus interest which were necessary or useful under the given circumstances, discharge him to the same extent from all obligations incurred and compensate him for any other damage at the discretion of the judge.* [2]*The agent is entitled to such indemnity and compensation even if the intended result has not been realized, provided he acted with due care.* [3]. . .

From the point of view of causation, the damage suffered by a person involved in a rescue operation can again be qualified as indirect or mediate, but it is considered as (sufficiently) adequate, i.e. not too remote to justify compensation.[35]

8. 'Kidney-transplant'
The case is quite close to the rescue hypothesis. The difference lies in the fact that P.'s generous donation of his kidney is a free and deliberate choice, while in the case of a person coming across an accident and assisting the victims, there may be a legal, but at least a moral duty to do so. It seems therefore doubtful that a Swiss court would grant compensation to the donor of an organ, even if he has submitted himself to such operation in favour of a specific person; as a matter of fact, organs which are used for transplantation usually come from unknown (frequently: dead) donors who are not indemnified.

Intervening events

9. Plumber-case
See case I/3 a).

10. Twice repaired ship
It seems unlikely that the owner of the damaged ship will get compensation for the full repair costs incurred after the additional damage suffered as a result of the heavy weather during the voyage to the US, even if this voyage was to some extent a consequence of the first collision. The heavy weather is either an event of force majeure or it is a characteristic and accepted risk of any voyage at sea. It would be neither sensible nor adequate to shift this risk over to the first tortfeasor.

---

35 Apparently K. Oftinger/E. W. Stark (supra note 34) § 25 no. 424, are of the opinion that a causal link in the sense of adequacy is not required for this specific kind of responsibility between the risk or fact which sets off liability and the damage suffered by the rescuer; in contrast to this view, we would admit that the explicit recognition of an obligation to compensate persons who are injured while assisting the victims of an accident, itself creates such a 'link of adequacy'.

11. Drunken driver and avalanche
The intervention of the drunken driver X will certainly not exonerate D as the person responsible for the car accident. But it seems again unlikely that D will have to provide compensation of the whole damage suffered by P., insofar as this damage consists of a measurable and separable prolongation of the time he needs for recovering. In principle, there will therefore ensue a joint and several liability of X and D (see also above point 1/3) which might conceivably allocate different proportions of liability for one and the other tortfeasor; it would indeed seem appropriate and 'adequate' to charge X in any case with 100 per cent because he bears a double responsibility, being liable as much for the objective risk of holding a motor car as for the gross negligence involved in driving under the influence of alcohol, while D – if he drove his car correctly or committed only a very slight fault – could be held liable only for 80 per cent (or even less). It will then be at the judge's discretion to determine that part of the whole damage which has to be definitely born by D and by X in their internal relationship as co-defendants or more particularly within the framework of a recourse action.

The avalanche, on the other hand, will probably be classified as a fortuitous event which is not imputable to D, with the consequence that he does not have to pay compensation for that part of the damage which results from this additional injury.

12. Collision between several vehicles
The case of an accident in which several persons are involved and cause damage to a third party or mutually to each other, are explicitly envisaged by article 60 and 61 of the RTA.[36] Where the liability of more than one person (car holder) in relation to a third party is at stake, these persons will be held jointly and severally liable; in their internal relationship, the damage will be divided between them 'in consideration of all circumstances' and particularly in proportion of their respective (additional) fault. In case of a collision of cars (and liabilities) the solution is similar: each of the involved car-holders has to assume a part of the damage suffered by the other ones and a part of his own damage; the division is made in proportion of the fault of each of them, except where special circumstances, in particular different degrees of risk (e.g. between a Citroën 2CV and a big truck) have to be taken into account.

This solution is generalized in article 27, 29 and 30 of the DGP (see also above point 1/3), with the difference that fault is no more considered as a preponderant criteria, but as one circumstance among others. Accordingly, article 28 DGP reads as follows:

III. Collision of liabilities	**Art.28**	*Where several persons mutually cause damage to each other, such damage will be supported by each of them according to all circumstances, in particular according to the gravity of fault and the intensity of the characteristic risk imputable to each of them.*

If D2 has been driving recklessly, it seems probable that he will be charged to a larger extent than Dl, and it could be – if the principle of solidarity (joint and several liability) is applied correctly – that Dl's part could be reduced (e.g. to 75 per cent) vis-à-vis P2 and P3.

36 *See* above (supra note 20).

13. Stolen wallet
If the driver D is not at fault, it seems quite evident that the theft of the wallet does not pertain to the typical and characteristic risk created by a motor vehicle. Thus, in terms of (adequate) causation, the intervention of the thief would have to be considered as an external cause (act of a third party) which is intensive enough to 'interrupt' the causal link. If D has committed additional negligence of some gravity or, even worse, if he knocked down P. intentionally, the solution could be different and one could perhaps envisage the partial liability of D also for the loss of the wallet.

14. *Heart attack*
The solution will depend upon the answer to the question of whether – from a medical point of view – the heart attack was a consequence of the accident or not. If the heart attack is a purely fortuitous event, D will probably be liable only for the loss suffered by P during the period running from the car accident until the heart attack. Again, we are confronted with a kind of 'overtaking causality', with the peculiarity, however, that the overtaking cause is not imputable to a person and with a second special feature insofar as the first cause only advances the occurrence of the loss which would have accrued anyway. One could also characterize this case as one of 'accelerating causality'.

The problem can also be seen in the context of damage: if damage is defined as the difference between the state of the assets of the injured person after the damaging event and the hypothetical state in which these assets would have been if the event had not occurred, it seems correct to conclude, that D's assets would in any case have diminished by the loss of income due to the heart attack.

15. *One-legged victim*
The case was discussed as No.6 of the Tilburg Hypotheticals.[37] From the 'causation' point of view, the problem is whether adequacy is 'slackened' or even interrupted by the elapse of a long time. Under Swiss law this is not the conclusion normally arrived at;[38] as long as the second accident was objectively foreseeable as a consequence of the first one, the damage resulting therefrom will be considered as imputable to the original tortfeasor.

In the present case however, prescription (statute of limitations) would come into play: according to art. 60, para. 1 SCO, the absolute period of limitation is ten years from the date on which the act causing the damage took place. Thus, after 11 years the claim for compensation would be barred. According to the DGP, this period shall be prolonged to 20 years, running from the date on which the damaging event took place or came to an end.

Loss of a chance

16. *Wrong diagnosis (loss of a chance)*
As we have already pointed out (above I/3 c), there is at present no jurisprudence referring expressly to the concept of *'loss of a chance'*. It could nevertheless be argued that the judge, as he is explicitly authorized to do with the assessment of damage by art.42 para.2 SCO, should also have the possibility to take into account a probability of causation and to deter-

37 The Swiss Report, in: J. Spier (supra note 30), p.206.
38 DFC 57 [1931] 41.

mine the compensation according to the percentage chance that loss would not accrue at all. In the present case, that would mean that the persons supported by B. (not necessarily his heirs) could bring a claim against Doctor A for 40 percent of their loss.

This solution is envisaged by art.49 DGP[39] and encouraged by a part of the legal literature.[40]

17. Increased rate of illness
The problem is that it is not possible to establish which of the persons falling ill is a victim of the (negligent) activity that increased the rate of occurrence of a particular disease. The case is one of uncertain causality. But if there is a reasonable probability that the activity in question is a potential cause of the disease, it would seem fair to impose partial liability upon D towards all victims in a definite area, corresponding to the difference between the normal rate and the abnormally high rate which can be connected to D's emissions.

Concurring causes

18. Collapsing wall
The case is one of alternative causation as the contribution of either Dl or D2, taken by itself, would not have been sufficient to cause the loss. If it is not possible to establish which contribution was decisive, one may opt either for joint and several liability perhaps with the possibility of recourse – or for the divided several liability of each tortfeasor.[41]

19. *Three hunters*
This again is a classical case of alternative causation with the difference – compared to the case of the collapsed wall – that (probably) one of the three shots was sufficient to produce the injury. Hence, the difficulty is essentially one of proof. As explained above, the traditional position in Switzerland would be that – for lack of evidence – none of the three hunters could be made liable. Recent tendencies in the literature advocate however a more satisfactory solution, either in line with German law (§ 830 para.1, 2nd sentence, BGB), which provides expressly for joint and several liability, or by rendering each of the persons involved liable for an equal quota.[42] It is, basically,[43] irrelevant whether or not the three hunters acted in concert; there is, however, a decision of the Swiss Federal Court in a criminal case in which it imposed a kind of joint and several (penal) liability upon two men who, acting in concert, had rolled down blocks of stone from a road onto the banks of a river where a fisherman was killed; the Court declared explicitly that it would have had to decide differently if the two tortfeasors had acted independently of each other.[44]

20. Poisoned river
In the present case, each single contribution of A and B is sufficient to produce the whole

39 *See* above I/3 b.
40 E. W. Stark (supra note 17).
41 *See* above I/3 c.
42 K. Oftinger/E. W. Stark (supra note 1) § 3 nos. 113 et seq. and 123 et seq.
43 Except where the hunters acted together with the intent to hurt a third person; in this case, art.50 SCO explicitly prescribes joint and several liability, independently of the exact contribution of each single wrongdoer.
44 DFC 113 [1987] IV 58.

damage (so called 'cumulative causation'). So there is no doubt that they will each be held jointly and severally liable for the whole amount of compensation and have to bear the risk of insolvency of the other in any recourse claim.

The question of the compensability of damage caused to fishing grounds is explicitly regulated in the *Fishery Act* 1991[45] where art. 15 states in para. 2 that:

> [2]*In calculating the loss, the reduced capacity of production of the polluted waters has to be taken into account*

And, according to para.3 of the same provision:

> [3]*The payee of the compensation received in order to restore the former situation, has to use it to repair the damage as quickly as possible.*

This is one of the rare examples in which the law obliges the victim to utilize the compensation in a particular way.

21. Defective drugs
At present, there is no known case in Switzerland in which 'market-share-liability' has been applied. It seems not impossible, however, that this idea could be introduced into Swiss law. Art. 49 DGP[46] is designed in such a manner as to allow the allocation of damages in conformity with market shares. In this context a quota-solution seems more likely to be adopted than joint and several liability of all manufacturers.[47]

22. Falling rocks
As the chamois cannot be made responsible for its part of causation, D may be held liable only for an appropriate (adequate) part of the damage. The reduction will be introduced on the basis of art. 43 / 44 SCO, which instructs the judge to take into account all relevant circumstances when fixing compensation. The chamois or more particularly its fortuitous contribution is such a circumstance.

23. *Ship crash*
The question is whether the bad weather conditions, fog and high sea can be considered as fortuitous events or even as force majeure which again would allow the judge to adjudicate only partial compensation. The answer depends very much on the strictness with which the negligence of the captain of ship A will be judged. If the 20 per cent mentioned in the hypothetical refers to the degree of imputation based on obviously slight negligence of the captain, then his part of the liability should not exceed this rate; otherwise it would become 'inadequate'.

---

45 Bundesgesetz über die Fischerei (federal statute on fishery, loi fedérale sur la pêche) SR/RS 923.0.

46 *See* above I/3 b.

47 Concerning the DES-case in the Netherlands, *see* 0. Guillod/A. Leuba, Causalité alternative et responsabilité du fait des produits: un pour tout, tous pour un, in [1994] *European Review of Private Law* (ERPL), 452 et seq. This contribution is one of a whole series of articles on the same case, beginning with a note by E. Hondius in ERPL 409.

Miscellaneum

24. Mass collision

This case of a collision between many vehicles and between liabilities is explicitly envisaged by art. 61 of the Road Traffic Act 1958 (RTA).[48] It states that, as far as personal injury is concerned, the damage will be divided between all car holders involved, taking into account their respective degrees of fault, except where special circumstances, in particular the difference of inherent risk between the vehicles involved, justify another apportionment of the damages.

On the other hand, liability between car holders for material damage is envisaged only to the extent to which the injured person can prove that the damage was caused by negligence or by temporary loss of capacity of the defendant car holder or of a person for whom he is responsible, or by a defect of the vehicle. Where numerous car holders have to compensate the damage suffered by another holder, they are jointly and severally liable towards him.

Art.28 DGP generalizes this solution for the whole field of tort law, but eliminates the priority of fault compared with other circumstances as criteria for the allocation of liability.[49]

48 Above case II/ 1; (supra note 27).

49 For the text of this provision *see* above case II/ 12.

United States

CAUSATION UNDER US LAW

Gary T. Schwartz

Keep in mind that American tort law operates as a federalism. Each state has the technical right to establish its own rules on tort issues such as causation. While the rules do tend to be the same from state to state, there can be differences.

Part I

Causation as a requirement

(a) Causation is generally required in American tort law.
(b) There tend to be two steps in causation. The first step is a test of 'actual cause' or 'but-for cause.' The second step is what is commonly referred to as 'proximate cause' or 'legal cause.' Both actual cause and proximate cause must be affirmed before liability can be imposed.

2. Proximate cause includes several themes. The most important of these themes is the foreseeability of harm. If the harm suffered by the plaintiff seems clearly foreseeable, then a finding of proximate cause is likely. But if the harm suffered by the plaintiff is deemed totally unforeseeable, a finding of proximate cause unlikely. In these latter cases, a causal relationship may well exist, but it is seen as merely coincidental. 'Directness' is also a factor that is taken into account. The more direct the harm, the more likely a finding of proximate cause. Yet even if harm is indirect, if it is clearly foreseeable, proximate cause can be affirmed. Within the doctrine of proximate cause, arguments from policy or principle are sometimes taken into account. One policy that is sometimes brought forward in support of the doctrine of proximate cause is that it prevents liability from becoming totally disproportionate to the extent of the defendant's negligence. While courts in proximate cause cases sometimes refer to proximity in space and time, these factors are of declining significance. For example, a defendant which manufactured a car in Detroit in 1993 can easily be held liable for an accident brought about by a defect in the car in California in 1998.

3. While there are many statutes relating to tort reform in recent decades, few of these address causation rules as such. However, the common-law doctrine of joint-and-several liability has been modified by statute in the majority of states. A few states have abolished joint-and-several liability altogether in favor of proportionate liability. Some states apply joint-

J. Spier (ed.), Unification of Tort Law: Causation, 123–126.

and-several liability to the plaintiff's economic losses, but not to pain and suffering. Some states apply joint-and-several liability only if the defendant's share of the overall fault exceeds some certain percentage.

4. The borderline between causation and causation or other factors

(a) This would be deemed a causation issue. Applying ordinary notions of causation, Y would be held liable. However, in limiting his liability, Y could refer to the horse's short life expectancy. Whether X could be held liable for having shortened that life expectancy is an undecided question.

(b) So long as A's asbestos is the but-for cause of the harm – that is, so long as X would have avoided disease had it not been for A's original asbestos – A could be held liable as a negligent cause. In such a case, however, one would need to consider how the rules of joint-and-several liability work.

(c) In such legal malpractice cases, C must win the 'case within the case.' That is, C must show that his appeal would have been successful.

(d) Negligence per se would not be available in this case as a method of proving the defendant's negligence. The purpose of the statute was not to protect against the particular harm suffered by the plaintiff. Nevertheless, P can recover if P can show – quite without regard to the statute – that the carrier was under an obligation imposed by general negligence principles to build pens so as to prevent disease. If, however, the ship sinks in the storm, any negligence in not building a pen becomes causally irrelevant.

Part II

Single event occurrences

1. Each plaintiff can recover in full. 'The defendant takes the plaintiff as he finds him.' This is one particular rule within the larger doctrine of proximate cause that pays little attention to the factor of foreseeability.

2. The plaintiff recovers in full. Again 'the defendant takes the plaintiff as he finds him.'

3. In such 'key in the car' cases, there are rulings in many jurisdictions; and these rulings are dramatically divided as to what result is appropriate.

4. As far as P2 and P3 is concerned, their losses seem merely economic. Their claims would therefore be barred by the rule - accepted in most states – that economic losses are not recoverable against a merely negligent defendant. P1, however, has suffered property damage. P1 can probably recover from D, though some courts would worry about the prospect of D's 'open-ended' liability.

5. American legal scholars have discussed this hypothetical. Their point is that the causal relationship is 'coincidental' rather than 'foreseeable.' Therefore, they argue, proximate cause should be denied. But there are no cases.

6. This would not be seen as an issue of causation, but rather a question of damages. P's costs would be deemed to be normal monetary losses, and hence recoverable in a property damage action.

7. In Judge Cardozo's phrase, 'danger invites rescue.' In C's suit against A, C can recover; proximate cause can be affirmed.

8. There are two American opinions denying recovery in such cases. I am aware that certain European cases affirm recovery. In my own analysis, the case raises in a dramatic new form an equivalent of the old idea that 'danger invites rescue'.

Intervening events

9. There are no cases. Many scholars would argue that the plaintiff can recover in full, since the earthquake was completely unanticipated at the time of the original fire. I am not sure I agree with this assessment.

11a. Most courts would say that the risk of being hit by a negligent driver is part of the risk of highway travel. Since D's negligence has exposed the plaintiff to that risk, the plaintiff can recover from D.

11b. Yet being on the highway does not increase the chances that you will be hit by an avalanche. The relationship between D's negligence and the avalanche harm is a coincidence. Most courts would deny liability for the additional harm.

12. Most courts would affirm D1's liability. D1's negligence created a situation that was full of potential risks. At no point did that risky situation really 'stabilize.' The particular details as to how P2 and P3 suffered injury would probably not be deemed especially relevant. Still, some courts might be impressed by the fact that D2's driving was reckless rather than merely negligent.

13. D would be held liable. D's negligence foreseeably exposed P to the risk of theft.

14. This seems about same as 9, above. I am unaware of cases.

15. American courts would probably find in favor of proximate cause here. If, however, the plaintiff has already sued and recovered for his original injury, there may be a problem of res judicata. And given the timing of that original injury, there may be a related problem concerning the statute of limitations.

Loss of a chance

16. This issue has divided American states. Those states that allow recovery would limit the amount of recovery to 40 per cent of the 'value' of B's life.

17a. I think American courts would be reluctant to assume that a 'cluster' as large as 100 is a mere coincidence. But this would be a question of fact for the jury to decide.

17b. It may have been I who contributed this hypothetical. American courts would probably (a) admit the statistical evidence, and (b) allow all three plaintiffs to recover in full. But there are an inadequate number of cases.

17c. I think that American courts would be inclined to deny liability here. However, they might be willing to send the issue to the jury, and the jury might 'cheat' and come in with a 'more likely than not' finding on the issue of causation.

Concurring causes

18. If the evidence shows that the wall would not have collapsed but for the pile of rubbish contributed by D1, then D2 can be held liable. But the various rules of joint-and-several liability here come into play.

19. P can probably recover from D1, assuming that D1 cannot carry the burden of proof and show that he was not the cause. The leading case concerns defendants who were hunting together; but that probably was not necessary for the result.

20. A would be liable. The pollution to the river would be deemed 'indivisible.' Also, *if* the law were to allow A to escape liability (on grounds that B was a sufficient cause), then the law would be required to exonerate B as well; and this would be seen as an unacceptable result.

21. These 'market share' issues have arisen in the United States in the context of manufacturers no one of which has a market share exceeding 50 per cent. In these circumstances, American courts are divided as to whether each manufacturer can be held responsible to individual plaintiffs under a partial-liability 'market share' doctrine. Some courts affirm the partial liability of each manufacturer; other courts apply conventional causation rules, and conclude that no manufacturer can be held liable at all. In this hypothetical, however, D1 has a market share of more than 50 per cent. I have not seen American courts explicitly consider this issue. But they might conclude that D1 is fully liable, since the chances of it being the relevant manufacturer are greater than 50 per cent. As for D2 and D3, in states rejecting the market share doctrine, they would be free of liability. Even states that accept the market share doctrine would need to consider whether that doctrine continues to apply when there is one manufacturer with a market share of more than 50 per cent.

22. Unless the evidence somehow permits a finding by the jury that it was D's rock that struck the plaintiff, the court would be required to rule in favor of D.

23. So long as the collision would not have occurred in the absence of the captain's negligence, the concurring causes are irrelevant; ship A is liable. And the joint-and-several liability doctrine would not be a problem here, since the other causes identified are not causes involving the negligence of any human beings (or corporations).

Miscellaneum

24. American states divide in situations of this sort. Most states would probably hold that D1 is liable for all the harm. When there is a traffic accident, all kinds of bad things can happen before the situation stabilizes. As for later motorists, each can of course bear liability only if their negligence can be established. One's guess is that in considering the extent of the liability of (say) the negligent D5, American courts would send the matter to the jury, relying on the jury's supposed good common sense.

Comparative Conclusions on Causation

Jaap Spier and Olav A. Haazen

1. Introduction

In this report we address issues of factual and legal causation from a comparative angle, based upon the country reports published in this book and the discussions during the plenary meetings of the European Group on Tort Law. In the more general sense the law of causation reveals many similarities throughout different jurisdictions. But it soon became clear that quite a number of specific issues are problematic either because they receive divergent doctrinal solutions or, in fact, because they still remain unclear or unresolved in many jurisdictions.

2. Condicio sine qua non and the two step approach to causation

Step 1: factual causation
All jurisdictions recognise causation as a requirement of tortious liability and all legal systems consider a *condicio sine qua non* as such as a first test. It seems that only in one jurisdiction, *viz.* Belgium, the *condicio sine qua non* is clearly officially regarded as the *sole* requirement for causation to be established. As a result, Belgium officially rejects the dual test, or two step approach, which all other jurisdictions take as a theoretical framework.[1]

According to the *condicio sine qua non*-requirement, also known as the but for-test, equivalence theory, 'cause-in-fact' or factual cause, one should, in order to determine whether an act or omission was a cause of the loss, eliminate the act or omission mentally and consider whether or not the loss would still appear. If the loss does not occur when the act or omission is eliminated, the act or omission is a *condicio sine qua non* for the loss. If the loss would still occur, even when the act or omission in question is disregarded, the loss has not been caused by this act or omission.[2] Another formulation has it that an act or omission is the cause in fact if, *ex post*, it is established that the damage would not have occurred without the act or omission judged *'on the basis of the best science and experience of the moment'*[3]. The highlighted phrase basically adds a rule of evidence to the *condicio sine qua non* formula. A third alternative formulation, still amounting to the same meaning, is the equivalence theory: between all causal events no distinction is made between adequate and inadequate, direct and indirect, or normal and abnormal causes; all causes are considered to be equivalent.[4]

When it comes to the application of the *condicio sine qua non* theory to particular cases, however, the real meaning of the term turns out to be ambiguous. This follows from the case of the Julian horse (case I.4.a) and the plumber case (case 9). Let us for the moment focus on the horse case.

---

1 *See* however, for French law, *infra*, paragraph 2.
2 *Cf.* J. Neethling, The South African Report: I.1. (Causation as a Requirement. Factual Causation.); under German law a slightly lower degree of probability is sufficient; *cf.* U. Magnus, The German Report: I.1.b. (One or Two Step Approach).
3 *Cf.* D. Busnelli/G. Comandé, The Italian Report, I.1. (Cause in Fact).
4 *Cf.* H. Cousy/A. Vanderspikken, The Belgian Report, 1.1.; H. Cousy/A. Vanderspikken, The Belgian Report, in: J. Spier (ed.), *The Limits of Expanding Liability* (1998) p. 81.

J. Spier (ed.), Unification of Tort Law: Causation, 127–154.

> X poisons a horse in stable with a slowly working poison. Before the poor animal dies, Y sets fire to the stable. The horse perishes in the flames. Who may be sued, X and/or Y, and why?

In the horse case, the more common approach among all jurisdictions holds X not liable for lack of *condicio sine qua non*. Most jurisdictions consider the damage *as it actually occurred (damage in concreto) as the relevant damage with which the wrongdoer's action must be causally linked. In the Julian horse case this damage consists, therefore, in death by burning or by suffocation, not simply death generally or health deterioration. As a result Y, who set the stable on fire, is the condicio sine qua non* for the horse's death, and, as Busnelli and Comandé put it,[5] Y is the *sole* cause. X is not considered a factual cause because it is not X's, but Y's wrongful act alone that caused the horse's *death by burning*[6].

For the purpose of the principles of causation it may well be argued that the only proper and consistent approach is to decline to follow the prevailing opinion as to X's and Y's liability. This point may be illustrated by turning to the position of Y. As Rogers rightly mentions,

> Y did kill the horse, but a much less valuable horse than it would otherwise have been, so he pays very little. Just as it is cheaper to kill a 90 year old than a 30 year old. While this is logical, it is hard on the owner, who a few hours ago had a good horse of which he has certainly been deprived.[7]

Similarly Schwartz:

> In limiting his liability, Y could refer to the horse's short life expectancy. Whether X could be held liable for having shortened that life expectancy is an undecided question.[8]

And Kerameus:

> If of course Y can prove that the animal would have died irrespectively of the fire, he would not be considered liable for that part of the damage[9, 10]

If Y is to be held liable only for killing a virtually valueless horse it would indeed be 'hard on the owner' in the case that Schwartz' 'undecided question' is decided with the argument that X is not liable because there is 'no law of attempted tort'.[11] However, one need not recognise attempted torts at all, as X's tort may be considered *complete*. At the moment Y

---

5 *Cf.* F. D. Busnelli/G. Comandé, The Italian Report, II. (Borderline between Causation and other Factors. Cases.a).

6 *Cf.* S. Galand-Carval, The French Report, I.4.a.; H. Cousy/A. Vanderspikken, The Belgian Report, 1. Question 4.a.; J. Neethling, The South African Report, I.3.a.; H. Koziol, The Austrian Report, I.3.b.; P. Widmer, The Swiss Report, I.4.a.

7 *Cf.* W. V. H. Rogers, The English Report, I 4.a.

8 *Cf.* G. T. Schwartz, The U.S. Report, I.4.a.

9 *Cf.* K. D. Kerameus, The Greek Report, I.4.a.

10 Under German law, X is liable for the total loss, while Y is only liable for the loss, if any, that resulted from the earlier death. *See* U. Magnus, The German Report, I.4.a.

11 *Cf.* W. V. H. Rogers, The English Report, I.4.a.

comes on the scene, X's actions had already sickened the horse irreversibly and therefore depreciated the animal to the extent that it had become almost valueless. Therefore, X ought to be liable for the real damage that he had already caused (*e.g.* 90 per cent).[12] Seen from this perspective it need not be considered a case of *hypothetical* causation. Carval's report indicates that there may, indeed, be some room for this approach towards X's liability under French law, *e.g.* in the event of Y being insolvent.

> In such a case, (. . .) it would be possible to argue that before Y's intervention, X's wrongful act had already caused a substantial damage, consisting in the diminution of value of the horse. Should this analysis be admitted, X would be liable to that extent.[13]

We might add that this solution[14] avoids the awkward reasoning of X's liability, or causation, *without condicio sine qua non*, since it saves the *condicio sine qua non*-test, which is unanimously adhered to by all.

One might argue that X is not liable because he did not cause the *damage* – which is the German view[15] – because with the wisdom of hindsight it is clear that the value-diminution would have happened anyway. This supposed reasoning, however, would lead to the unsatisfactory conclusion that if a man actually *kills* a horse, he will not be liable if Y shoots the horse in the head afterwards. If we add Z, who shoots it after Y did, and later A, B, C . . ., all but the last shooter would be exempted from liability, thus creating a legal perpetuum mobile. After all, one should have to argue just as well that with the wisdom of hindsight the damage would have happened anyway. Taken to the extreme, no tort is ever a tort, for in the future there could always be a subsequent event, such that in retrospect it may be said that the damage would have happened anyway.[16]

The following hypotheticals may shed light on the difficulties one faces:

> Farmer P owns a horse. For several years, P has allowed Y, one of P's neighbours, to ride his horse. Y is not particularly attached to the horse. One day when P takes the horse out of the stable, X – negligently driving his car – collides with the horse and causes serious injury to the animal. During the next six hours the horse is in agonizing pain while its death is slowly, but inevitably, on its way. Moved to tears, Y, who is to the driver's knowledge cold, unsympathetic towards animals and normally not at all impulsive, proposes P to end the horse's suffering. P refuses (on religious grounds). Five minutes later, Y can suddenly no longer bear the sight of the dying animal and decides for mercy-killing.
>
> Under the laws of the relevant jurisdiction any killing of an animal without the consent of the owner is considered a serious crime punishable with imprisonment; in

12 *Cf.* H. Koziol, The Austrian Report, I.4.a., and P. Widmer, The Swiss Report, I.4.a., even suggests that X and Y might be held jointly and severally liable.

13 *Cf.* S. Galand-Carval, The French Report, I.4.a.

14 Incidentally, this is also the prevailing, but not the unanimous opinion in the Netherlands: C. Asser, *C. Asser's handleiding tot de beoefening van het Nederlands Burgerlijk Recht, Verbintenissenrecht, Deel I: De verbintenis in het algemeen* (1996) nr. 440.

15 *Cf.* U. Magnus, The German Report, I.4.a.

16 *See infra* the rest of this report.

other words, also given the drivers's knowledge about Y's characteristics, the mercy-killing is far from reasonably foreseeable.

P is the owner of a dwelling house to which X sets fire. When the house is all but destroyed, except for the remains of some walls, Y, a terrorist, throws a fire bomb into the ruin which destroys everything.

As to the latter case, it would be unattractive to let X escape liability on the basis of the argument that his act of arson is not a *condicio sine qua non* since in the absence of it, the house would have been destroyed anyway. The better reasoning seems that X had completed his tort and is liable to the extent of the loss that he has caused, while Y, the terrorist, is liable as a subsequent tortfeasor only to the extent that his act caused any additional damage.

Similarly, in the horse case, the Group is inclined to think that the driver could only be held liable for the additional loss caused by Y's mercy-killing if such a subsequent tortious act may, after careful balancing of several factors, reasonably justify the imputation of the consequences to the tortious act.

Step 2: legal causation and reasonable imputation

Factual cause is generally seen as an insufficient basis for imputation of the loss to the tortfeasor's act or omission. As said above, Belgium is the only system which, theoretically, applies the equivalence theory, *i.e.* a one step-approach. Though in Austria the theory of equivalence also prevails, Austrian law nevertheless takes a two step-approach. Austrian law considers its second step (adequacy) not as a part of causation but instead as an independent doctrine designed to limit liability. Is it not merely a matter of semantic taste to restrict the use of the term 'causation' in this way rather than to apply it in a more general sense so as to include adequacy or any other limiting factors? In these Comments the latter approach is taken, which conforms to the common use of the term causation.[17]

We may roughly distinguish four approaches: (a) *condicio sine qua non* as the sole test, (b) the theory of proximate cause, (c) the theory of adequate causation, and (d) an openly flexible approach.

(*a*) condicio sine qua non *as the sole test*

The Belgian position was already explained above. Here, we must recall Cousy's and Vanderspikken's illuminating observations with regard to the meaning of *condicio sine qua non* in practice. Although as such the theory of the equivalence of causes should logically lead to a very liberal, plaintiff-friendly verdict on causation issues, in practice much more manoeuvring room is available to the courts. Application of the equivalence theory in Belgium does not really lead to outrageous results, for somehow – and mostly via other ways than by openly declaring a departure from the official equivalence theory – the courts manage to reintroduce most of the limitations which are sought by other theories.[18] Two other possible explanations why such an impractical doctrine actually works quite well in Belgium might be, as Cousy and Vanderspikken mention, that (1) Belgian plaintiffs simply omit seek-

17 *Cf.* Preliminary Observations, in: J. Spier (ed.), *The Limits of Liability* (1996) p. 5.

18 *Cf.* H. Cousy/A. Vanderspikken, The Belgian Report, 1.3.; *see* also The Belgian Report, in: J. Spier (ed.) (supra note 4) pp. 82 and 86 (courts tend to 'invent' intervening causes).

ing compensation from remote tortfeasors and (2) in a small country there may simply not be enough published case law to hold many illustrations of clearly unsatisfactory results.[19]

The Belgian approach seems less appealing as a basis for the principles of causation. First, Belgian practice itself may be less loyal to official doctrine in this respect.[20] Secondly, Belgium stands virtually alone in its adherence to the equivalence theory. Thirdly, the Belgian approach could not possibly be taken as common starting-point for European principles because other jurisdictions may not at all, or not to the same extent, share the particular Belgian legal culture.[21] Fourthly, factors that turn out to be relevant but are not openly admitted, would give little guidance to parties and courts, as is also stressed by Cousy and Vanderspikken.[22]

In this context one must also point at the French situation. French case law is divided and alternates between the equivalence theory and a conception of causation which distinguishes between direct and indirect causes, for which it seems to find inspiration in the 'adequacy theory.' In other words, judges freely apply two contradictory doctrines, so that not infrequently French cases show opposite results on very similar facts, a situation which is widely considered among French scholars and lawyers to be unsatisfactory.[23]

(b) proximate cause and remoteness

The Common Law's second step is usually referred to as 'proximate cause.' The word 'proximate' means nothing more than 'near' or 'immediate'. When it was first taken up by the English courts, it had connotations of proximity in time and space which have long disappeared.[24] In the United States, proximate cause nowadays includes several themes, such as foreseeability of harm, directness, proximity in space and time (and as such a factor of declining significance) and policy (including the floodgates argument or the fact that liability would become totally disproportionate to the defendant's negligence). Most weight is given to foreseeability.[25] Similarly, while English law speaks of 'remoteness' or 'proximate cause,' it uses foreseeability as the leading test of remoteness. Most of the other factors, such as fairness and reasonableness, proximity, the protective purpose of the violated rule,[26] and policy can be found in English cases.[27]

As we shall see *infra*, this multi-factor approach bears considerable resemblance to that of the theory of adequacy, as well as the openly flexible approach of reasonable imputation chosen for these principles of causation.[28]

---

19 *Cf.* H. Cousy/A. Vanderspikken, The Belgian Report, 1.4.

20 *Cf.* H. Cousy/A. Vanderspikken, The Belgian Report, 1.8.

21 Claim cultures, especially today, are subject to change and differ to some extent within Europe. *See* O. A. Haazen/J. Spier in: A. T. Bolt/J. Spier (eds.), *De uitdijende reikwijdte van de aansprakelijkheid uit onrechtmatige daad*, Handelingen, Preadvies voor de Nederlandse Juristen-Vereniging (NJV) 1996-I, pp. 7 et seq.

22 *Cf.* H. Cousy/A. Vanderspikken, The Belgian Report, 1.8.

23 *Cf.* S. Galand-Carval, The French Report, I.2.(iii).

24 *Cf.* Prosser and Keeton on Torts, § 42, p. 273.

25 *Cf.* G. T. Schwartz, The American Report, I.2.

26 Although the protective purpose-rule is not in analytical terms a matter of causation. But the effect is the same as a second stage rule of causation, to limit the defendant's liability; *cf.* W. V. H. Rogers, The English Report, I.2.

27 *Cf.* W. V. H. Rogers, The English Report, I.2.

28 *See under* (d).

(c) the test of adequate causation
Quite a few legal systems apply the so-called 'theory of adequate causation' or 'adequacy-test'. France, Germany, Greece, Austria and, to some extent, Switzerland may be seen as adequacy jurisdictions.

French case law essentially appeals both to the theories of equivalence and adequacy, although no reference is made to explicit terminology of 'adequate' or 'inadequate' causes. Thus, *e.g.* in case 7 C's coming to rescue would be considered as 'a normal consequence' of the dangerous situation created by A[29] The theory of proximate cause and in particular the idea of proximity in time, is generally rejected in France. It should be noted, however, that, not unlike the application given to proximate cause in Anglo-American law, French law uses factors such as *immédiat, direct* and *prévisible*. The distinction between direct and indirect consequences is clearly factored into the French approach when it comes to damages such as those at stake in case 4 ('dommages par ricochet'). 'Dommages par ricochet' are not 'indirect' as such, but courts do distinguish between losses suffered by the victim's family (as a result of the victim's own loss) and losses suffered by other persons like business clients, workers *et cetera*. Losses suffered by family are always regarded as direct.[30] Though foreseeability is not a formal requirement of causation, it is evident that the courts do appeal to foreseeability in their evaluations of adequate causation.[31]

It seems quite clear, then, that the French body of cases are not sufficiently understood when described as mere application of the equivalence theory. French judicial reasoning goes much further than mere pointing at all necessary, 'equivalent causes.' When the need arises, directness, foreseeability, adequacy and 'the normal consequences' start playing a role. The courts furthermore take into account the gravity of the respective faults in the context of contributory negligence,[32] the nature of the loss (personal injury),[33] and policy arguments.[34]

Under German law, courts normally analyse the adequacy of causation as a second step: the chain of causation is established if the fact generally and not only under abnormal, completely improbable and in the ordinary course of things negligible circumstances could have led to the occurrence of the result that happened. The degree of probability is, in other words, decisive. Causation is lacking if the act results in a very unexpected, unforeseeable consequence that nobody had to reckon with. The standard is set by an objective, optimal or at least experienced observer. That observer knows, for example, that a vaccination damage can happen even if the statistical probability lies under 0.01 per cent. Only very rarely does he not foresee that damage could occur.[35]

In Austria adequacy is established if the damaging event was generally suitable for

---

29 *Cf.* S. Galand-Carval, The French Report, II.2.c. (Case 7).
30 *Cf.* S. Galand-Carval, The French Report, II.1.b. (Case 4).
31 *Cf.* S. Galand-Carval, The French Report, I.2.(ii) et seq.
32 *Cf.* S. Galand-Carval, The French Report, I.2.(ii).
33 *Cf.* S. Galand-Carval, The French Report, I.4.b. (The Asbestos Case).
34 *See*, e.g. S. Galand-Carval, The French Report, I.4.c. on the omitted appeal case ('damages are awarded, even if the chance to win the appeal is slight and this is generally thought to be a means of penalizing negligent lawyers'); *see also* S. Galand-Carval, The French Report, II.2.c. (case 8), where regard may be had to fairness and policy arguments.
35 Much criticised due to its imprecision. *See* U. Magnus, The German Report, I.1.b.

increasing, to a considerable extent, the possibility of such a damage as in fact occurred.[36]

The Swiss Federal Court considers a cause to be adequate if, according to the ordinary cause of things and the general experience of life, the cause in question was apt to entail a result of the kind of that which has effectively occurred, in such a way that the occurrence of this result appears as generally favoured by the cause referred to.[37] It follows that, in principle, only ordinary, natural or common results for which the event was 'generally suitable' should be taken into account. It turns out, however, that, also according to the Swiss Federal Court, a cause can also be considered as adequate when it generates a *very uncommon* result. It seems then – and this holds true for the adequacy-test in general, not just for Swiss law – that afterwards, and overlooking the whole causal development, one can indeed always say that there has been a certain aptitude of a certain event to cause even a quite unusual loss. Add to this the importance played by factors such as foreseeability, a low degree of culpability such as slight fault, intent, the protective purpose of the rule, the unforeseeable dimensions of the damage for *this* particular person,[38] and adequacy as officially defined loses a lot of its distinctiveness and comes very close indeed to the flexible approach discussed below.

Such is indeed the conclusion drawn by the Swiss Federal Court, namely that the essential aspect is a political one and one of common sense and equity.[39] The aim is to limit liability to a *reasonable extent*. This accords with the view that the 'adequacy'-test as such would be too strict and inflexible and is, therefore, in need of a more flexible interpretation in order to establish a reasonable restriction of liability.[40]

(d) An openly flexible approach

A comparable pattern emerges if we consider the South-African experience with the remoteness-test. Following the steps of English law South-Africa has traditionally applied the doctrine of remoteness of damage. As with Anglo-American law, reasonable foreseeability played a predominant role but adequate causation, direct consequences and fault had also been taken into account. The Appellate Division, however, has now expressed itself in favour of a *flexible approach*, which asks the question if there is a sufficiently close relationship between the wrongdoer's conduct and its consequence that such consequence may be imputed to the wrongdoer in view of policy considerations based on reasonableness, fairness and justice. The criteria for legal causation, which already exist, such as adequate causation, direct consequences and reasonable foreseeability, may play a subsidiary role in determining legal causation within the framework of this elastic approach.[41]

Italian law also indicates that flexibility is necessary. While adequacy, remoteness, proximity in time, foreseeability and immediate and direct consequences play their roles, the

36 *Cf.* H. Koziol, The Austrian Report, I.2.a. (Adequacy).
37 *Cf.* P. Widmer, The Swiss Report, I.2. (Relevant Factors/Reasons/Criteria).
38 All or some of these factors mentioned by P. Widmer, The Swiss Report, I.2. (Relevant Factors/Reasons/Criteria), H. Koziol, The Austrian Report, I.2. (Relevant Factors in Restricting Liability for Caused Damage) and S. Galand-Carval, The French Report, I.2.(ii), I.4.c. (The Appeal Case), I.4.d. [The Carrier Case (i)].
39 *Cf.* P. Widmer, The Swiss Report, I.2. (Relevant Factors/Reasons/Criteria).
40 *Cf.* H. Koziol, The Austrian Report, I.2.c. (The Flexibility of the Criteria).
41 *Cf.* J. Neethling, The South African Report, I.1.(i)–(v).

courts, in fact, go beyond the strict sense of 'immediate and direct consequences' to include those damages that can be considered consequences of the tort according to an evaluation of the relationship between cause and effect carried out on the basis of the so-called *suitable causality* criterion.[42]

The Dutch Civil Code of 1992 takes the view that damages are only recoverable for losses which stand in relation to the defendant's act or omission in such a manner that the damage, also taking into account the nature of the damage and that of the liability, can be imputed to the defendant as a result of his act or omission. This is generally understood to be a flexible 'reasonableness'-approach.[43]

Similarly, in Germany, while the adequacy-test is much criticised, the courts apply policy considerations as a *third* step. These policy considerations are partly connected with the 'protective purpose of the rule,' so that the German approach is effectively a flexible approach, which takes into account at least foreseeability, proximity, adequacy, policy and the protective purpose as a factor.[44]

Likewise, the French 'adequacy'-test does not preclude the relevance of factors like foreseeability, directness, the degree of fault, the nature of the loss and policy, as was mentioned in the previous paragraph. French law, however, clearly denies relevance to factors as the exceptional magnitude of the loss and proximity in time, while the protective purpose of the rule is virtually unknown in France.[45] Taking into account that openly recognising what is being done has a clear advantage, the openly flexible, multi-factor approach could serve as the prevailing test of legal causation. The flexible approach takes several factors and theories into account, but always weighs them in light of policy, reasonableness, justice and common sense.[46] By adopting a flexible approach, it is not intended to travel the road of least resistance, *i.e.* achieving unification of truly distinct solutions by 'die Flucht in Generalklauseln' (falling back on standards so vague as to conceal real differences in order to accommodate all or most legal systems). It is submitted that the flexible multi-factor approach effectively represents a real common core.

3. Relevant factors

Table 1 shows the relevance of several factors all through the different legal systems. Those which are mentioned in table 1, with the exception of disproportionate loss, are all recognised by quite a number of jurisdictions as relevant factors.

Disproportionate loss is rejected as a relevant factor at least in England and France and only explicitly recognised as one in South-Africa. Four other jurisdictions, notably Italy, the Netherlands, Sweden[47] and Switzerland see possibilities of taking into account the dispropor-

42 *Cf.* F. D. Busnelli/G. Comandé, The Italian Report, I.2. (The Second Step: Legal Cause).

43 *See* R. J. B. Boonekamp, *Schadevergoeding* art. 98.

44 *Cf.* U. Magnus, The German Report, I.1.a. and I.1.b.

45 *Cf.* S. Galand-Carval, The French Report, I.2.(ii) and I.4.d. [The Carrier Case (i)].

46 'Causation is to be understood as the man in the street and not as either the scientist or the metaphysician would understand it, *Yorkshire Dale Steamship Co.* v. *Minister of War Transport*, *per* Lord Wright, cited in W. V. H. Rogers, *Winfield & Jolowicz on Tort* (15th ed.), p. 208.

47 *See* The Swedish Report, in: J. Spier (ed.) (supra note 4) pp. 62 and 189.

tionate character of the damage done; they normally approach that issue, however, under the heading of *ad hoc* mitigation.[48]

The cases 1 (US attorneys) and 21 (DES) need some specific attention, in that the obligation to compensate the entire amount of damages may well be a heavy burden for the defendant.[49] We therefore have to ascertain whether or not this were to be a relevant factor in the sphere of causation.[50]

It follows from the answers to these cases and also from another case previously considered by the Group[51] that, in most jurisdictions, the mere circumstance that the loss at stake is disproportionate is in itself no sufficient reason to deny legal causation, though it still remains a factor to be taken into account. *The Limits of Liability* reveals that *ad hoc* mitigation is an instrument provided by Swiss and Dutch law,[52] while in the United States it comes into play in arguments of policy, which is a factor in the context of causation.[53] It does not seem totally impossible to recognise this factor under Belgian and Austrian law, where it plays a role in a more concealed way.[54] The same is true for Portugal and in certain cases Sweden.[55]

In particular remoteness/proximity, foreseeability and, except under Austrian law, directness are widely considered to be of great importance. A similar conclusion holds true for adequacy, with the exception of the Common Law, while it plays a concealed role in Belgium. Factors as the *degree of foreseeability* of the loss at the time of the wrongful act or omission and the *closeness in time or space* between the wrongful act or omission and its consequence are clearly relevant. Regard is also to be had to the *nature of the loss* (in the sense that, *e.g.*, imputation of personal injury extends wider than of damage to property, imputation of damage to property extends wider than pure economic loss and imputation of personal injury extends wider than of losses consisting in pain and suffering, loss of consortium, emotional harm *et cetera)*, as well as the *nature of the liability* (in the sense that in case of an intentional or grossly negligent act or omission imputation may extend much wider than it does when liability is based on negligence, strict liability or vicarious liability). Further relevant factors to be balanced should be the *extent to which the normal risks of life are increased* (in the sense that dangerous activities, notably ultrahazardous activities give rise to wider imputation) and, as already stated, the *character of the loss* (in the sense that impu-

---

48 *Compare* the view of G. Viney in Preliminary Observations, in: J. Spier (ed.) (supra note 17) p. 15.

49 This would especially be true in case of joint and several liability in cases like DES. Dutch law [Hoge Raad (Supreme Court, HR) 9 October 1992, [1994] *Nederlandse Jurisprudentie* (NJ), 535] and possibly Italian law (F. D. Busnelli/G. Comandé, The Italian Report, 3. Case 21) opt for joint and several liability in those cases.

50 *See*, explicitly, J. Neethling, The South African Report, I.1. Conclusions.

51 *See* The Country Reports in: J. Spier (ed.) (supra note 4) pp. 21 and 80 (The Austrian Report), pp. 90–91 (The Belgian Report), p. 105 (The English Report), pp. 117–118 (The French Report), pp. 126–127 (The German Report), pp. 152–153 (The Italian Report), pp. 170–171 (The Dutch Report), p. 187 (The Portuguese Report), p. 196 (The Swedish Report), pp. 208–209 (The Swiss Report) and pp. 237–238 (The U.S. Report).

52 *Cf.* J. Spier (ed.), (supra note 17) p. 110 (The Dutch Report) and p. 156 (The Swiss Report); *see* iure constituendo *also* p. 15.

53 *Cf.* G. T. Schwartz, The U.S. Report, I.2.

54 *Cf.* Preliminary Observations, in: J. Spier (ed.) (supra note 17) p. 9.

55 *Cf.* J. Spier (ed.) (supra note 4) Preliminary observations, para. 7.2 and p. 196.

Table 1

	Jurisdiction			
	Ger	A	B	Eng
Factors				
remoteness/				
proximity	x	x	(x)	x
adequacy	x	x	(x)	–
policy		x (Koziol)		x
degree of fault	x (intent)			x
disproportionate loss		x (Koziol)		
nature of loss	x (pers. injury, pure economic loss)			x (pure econ.)
directness		–	(x)	x
foreseeability	x	x	(x)	x

tation is less likely if the magnitude of the harm is, *per se* or in relation to what would be the normal consequences of the wrongful act or omission, out of proportion). It should be stressed that these factors may point in opposite directions. Strict liability will, *e.g.*, often be a factor with the effect of 'mitigating' imputation. However, increasing the normal risks of life will be reason for wider imputation. Strict liability has been established in connection with various kinds of increase of risks (*e.g.* in relation to damage caused by dangerous substances).

Finally, there is all the more reason for wide imputation of the loss to the tortfeasor's wrongful act or omission if the type of loss at stake, the person or persons suffering the loss, or the particular wrongful act or omission involved is such as was, explicitly or implicitly, covered by the *protective purpose of the rule* that has been violated.

4. The protective purpose of the rule

The issue of 'the protective purpose of the rule' (the 'scope of the rule', *Schutzzweck der Norm, Schutznorm-theorie, normbestemmingsleer, relativiteit*) is one of the most difficult topics for the ultimate drafting of our principles. The comparative reports of Sinde Monteiro, Rogers and Koziol in *The Limits of Expanding Liability* show that the protective purpose

F	Gr	I	NL	SA	CH	US
(x)[56]		x	x	x	x	x
x	x	x	x	x	x	–
x	x	–	x	x	x	x
x (contrib. negligence)				x	x	x
–	–	x	x/– (ad hoc mit.)	x/– (ad hoc mit.)	x	x/– (ad hoc mit.)
x (pers. injury)[57]			x		x	x
x (par ricochet)		x	x	x	x	x
x (cases 1 & 9)	x	x	x	x	x	x

truly serves as a causation negating doctrine in several legal systems. It seems convenient to summarise the results briefly by means of Table 2.

As was well put by Koziol,[58] we might distinguish three rules: (a) the wrongdoer must compensate only the loss of those *persons* which the law is intended to protect; the plaintiff must be within the category of persons envisaged by the rule; (b) the wrongdoer is to compensate the plaintiff only for the loss which the violated rule is intended to avoid; the *loss* must be of the type envisaged by the rule; and (c) the wrongdoer is held liable only if he caused the loss in a *manner* that the rule forbids; the particular *conduct* (act or omission) must be of the type envisaged by the rule.

56 *See* The French Report, in: J. Spier (ed.) (supra note 17) p. 111; in as far as remoteness/proximity means the same as indirectness/directness, *see* S. Galand-Carval, The French Report, I.2.(ii), I.4.b. (The Asbestos Case), I.4.d (The Carrier Case) (ii) and II.1.b. (Case 4); proximity in time is irrelevant.

57 *Cf.* S. Galand-Carval, The French Report, answer to case I.4.b (The Asbestos Case).

58 *Cf.* H. Koziol, The Austrian Report, I.2.b. (Protective Purpose).

Table 2

Jurisdiction	Basic rule	Conclusions	Issue
Austria	* if a protected statute prohibits a certain behaviour in order to protect certain assets, the wrongdoer must indemnify even remote damage	positive factor	causation
	* if P is *not* within category of protected persons, then 'causation'[59] less likely	no liability (negating factor)	'causation'
	* if *not* within category of damage envisaged, then 'causation' less likely;	'no causal link' (negating factor)	'causation'
	* if *not* envisaged manner/type of conduct, then 'causation' less likely	'no causal link' (negating factor)	'causation'
Switzerland (Widmer's view)	* if *not* within category of damage envisaged, then causation less likely; (ex. of drunken victim, Widmer, p. 4–5)	no causal link (negating factor)	causation
	* if *not* within category of persons, then less likely; (ex. drunken victim)	no causal link (negating factor)	causation
	* if *not* envisaged manner/type of conduct (sheep case), then no causal link (adequacy)	no causal link	causation
South Africa	* if *within* type of damage envisaged, then causal link (adequacy)	causal link	causation
	* if *not* within category of damage envisaged, then causation less likely (adequacy; Neethling p 3)	no causal link (negating factor)	causation
	* if *not* protected conduct and damages, then no wrongfulness (sheep case)	no wrongfulness	wrongfulness
Netherlands	* if *within* category of damage envisaged, then merely a matter of causation	neutral on causation	causation
	* if P is *not* within category of protected persons, then not wrongful to P (or not at all)	no wrongfulness	wrongfulness
	* if *not* within category of damage envisaged, then no violation of Schutznorm(in practice probably causation)	no wrongfulness	wrongfulness

59 'Causation' in the sense that the term is generally used. We are, of course, aware that under Austrian law, the term has a very specific meaning and is limited to what is otherwise known as 'factual causation.' *See supra* 2. Condicio Sine Qua Non and the Two Step Approach to Causation. Step 1: Factual Causation. In Austria, therefore, these issues are clearly *not* regarded as issues of causation but of 'adequacy,' 'restriction of causation' or 'policy.'

Jurisdiction	Basic rule	Conclusions	Issue
	* if *not* envisaged manner/type of conduct, then not wrongful	no wrongfulness	wrongfulness
England & Wales	* if *not* envisaged manner/type of conduct, then not negligent *per se*	no 'wrongfulness'	'wrongfulness'
US	* if *not* envisaged manner/type of conduct, then not negligent *per se*	no 'wrongfulness'	'wrongfulness'
Belgium	* no protective purpose rule, though it plays a role sometimes[60]	-	-
France	* no protective purpose rule[61]		
Germany	* depending on whether a consequence of some category or source belongs to those effects that the violated provision is designed to protect	-	-

So far it seems clear that most jurisdictions reveal a tendency to take the protective purpose into account one way or another, though in different areas and sometimes only partially. Consequently, we suggest incorporation of the protective purpose rule in the principles of tort law. All jurisdictions that do recognise the protective purpose rule somehow, draw the logical conclusion that, once a particular case is judged to fall *within* the protective purpose of the rule, it is not, or no longer, an issue of *wrongfulness*. One must, therefore, move on and see if the case becomes an issue of *causation*. We assume that it is also implicit in those jurisdictions whose reports did not explicitly state this, that the issue is about causation once it is established that the tort falls within the protective purpose.

A rule of thumb might be the Austrian 'rule' that if a protective statute forbids a certain behaviour in order to protect certain assets, the wrongdoer who violates such a law must indemnify even remote losses. In other words: if the case does fall under the protective purpose the loss is not likely to be too remote.[62] Though no support can be found in any of the other reports, this rule of thumb seems little controversial and relatively unproblematic.

The differences come to surface where cases do *not* fall within the envisaged category of victims, conduct or loss. Here our question is if the issue is one of causation or wrongfulness. More or less explicit answers are provided by the Austrian and Swiss reports. *See* for Austria above under (a)-(c). Treating the issue under the heading of adequacy, Widmer favours the attempt to bring compensation into line with the *range* of a norm founding liability.

It may turn out that the person hit by a car or a train was dead drunk so that this drunkenness has to be regarded as the prevailing or at least a 'concurrent' cause of the accident. Seen under the aspect of the *range of the norm*, this means that one considers that the *characteristic risk* of a motorvehicle or of a train *does not include (or does not fully include) damage to persons* who expose themselves to danger in an unreasonable way.[63]

60 *Cf.* H. Cousy/A. Vanderspikken, The Belgian Report, 1.6.

61 Except for application of the rule in the area of civil liability for the commission of a criminal offence; but even here its use is in decline, *cf.* S. Galand-Carval, The French Report, I.2.(ii).

62 *Cf.* H. Koziol, The Austrian Report, I.2.a. (Adequacy).

63 *Cf.* P. Widmer, The Swiss Report, I.2. (emphasis added).

Although the case involved strict liability, Widmer's reasoning seems no less valid in general. His argument goes to both the *damage* and the *persons*. As to *conduct* which the rule seeks to prevent we turn to the sheep case, where it can be argued that the violated statute *did not aim* at the security of the animals in the eventuality of a storm (but was intended to prevent the spreading of diseases), the *violation of this norm is irrelevant for this particular accident*.[64]

This to Widmer means nothing else than to say that the plaintiff's wrongful act or omission was not *adequately causal* for the accident. But he recognises, of course, that the theory of adequacy is very close to the protective purpose doctrine, in that both of them try to determine the extent of liability in function of the aim of the applicable norm. Conclusion: call it the protective purpose rule or adequacy or causation, when the protective purpose is not met, the issue is, in any case, one of causation.

Other jurisdictions, however, are inclined to address the problem from a *wrongfulness* perspective. Thus, in the Netherlands, there is no wrong done in relation to the plaintiff (relativity) or none at all[65] if (a) the defendant did not violate a duty which was intended to protect the plaintiff, (b) the losses incurred were not of a type as envisaged by the violated rule, or (c) the manner of infliction of the harm was not envisaged by the violated rule.[66]

Neethling suggests that the situation in South-Africa is somewhat more ambivalent. If the incurred losses are not those which the rule intended to protect, this is to be seen as a factor that tends to negate adequacy and, thus, *causation*.[67] Turning to the sheep case, however, the South-African answer seems to be that the loss of the sheep was not in breach of a statutory duty because the nature of the harm and the nature in which it occurred were not such as was contemplated by the statute. Therefore, there is no *wrongfulness* to begin with.[68]

The difficulty continues when we turn to England and the United States. At first sight it might appear a bit of a theoretical stretch to recognise a rule that the protective purpose negates wrongfulness in Anglo-American law. After all, there is no general doctrine of protective purpose nor can wrongfulness be seen as a clear requirement in the first place. However, the protective purpose rule negating wrongfulness appears to us as the closest analogy to Anglo-American reasoning. This is one of those areas where the South-African perspective is of tremendous help to the comparative lawyer engaged in unification efforts. Anglo-American law (obviously, as our sheep case was derived from *Gorris v. Scott*) recognises the rule that the injury must be of the kind which the statute intended to prevent.[69] Anglo-American law treats this case under *remoteness of damages* or *proximate cause*,[70] which suggests that it is an issue of causation, but also a matter of *breach* of statutory duty.[71] Negli-

64 *Cf.* P. Widmer, The Swiss Report, I.4.d. (Shipwrecked Animals), (emphasis added).
65 HR 30 September 1994, NJ 1996, 196.
66 Parl. Gesch. (Travaux préparatoires) Bk 6, p. 637.
67 *Cf.* J. Neethling, The South African Report, I.1. Legal Causation. (ii).
68 *Cf.* J. Neethling, The South African Report, I.3.d.; Neethling, Potgieter and Visser, *Deliktenreg*, p. 71; Van der Walt, *Delict: Principles and Cases* (1979) p. 39.
69 W. V. H. Rogers (supra note 46) *Gorris v. Scott*, pp. 217 and 261.
70 Charlesworth and Percy on Negligence (8th edn.), nos. 4–41, p. 306. *See also Prosser and Keeton on Torts* (5th edn.), pp. 283–284.
71 W. V. H. Rogers, *Winfield & Jolowicz on Torts* (14th ed.), p. 199–200; *Prosser and Keeton on Torts*, p. 225.

gence *per se* (breach of statutory duty) is close enough to the civil law rule that the mere breach of statutory duty entails wrongfulness. It is precisely *because* there is no general requirement of wrongfulness under Anglo-American law, that the issue *could not* have been categorised as one of wrongfulness. Since our Group has decided on such a requirement, we feel that it is in accordance with the spirit of Anglo-American law to conclude that even Anglo-American law would have considered it a wrongfulness problem, had it had a wrongfulness requirement.

This interpretation is supported by the experience of South-Africa, where the law has had to accommodate the Civil law wrongfulness requirement with English tort law (mainly negligence). Indeed, it is particularly indicative that Van der Walt[72] treats *Gorris v. Scott* as a wrongfulness case. Perhaps, therefore, the issue of losses falling *outside* the scope of the rule may be dealt with in the context of the wrongfulness requirement.[73] Under which doctrinal heading the issue of the protective purpose of the rule is ultimately best dealt with is, however, a question that will finally be tackled in a later stage.

5. Multiple causation

Our treatment of multiple causation will immediately include the answers to the questions provided by the members of our Group, as well as those to hypothetical 6.[74]

We have sought to systematise the subject-matter as follows:

(1) one time loss
- (a) **identical** loss subsequently caused by
  - (i) natural cause (plumber case)
  - (ii) liable third party (terrorist case)
- (b) **aggravated** loss subsequently caused by
  - (i) natural cause (horse plus lightning)
  - (ii) liable third party (Julian horse case)

(2) continuous loss
- (a) **identical** loss subsequently caused by
  - (i) natural cause (heart attack)
  - (ii) liable third party
- (b) **aggravated** loss subsequently caused by
  - (i) natural cause (avalanche case)
  - (ii) liable third party (ambulance plus drunken driver case)

(1) (a) (i) one time loss – identical loss – natural cause: the plumber case (case 9)

D, a plumber, negligently causes fire in P's house. Before repair, the house is completely destroyed by an earthquake. D argues that P did not suffer any damage as a result of D's act or omission, as P's house would have been destroyed anyway.

72 Van der Walt (supra note 68) p. 39.

73 We propose the same for strict and vicarious liability.

74 For which we refer to J. Spier (ed.) (supra note 4) pp. 20 and 78 (The Austrian Report), p. 89 (The Belgian Report), pp. 102–103 (The English Report), pp. 114–115 (The French Report), pp. 124–126 (The German Report), p. 134 (The Greek Report), pp. 148–150 (The Italian Report), pp. 167–168 (The Dutch Report), pp. 183–185 (The Portuguese Report), p. 195 (The Swedish Report), p. 206 (The Swiss Report) and pp. 228–235 (The U.S. Report).

In this type of situation, where the damage hypothetically done to the plaintiff's person or property by natural cause or occurrences in the personal sphere and risk of the plaintiff[75] is *identical* to the loss caused by the defendant, our legal systems reveal nearly complete consensus: the defendant is liable in full. This issue is addressed in the plumber case (case 9).[76]

Assuming that P's house was already *entirely* destroyed by the fire, we are dealing with a case of (hypothetically) identical and subsequent damage. This, in any case, is how it was understood in the reports and how the case was meant, though its wording is admittedly unclear in this respect.

English law (and probably German law and possibly Swiss law[77] as well), however, provide a deviant answer: for lack of *condicio sine qua non*, D is probably not liable except for loss of use before the earthquake, since there is no factual causation of P's loss for the period after the earthquake – it would have happened anyway.[78]

Most others say that liability is established once all the elements of a tort are present. Thus,

> [D's] wrongful act produced its damaging effect (the destruction of the house) before the earthquake, and P's right to compensation *arose at this time*. The earthquake is *not* an *intervening* event but a subsequent event, which has no [exonerating] effect on causation.[79]

To be very precise, the tort will be deemed complete once the loss is complete.[80]

The United States and Greece achieve the same result on a different ground. They argue that the earthquake was, at the time of the original fire, 'completely unanticipated' and 'neither a usual nor a foreseeable event'.[81] We are not sure if we fully understand why the foreseeability of the natural cause would make a difference, since in *this* case the natural cause does not have the effect of making things worse. Magnus points out that in such a case 'the protected interest is predisposed to be certainly damaged'.[82] Probably Schwartz and Kerameus did, understandably, assume that the original damage was not yet complete, so that the foreseeability of *additional* damage becomes an issue.

The completeness-argument being decisive in other jurisdictions, we propose to go with that majority solution.

---

75 Hereinafter referred to as 'natural cause.'

76 It is possible to argue that the heart attack case ought to be classified in this category as well. *See* what is discussed *infra* (2).(a).(i).

77 *Cf.* P. Widmer, The Swiss Report, I.4.a. (Death of a Horse).

78 *Cf.* W. V. H. Rogers, The English Report, I.4.a and II. Case 9; U. Magnus, The German Report, II. Case 9.

79 *Cf.* S. Galand-Carval, The French Report, II.2.a. Cases 9, 10, 5 – especially Case 9 (emphasis added).

80 *See* also more or less explicitly J. Neethling, The South African Report, II. Case 9; H. Koziol, The Austrian Report, II. Case 9 (see also Case 10); F. D. Busnelli/G. Comandé, The Italian Report, II. Case 9; H. Cousy/A. Vanderspikken, The Belgian Report, II. Cases 9 and 10; P. Widmer, The Swiss Report, II. Cases. 9 (Plumber Case).

81 *Cf.* G. T. Schwartz, The U.S. Report, II. Case 9, and K. D. Kerameus, The Greek Report, II. Case 9 respectively.

82 *Cf.* U. Magnus, The German Report, II. Case 9.

(1)(a)(ii) one time loss – identical loss – liable third party: the terrorist case

In this type of situation, the damage 'done' to the plaintiff's person or property by the act or omission of a liable third party is hypothetically identical to the loss which was caused by the first tortfeasor. We may refer to the case of the terrorist, mentioned in step 1 above, who destroys an already burnt down house. We may imagine that not the terrorist should be liable in tort but instead the first tortfeasor to the full extent, for he already caused all the damage. No relevant difference with the plumber case (case 9) is involved.[83] Therefore, it is difficult to see why it should make a difference whether the subsequent hypothetical cause is a natural one or another liable party's wrongful act or omission or an act or omission for which no one is liable.

(1)(b)(i) one time loss – aggravated loss – natural cause: the Julian horse is struck by lightning

In this type of situations the subsequent natural cause results in additional damage to the plaintiff's person or property, over and above the damage already done by the defendant.

In the ship case (case 10) heavy weather caused extensive damage to a ship on its way to the United States, after being already damaged by the defendant's ship. Only French law might hold D liable under application of the equivalence theory, while under German law D might be liable if the ship had to cross the ocean for repair.[84] But that is not even sure because the courts might apply the adequacy theory and judge the causal link interrupted. Under Dutch law, applying the flexible approach, the answer is also unclear.

A fortiori, imagine a car that was involved in a car crash for which D is liable, not resulting in a total loss. If subsequently a tree, struck by lightning, falls onto the car and causes a total loss, there is reason to hold D liable for the partial loss only and little reason to hold him liable for the *additional* loss.

(1)(b)(ii) one time loss – aggravated loss – liable third party: the Julian horse case (case I.4.a)

Imagine the same car crash example. This time, however, the car is totalled by D2's totally unrelated subsequent negligence; it seems that D2, *not* D1, should pay the additional damage. In as far as the subsequent negligent driving is not unrelated but rather reasonably imputable to D1's negligence, D1's liability extends to the additional loss, too.

Incidentally, this solution would be in line with the one suggested to the Julian horse case and the case of the mercy-killing of an all but dead horse. Are not these cases really about *aggravated* damages (loss of the value of a dying horse v. loss of the value of a dead horse)? From that perspective, the first defendant would be liable for making the horse *almost* valueless and the second defendant for the remainder, the actual death.

(2)(a)(i) continuous loss – identical loss – natural cause: the heart attack case (case 14)

This problem is addressed in the heart attack case and receives two conflicting types of solutions. One approach, which is taken by a slight majority, holds the defendant fully liable

83 *Cf.* P. Widmer, The Swiss Report, I.4.a. (Death of a Horse) however, stresses the importance of intent.

84 *Cf.* U. Magnus, The German Report, II. Case 10.

for the entire damage. Many reports take note of the similarity of this case with the plumber case (case 9). The heart attack case is perceived as one of a *one time* damage, a permanent inability to work, and, therefore, of a *completed* loss.[85] A subsequent heart attack does, therefore, not at all diminish the inability to work any further. As a result the chain of causation has not been broken.

The other approach, of a large minority, categorises the loss as one *progressing* through time. The damage emerges, so to speak, every day that the victim misses income by not working or fails to make profit by virtue of the person's forced inactivity. A subsequent heart attack does change the chain of causation and denies liability from the moment of the heart attack.[86] The defendant does not have to compensate the whole loss of income because he only caused the loss of income at an earlier date, *i.e.* exactly the time between the car accident and the heart attack.[87]

We might describe the difference as such that the *first approach* focusses on *loss of earning capacity*, while the *second* on *loss of income*. These two characterisations might explain the difference in approach. The car accident took away the earning capacity entirely, but it cannot be said to have taken away the plaintiff's entire income. After all, that future income has not yet accrued.

As a matter of fact, in most jurisdictions a victim is not obliged to settle for a lump sum. This means that the principles of causation will at least have to be compatible with compensation payable in instalments. In cases of temporal or permanent disability to work, the tortfeasor's wrongful act or omission continuously causes the victim's loss of income to accrue so to speak from day to day. This implies that when a subsequent, totally unrelated natural event or wrongful act or omission *also* has a disabling effect, the natural event or wrongful act or omission may equally be said to cause the victim's loss of income to accrue as time goes by. To the extent that this loss of income resulting from the subsequent cause fully or partially overlaps with the already daily accruing loss of income, the situation is analogous to the fact-pattern of *concurrent* causes (*see infra*, paragraph 6). Following this analogy, there would be liability *in solidum* for all those who cause the victim's loss of income, which of course leaves only the one tortfeasor in case of a subsequent natural event. If, on the other hand, the continuously accruing loss of income may be imputed also as the consequence of a subsequent tortfeasor's wrongful act or omission, both tortfeasors are jointly and severally liable.

There seems to be little reason to give a tortfeasor so to speak the 'windfall' of a subsequent heart attack. This, in any case, does not happen if a plaintiff has been awarded a lump sum before he suffers the heart attack. On the other hand, the argument may be turned against the victim as well: why should the victim have the windfall of full compensation for loss of income which he would have suffered as a result of his heart attack anyway? Such a subsequent natural cause can be taken into account in *special circumstances* such as the following. If we imagine a case still pending in court, where the judge is asked to decide on

85 *Cf.* K. D. Kerameus, The Greek Report, II. Case 9 and S. Galand-Carval, The French Report, II.2.c. (Case 14).

86 *Cf.* W. V. H. Rogers, The English Report, I.4.a. (The Horse).

87 *Cf.* H. Koziol, The Austrian Report, II. Case 14.

liability in a situation similar to the car accident mentioned above. Imagine further that halfway through the litigation it is brought to the judge's attention that the plaintiff has deceased a week ago as the result of a heart attack. Such a judge is unlikely to disregard the heart attack and instead calculate the deceased plaintiff's loss of future income on the basis of his prospective retirement date as if nothing had happened. There is little reason to calculate future income on the basis of statistical estimation of how long the plaintiff could probably have worked *once it is known precisely* that he *could not* have worked beyond that point. It is one thing to say that the chain of causation has not been broken by the subsequent heart attack. But the judge would still have to decide on the extent to which, under these circumstances, future losses of income may still be reasonably imputed to the original wrongful act or omission, in light of the balance of all relevant factors such as those mentioned above. After all, it must always be decided to what extent certain losses are reasonably imputable to the tortfeasor's wrongful act or omission, once the first step of *condicio sine qua non* has been taken. This is no more than the general rule. Besides, it could be argued that the plaintiff does not suffer any loss. That topic, however, will be addressed within the framework of damages.

(2)(a)(ii) continuous loss – identical loss – liable third party

It follows from paragraph (2) (a) (i) that the previous and the subsequent tortfeasors are jointly and severally liable, if, and to the extent that, they caused the same loss.

(2)(b)(i) continuous loss – aggravated loss – natural cause: the avalanche case (case 11.b)

> P is seriously injured in a car accident caused by D, such that it would take him a year to recover from his injuries. While an ambulance brings him to the hospital, the ambulance is hit by an avalanche, causing additional injury. P now needs three years to recover. To what extent is D liable?

A natural cause, like an avalanche crushing the ambulance in which the victim of a car accident is being driven to the hospital, does not result in the tortfeasor's liability for the *aggravated* loss, unless, following the general principles of causation, such a consequence may reasonably be imputed to his negligent act.

(2)(b)(ii) continuous loss – aggravated loss – liable third party: the ambulance plus drunken driver case (case 11.a)

In this type of situations the subsequent act or omission of a third party results in *additional* damage to the plaintiff's person or economic interests, over and above the damage already done by the first tortfeasor.

Thus, in case 11.a, a drunken driver causes P to need two extra years to recover. It seems obvious and in line with the above that the drunken driver is liable for the two additional years. As to the first tortfeasor (D), the opinions are divided. Four jurisdictions answer in the affirmative; five answer in the negative, whereas the Swiss position is somewhat in between.

Austria and Germany are of the opinion that the first tortfeasor did not increase the general risk that the plaintiff might be involved in a car accident, so adequacy has to be negated.[88] Furthermore the rule violated by D does not have the purpose of avoiding accidents which are part of the general risks of life, under which confrontations with drunken drivers also fall.[89]

Similarly, both England and South-Africa find the appearance on the scene of a drunken driver a 'mere coincidence' or, at least, 'probably not reasonably foreseeable,' therefore no legal cause.[90]

Driving in the United States is a different matter and, apparently, so is drunken driving. Most United States courts would say that the risk of being hit by a negligent driver is part of the risk of highway travel.[91] As a result, D is liable to the full extent.

Liability is further imposed in France, Switzerland, the Netherlands and probably Belgium. Swiss law holds that the intervention of the drunken driver will certainly not exonerate D as the responsible person for the car accident, even though he may not be held liable to the full extent.[92]

As to Dutch law, virtually all causes will be imputed when it comes to violation of traffic and safety rules and/or personal injury.

For reasons of comparison and convenience we include Table 3 (pp. 148–149).

6. Concurrent causes

Case 20 (waste discharge) is about concurrent causes, which take place at the same time and which would have caused the entire damage, the other cause or causes thought away. Although it could be argued that the *condicio sine qua non*-test fails as to each individual occurrence,[93] all jurisdictions would unanimously hold the tortfeasors jointly and severally liable.

7. Insufficient causes

Unanimity disappears in the following cases:
(a) acts or omissions which occurred more or less *at the same time* and *together* cause the damage, which would not have been brought about if one or more of these acts or omissions would not have occurred [rubbish case (case 18), as it was meant; a similar problem is at stake in the colliding ships case (case 23)];
(b) *subsequent* acts or omissions, which *together* cause the damage (the asbestos case, I.4.b).

(a) concurring causes
We now turn to the rubbish case. Under the laws of Italy, Germany, Belgium, Greece, France, Austria, and South-Africa, D1 is held *liable for the entire damage*. The same is

88 *Cf.* H. Koziol, The Austrian Report, II. Case 11; U. Magnus, The German Report, II. Case 11; K. D. Kerameus, The Greek Report, II. Case 11; F. D. Busnelli/G. Comandé, The Italian Report, I.3. (Relevant Factors) and II. Case 11.
89 *Cf.* H. Koziol, The Austrian Report, II. Case 11.
90 *Cf.* W. V. H. Rogers, The English Report, II. Case 11; J. Neethling, The South African Report, II. Case 11.
91 *Cf.* G. T. Schwartz, The U.S. Report, II. Case 11a.
92 *Cf.* P. Widmer, The Swiss Report, II. Cases. 11 (Drunken Driver and Avalanche).
93 *See*, e.g., J. Neethling, The South African Report, II. Case 20.

probably true for most of the United States.[94] Dutch and Swiss law[95] may be different, but the situation is unclear. As to Dutch law, the answer depends on the question whether the damage has to be perceived as 'indivisible' or 'the same damage' (article 102 Book 6 BW).[96]

Thus, the majority would hold each tortfeasor jointly and severally liable with the other. It should be noted that in these types of situations, each tortfeasor's act or omission is insufficient to cause any harm; without the contribution of the other tortfeasor, there would have been no loss at all and hence no liability. Compared to that situation, it is then, in fact, *another* tortfeasor's appearance on the scene that has the effect of turning no liability into joint and several liability. This is somewhat harsh on each tortfeasor, given that the conduct of each without the other would not have led to legally redressible damage. In weighing the interests of an innocent victim and a negligent tortfeasor, however, we are inclined to accept that the interests of the former should prevail.

The victim's interests, of course, constitute an important consideration. Nonetheless, it must be recognised that a strict application of this principle may lead to unsatisfactory results, in particular in case of mass tort litigation or when the causal contribution of one of the tortfeasors is really only minimal. After all, it is hard law to oblige a tortfeasor, whose negligence and contribution to the damage is only minimal, to compensate for all losses and to bear them without recourse in case the other defendants have become insolvent.[97] It is then not necessarily justified to sacrifice the defendant for the plaintiff's sake. Under these circumstances the flexible approach to imputation may serve to put a restriction on the extent to which the minimal contributor is to bear all consequences.

(b) subsequent occurrences

We now turn to the asbestos case (case I.4.b). We find four different solutions:
(i) According to Greek, German, Swiss, French, Austrian, Belgian and probably Italian law, A is *liable in full*;
(ii) The Netherlands[98] opt for *proportional liability*;
(iii) The outcome is *uncertain* in the US; the plaintiff will have to take the but for-hurdle anyway; in England the answer is also uncertain and will turn on whether the damage is indivisible or progressive.
(iv) *Causation* is *denied* under South-African law.

According to Widmer, this is 'a simple situation of concurrent' tortfeasors 'and that means also: joint and several liabilities'.[99] Koziol mentions that A, B and C are *condiciones sine quibus non*,[100] which means that they are *jointly and severally liable*, assuming that 'they

94 *Cf.* G. T. Schwartz, The U.S. Report, II. Case 20.
95 *Cf.* P. Widmer, The Swiss Report, II. Cases. 18 (Collapsing Wall).
96 *See* for different opinions: J. Spier, *Schadevergoeding* (Boonekamp) art. 98 aant. 22 and art. 102 aant. 6.2.; *see also* J. Spier, *Sluipende schade. Rede uitgesproken bij de aanvaarding van het ambt van hoogleraar in het Privaatrecht aan de Katholieke Universiteit Brabant op 21.09.1990* (1990). We adhere the view that the damage is the amount to be paid for repair or the lesser value of the damaged property. That damage can easily be divided in parts.
97 *See* for a different view H. Lange, *Schadensersatz* (2nd ed., 1990) p. 169.
98 *See* J. Spier, Sluipende schade and Mon. *Nieuw Burgerlijk Wetboek* (Nieuw BW)-36, nr. 52.
99 *Cf.* P. Widmer, The Swiss Report, I.4.b. (The Asbestos Case).
100 *Cf.* J. Neethling, The South African Report, I.3.b. (The Asbestos Case).

Table 3

	Case			
Jurisdiction	9. (Plumber)	14. (Heart attack)	10. (Ship)	11. (Ambulance drunken driver)
A	in full, tort complete	no, no adeq.	no, no adeq.	no adeq. causation
	Koziol: no	Koziol: no	not within scope of rule	not within scope of rule
B				
CH			no, not adeq., not sensible	in full (j&s)
Eng	no, no csqn for rest	no	no legal cause	no legal cause, mere coincidence
F	in full, tort complete	in full	yes (equivalence theory) maybe not (adeq. theory)	in full
Ger				
Gr	in full, tort complete	in full	no, no adeq. causation	no
I	in full	in full	no legal cause b/c damage by weather avoidable	no
NL	in full, damages complete	no, no legal unclear cause (interrupted)	in full	in full (j&s)
Por				
SA	in full, tort complete	in full	no legal cause, b/c maybe reasonably foreseeable and unfair, unreasonable	no legal cause, probably not reasonably foreseeable
US	in full, b/c earthquake unanticipated			in full, negligent drivers are normal risk

	Avalanche	12. (Highway parking)	13. (Victim's wallet)	15. (One leg)
A	causation not within scope of rule	in full, causation within scope of rule	no, only slight adeq. and scope doubtful, only if gross negligence	in full, adequacy
B				in full, csqn
CH	no legal cause (fortuitous)	in full (j&s)	no adeq. cause (interrupted)	in full, adequate causation
Eng	no legal cause, mere coincidence	no, recklessness broke chain	no, only if 3rd party's wilful wrongdoing very likely	no legal cause, too remote, prox. in time relevant factor
F	in full	in full	in full	not certain, proximité temporelle no decisive factor
Ger				in full, (adeq., b/c not very unlikely)
Gr		no, adequate cause interrupted	no	no legal cause
I	no	in full (j&s)	no, not regular, direct, immediate, normal	
NL	no, cause interrupted	in full	in full	in full (maybe *ad hoc* mitigation)
Por				probably no adeq. cause unlikely
SA	no legal cause probably not reasonably foreseeable	probably not, improbable, not reasonably foreseeable, unfair and unreasonable	probably not, not reasonably foreseeable, unfair and unreasonable	no, not reasonably foreseeable, too remote
US	in full, b/c coincidence	in full, but maybe recklessness taken into account	in full, theft reasonably foreseeable	in full

acted in fault'[101] (and assuming, we suppose, that the second step is also successfully taken).

Neethling points out that it is doubtful whether A is a *legal* cause. The damage was 'probably not reasonably foreseeable when X left A's employment.' It does not seem reasonable and fair to him to impute the damage to A.[102]

Neethling's observation seems the more attractive approach from the point of view that, to the extent possible, it is to be avoided that someone is liable for damage he *cannot* have caused.

Joint and several liability is less appropriate in specific cases. As already mentioned, it may be a fair solution in average cases. To give a rather extreme example: X was just one day employed by A and then got a better offer from B. He was employed by B for decades. If B went bankrupt, possibly because his wages were too high, it does not appeal to the sense of justice that A would have to compensate X entirely.[103] The same holds true for mass torts.

This issue is almost unanimously perceived as one of *causation*.[104] It could equally be argued that it is about damages.

At this stage, we do not touch upon the intriguing question whether, seen from the perspective of damages, A has to compensate X for his entire loss. We stick to the observation that, when X left A's service, he was not yet ill and he would never have become ill, if he would not have engaged in subsequent dangerous activities. So it may need further justification why A should have to pay X's full loss, given that there was no loss at all when X left A. In other words: the mere fact that the causation hurdle will be taken by X, does not necessarily mean that his claim may not founder on the damages obstacle.[105]

This brings us to the question as to whether there should be any difference in treatment between simultaneous and subsequent causes when these are each, taken separately, insufficient to cause a victim to suffer loss. It becomes difficult to justify a negative answer; hence, all those contributing to the loss ought to be held jointly and severally liable.

8. Uncertainty of causation

In this part we discuss cases 16 (omitted diagnosis case), 17 (emissions case), 19 (hunters case), 21 (DES case) and 22 (falling rock case), all of which deal with uncertainty of causation: alternative causation and/or loss of a chance. We should immediately stress that 'loss of a chance' might also be seen as a matter of damages (*see below*), and that alternative

101 *Cf.* H. Koziol, The Austrian Report, I.4.b.

102 *Cf.* J. Neethling, The South African Report, I.3.b.

103 *Cf.* H. Cousy/A. Vanderspikken, The Belgian Report, 1. Question 4.b.

104 *Cf.* J. Neethling, The South African Report, I.3.b.; F. D. Busnelli/G. Comandé, The Italian Report, II. Cases.b.; H. Koziol, The Austrian Report, I.4.b.; P. Widmer, The Swiss Report, I.4.b. (The Asbestos Case); S. Galand-Carval, The French Report, I.4.b. (The Asbestos Case); G. T. Schwartz, The U.S. Report, I.4.b.; U. Magnus, The German Report, I.4.b.(The Asbestos Case); H. Cousy/A. Vanderspikken, The Belgian Report, 1. Question 4.b.

105 This approach (A's contribution does not constitute a *loss*) would also have its downsides. It could mean that *C* must be considered to have brought about the entire loss since there was then no loss when X started working for C and there was when he left. This would even be true if C's 'contribution' would be minimal. Understandably, it is stressed by P. Widmer (I.4.b.) and H. Koziol (I.4.b.), that the (mere) fact that X crossed the fatal threshold, when employed by C, is irrelevant.

causation covers several subcategories, *viz.* alternative defendants, alternative plaintiffs or both.

Prima facie one can put the issues this way:

(1) Alternative causation may be the term used for a *certain* (single) defendant of whom it is certain or likely that he caused damage, while it is *uncertain* precisely to whom. This is the fact-pattern of case 17 under a (possibly also b and c), the emissions case.

(2) Alternative causation may also refer to the situation that the plaintiff is a *certain* person with a *certain* loss but it remains *uncertain* if it was *this particular* defendant who caused the loss. Case 19 (the hunters case) is an illustration of this type of situation, as it is clear that the victim was shot, but unclear which of the hunters fired the fatal shot. Also case 22 (falling rock) is in fact a variation of the hunters' case, the only difference being that the action of one defendant is substituted by a natural cause.

(3) Finally, uncertainty may exist as to both plaintiff and defendant. Thus, we find in the DES case (case 21), that both uncertainty as to possible defendants and uncertainty as to the plaintiffs are at stake.

(4) In cases of 'loss of a chance' the plaintiff and the tortfeasor are readily identifiable, but it is uncertain whether or not the plaintiff actually suffered *a loss* which was *caused* by the defendant (case 16).

It is felt that legal causation is a necessary step to achieve a more just, more precise, and well-balanced decision. Its purpose cannot be described as merely to limit liability, even though many legal systems see it that way. Traditionally, doctrinal classifications deal with (4) separately. Doctrinal analysis, however, becomes almost arbitrary and breaks down in this context. First, it was repeatedly stated that the *condicio sine qua non*/but for-test is way too broad in that it can treat almost every physical cause as equivalent; for that reason it is said that the but for-test needs the 'second step,' legal causation, whose purpose or function it is said to be to limit the otherwise boundless number of relevant causes. In the cases discussed here, the but for-test cannot be applied: because of the very fact of uncertainty it is impossible to say whether or not the damage would have occurred *but for* the cause in question. As a result, the but for-test does not point at a multitude of *condiciones sine quibus non*, which are to be *restricted* by legal causation. On the contrary, legal causation serves to *expand* imputation.

Secondly, the distinction between loss of a chance and alternative causation is somewhat arbitrary.[106] Characteristic of both is uncertainty. When a physician fails to diagnose cancer, the early diagnosis of which may or may not have saved the victim, we may ask 'Did the physician's omission cause the patient to die, or did he die as the result of his disease only?' Thus, case 16 is one of alternative causality. Equally justified, however, is the doctrine that asks 'How likely is it that the omission caused the death?' It is then merely a matter of proof. Or, alternatively, 'Did the physician diminish the patient's chance of survival?' The latter question may be judged an issue of *damages*,[107] in which case *causation* is not uncertain but the damages and their amount are.

This point may also be argued in another way. If someone plays the lottery which gives

---

106 The Dutch Supreme Court, *e.g.*, realising that they amount to the same thing, probably treats both questions as identical: HR 24 October 1997, NJ 1998, 257.

107 *See*, e.g., H. Cousy/A. Vanderspikken, The Belgian Report, II. Case 16.

him a one percent chance of winning, he has a 99 per cent risk of losing. If a patient, suffering from a lethal disease, has a 40 per cent chance of being cured through proper treatment, he bears a risk of death amounting to 60 per cent. When the physician fails to diagnose, he takes away the 40 per cent chance of cure. Of course, he may also be said to have increased the risk of dying by 40 per cent (from 60 per cent to 100 per cent). The Italian courts have recognised this complementary character of chance and risk, using a test for loss of a chance which asks if the defendant's behaviour 'certainly increased the risk to damage a given plaintiff'.[108] When only two alternatives are possible (winning/losing, death/survival, catching a disease/remaining unaffected), questioning the increase of a risk is identical to the inquiry after the chance of the opposite outcome.

The Italian report takes the loss of a chance approach with regard to the omitted diagnosis, but denies that case 17a (emissions) falls into the same category. It seems merely a matter of preference and tradition, not of logically compelling argument, whether one asks:
(a) 'Did the factory cause the illnesses or were they due to natural causes?' Answer: 95 per cent caused by factory, 5 per cent due to natural causes); or instead
(b) 'How likely is it that the emissions caused the death of a particular individual?' Answer: chances are 95 per cent; or
(c) 'Did the emissions (certainly) increase the risk of illness?' Answer: yes, by 95 per cent; or
(d) 'Did the emissions decrease the chance of remaining unaffected?' Answer: yes, by 95 per cent.

Though the Italian report denies that the emissions case is about loss of a chance, the Italian courts still use the same test of 'certainly increase the risk.' This exactly hits the mark. All cases are, in one way or another, about increasing risk. It seems reasonable to attach a price to such an increase. It does not appeal to our sense of justice either to leave the victim empty-handed (by denying loss of a chance), or to fill his bank account with more than his damage *could* have been (by disregarding the *chance* and converting it into a 'certainty').

Besides these doctrinal issues, we also face oftentimes radically diverging outcomes of the remaining cases throughout our legal systems. It follows from the reports that the opinions are strongly divided. It does not seem likely to persuade one or more countries that their solutions are completely wrong in relation to such an important matter, the less so, because both extremes can reasonably be justified.

Let us first take the Common Law's 'more likely than not'-test as a matter of proof, adhered to in England, South-Africa and the United States. Especially in cases like personal injury, it may seem fair to compensate a potential victim if the defendant's acts increases the chances to a considerable extent. The tortfeasor is to bear the odds, because he can either be blamed or at least his acts or omissions invoke liability. The plaintiff is entirely innocent. It could be argued that, weighing both interests, the plaintiff's interests should prevail.

Yet, it is harsh to apply the 'more likely than not' test (balance of probabilities) if one feels that there is no significant difference between 50 per cent and 49 per cent or 51 per cent. Some examples: 40 per cent in the omitted diagnosis case (case 16) does not establish the balance of probabilities in the plaintiff's favour in England; a 50 per cent increase in the emissions case (case 17c) leads to the conclusion that the factory *clearly* caused one third

108 F. D. Busnelli/G. Comandé, The Italian Report, II. Case 16.

of the damage (Koziol). The 300 per cent increase in case 17b should be a clear balance of probabilities, but imputation of legal cause is nevertheless unclear in England (Rogers); in the same case 17b causation is 'more likely than not' in the United States, while the 50 per cent increase in case 17c is probably not; finally, though 50.01 per cent would constitute a balance of probabilities, there is still no liability in South-Africa (Neethling).

Given the fact that the great majority of jurisdictions hold the physician in case 16 liable in part,[109] and given that we have just explained case 17's similarity, we incline to the view that *proportionate liability* should be extended to that case and, in fact to the other cases by the same token. Not only does this constitute a middle ground for the litigants, which is less arbitrary than the 50 per cent barrier, but also does it make a compromise between the various solutions of our legal systems. *See, e.g.*, the answers to the cases 19 and 21. As one can see from Table 4 all answers are minority opinions.

Only in case 22 (falling rock) there is a clear majority arguing against causation. But it is not easy to understand why the hunter case (case 19) and the case of the falling rock would deserve different treatment. In both fact-patterns it is unknown which of the two possible causes was the actual cause. The only distinction (natural cause + human cause v. human cause + human cause) seems a distinction without a difference, a distinction to which we also denied decisiveness, or even relevance in the context of hypothetical causation (identical, additional or aggravated loss) and insufficient causes.[110] The question remains: what caused the damage?

It follows from the above that establishing a causal link is de facto a first step. This leaves untouched that the factors, mentioned supra 3., could play a role in the final question of imputation of the consequences to the original act or omission, be it for the purpose of restricting or expanding causation. Such an additional test seems useful, if not necessary, if one takes into account that the condicio sine qua non test in these cases has not been met.

Case 17a touches upon the question whether or not small 'chances' (percentages) at both extreme sides of the spectrum have to be disregarded. In line with the Austrian report, it is suggested that we should answer the question in the negative if a sufficiently reliable estimate of the 'chance' can be made.[111] It is very open to debate whether a very small percentage is to be neglected. But this probably is often mere theory, since in those cases either causation, or the absence of a causal link, is so overwhelmingly plausible, that it can be either fully affirmed or entirely denied.

The above suggests that evidence on the basis of statistics are to be admitted. This, however, does not answer the question under what circumstances such evidence is sufficiently reliable.[112] In particular in the above-mentioned situation of loss of a chance of only

---

109 K. D. Kerameus, The Greek Report, II. Case 16.; G. T. Schwartz, II. Case 16 (states are divided); S. Galand-Carval, The French Report, II.4. Case 16; H. Koziol, The Austrian Report, II. Case 16; F. D. Busnelli/G. Comandé, The Italian Report, II. Case 16; P. Widmer, The Swiss Report, II. Cases 16 (Wrong Diagnosis); for the Netherlands, *see* HR 24 October 1997, NJ 1998, 257.

110 *Cf.* P. Widmer, The Swiss Report, II. Cases 22. (Falling Rocks).

111 *Cf.* H. Koziol, The Austrian Report, II. Case 17a. This is also a kind of compromise to those legal systems which require a substantial chance of at least 50% or more.

112 *Cf.* K. D. Kerameus, The Greek Report, II. Case 17a; G. T. Schwartz, The U.S. Report, II. Case 17a; H. Cousy/A. Vanderspikken, The Belgian Report, II. Case 17a.

a few percent, the risk of statistical error is so high that, as was said above, the judgement should be 'all or nothing' (in this case nothing). This topic is dealt with in cases 17.b and 17.c. It seems in line with the reports to consider this matter as factual. It seems hardly possible to draft principles in this respect, which is only marginally a matter of substantive law.

Table 4

	Case				
	16. (omitted diagnosis)	17. (emissions) a.	b.	c.	19. (hunters)
Jurisdiction					
A	in part (%), not loss of chance, but altern. causation	95% altern. causation	2/3 altern. causation	1/3 clearly caused	yes, if highly dangerous, in full (j&s), altern. causation
B	in part (%), loss of a chance (with minimum of 50% in medical malpractice)	legal certainty required	unclear, but statistical evid. probably admitted	unclear, but statistical evid. probably admitted	causation has to be certain, unless defendants acted in concert
Eng	probably not, balance of probabilities (only 40%)	yes, but unclear	unclear, even though balance of probabilities	unclear	yes, in full (maybe)
F	in part (%) (actually the *entire* lost chance)	no, b/c possibly coincidence	probably not, statistical evidence insufficient	probably not, statistical evidence insufficient	yes, in full as collective fault
Ger	probably insufficient probability	yes, b/c probably not coincidental	no, 50% increase not sufficient		liable in full, irrespective of whether or not acting in concert
Gr	in part (%), loss of chance is separate damage		mere statistics insufficient	mere statist. insuff.	no
It	in part (%), loss of chance, b/c risk certainly increased	yes, risk certainly increased	yes	yes, risk more likely than not increased	probably not
NL	in part (%), loss of chance	yes, 95%	probably not statistics may be unreliable	no	yes, in full (j&s)
SA	yes, in full, b/c probable cause (40% deemed preponderance)	yes, b/c extremely high % (prima facie+ shift burden)	yes, b/c more probable than not	no, b/c not preponderance	no, if no proof no preponderance of probabilities
US	divided: yes: in part (%) no	yes, probably not coincidental in full/part?	yes, in full	probably not	probably yes (but question of proof)

Index

www.ingramcontent.com/pod-product-compliance
Lightning Source LLC
Chambersburg PA
CBHW071343230926
51846CB00002B/432
9789041113252